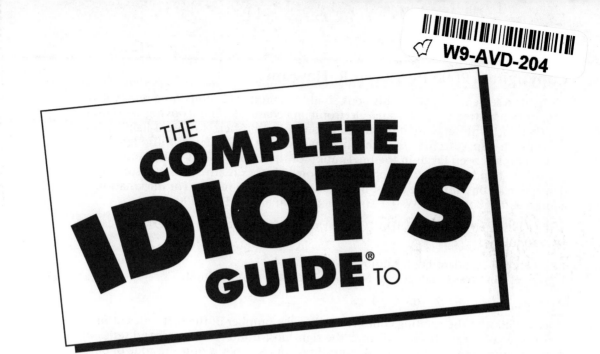

THE COMPLETE IDIOT'S GUIDE® TO

Intermediate Spanish

by Steven R. Hawson

alpha books

A Pearson Education Company

THE COMPLETE IDIOT'S GUIDE TO and Design are registered trademarks of Pearson Education, Inc.

International Standard Book Number: 0-02-863924-3
Library of Congress Catalog Card Number: Available upon request.

03   02   8   7   6   5   4   3

Interpretation of the printing code: The rightmost number of the first series of numbers is the year of the book's printing; the rightmost number of the second series of numbers is the number of the book's printing. For example, a printing code of 00–1 shows that the first printing occurred in 2000.

Printed in the United States of America

Note: This publication contains the opinions and ideas of its author. It is intended to provide helpful and informative material on the subject matter covered. It is sold with the understanding that the author and publisher are not engaged in rendering professional services in the book. If the reader requires personal assistance or advice, a competent professional should be consulted.

For marketing and publicity, please call: 317-581-3722

The publisher offers discounts on this book when ordered in quantity for bulk purchases and special sales.

For sales within the United States, please contact: Corporate and Government Sales, 1-800-382-3419 or corpsales@pearsontechgroup.com

Outside the United States, please contact: International Sales, 317-581-3793 or international@pearsontechgroup.com

Irregular Preterite Verbs

While most verbs are regular in the preterite, a few have irregular forms. Most of these verbs are quite common, so you'll be using them often when you speak Spanish. There are no real tricks to memorizing these—you'll just have to bite the *bala* (bullet) and learn them if you have not already done so:

➤ *andar* (**to walk**): *anduve, anduviste, anduvo, anduvimos, anduvisteis, anduvieron*

➤ *caber* (**to fit**): *cupe, cupiste, cupo, cupimos, cupisteis, cupieron*

➤ *dar* (**to give**): *di, diste, dio, dimos, disteis, dieron*

➤ *decir* (**to say**): *dije, dijiste, dijo, dijimos, dijisteis, dijeron*

➤ *dormir* (**to sleep**): *dormí, dormiste, durmió, dormimos, dormisteis, durmieron*

➤ *estar* (**to be**): *estuve, estuviste, estuvo, estuvimos, estuvisteis, estuvieron*

➤ *hacer* (**to do**): *hice, hiciste, hizo, hicimos, hicisteis, hicieron*

➤ *ir* (**to go**): *fui, fuiste, fue, fuimos, fuisteis, fueron*

➤ *haber* (**helping verb for "to have"**): third person is *hubo* (the others are very rare)

➤ *morir* (**to die**): *morí, moriste, murió, morimos, moristeis, murieron*

➤ *poder* (**to be able**): *pude, pudiste, pudo, pudimos, pudisteis, pudieron*

➤ *poner* (**to put**): *puse, pusiste, puso, pusimos, pusisteis, pusieron*

➤ *querer* (**to want**): *quise, quisiste, quiso, quisimos, quisisteis, quisieron*

➤ *saber* (**to know**): *supe, supiste, supo, supimos, supisteis, supieron*

➤ *sentir* (**to feel**): *sentí, sentiste, sintió, sentimos, sentisteis, sintieron*

➤ *ser* (**to be**): *fui, fuiste, fue, fuimos, fuisteis, fueron*

➤ *tener* (**to have**): *tuve, tuviste, tuvo, tuvimos, tuvisteis, tuvieron*

➤ *traducir* (**to translate**): *traduje, tradujiste, tradujo, tradujimos, tradujisteis, tradujeron*

➤ *traer* (**to bring**): *traje, trajiste, trajo, trajimos, trajisteis, trajeron*

➤ *venir* (**to come**): *vine, viniste, vino, vinimos, vinisteis, vinieron*

Remember that compound verbs (*convenir, extraer, retener,* and so on) will conjugate exactly the same as their basic root verb.

alpha
books

Irregular Tú Command Forms

For most verbs, use the third-person singular form of the verb. For the others, look here:

Irregular Tú Forms

Verb	Tú Command	Example	Definition	Verb	Tú Command	Example	Definition
hacer	haz	Hazlo.	Do it.	salir	sal	¡Sal de ahí!	Get out of there!
ir	ve	Vete.	Go away.	poner	pon	Ponlos aquí.	Put them here.
decir	di	Dímelo.	Tell me it.	venir	ven	Vente.	Come here.
tener	ten	Ten cuidado.	Be careful.	ser	sé	Sé feliz.	Be happy.

Irregular Future and Conditional Stems

Most verbs simply place the future or conditional ending right after the *–ar*, *–er*, or *–ir* ending. But some verbs require irregular stems. Here is a list of the main verbs in this category:

Verb	Stem	Example	Verb	Stem	Example	Verb	Stem	Example
poner	pondr–	pondría	venir	vendr–	vendríamos	decir	dir–	diría
poder	podr–	podríais	valer	valdr–	valdrían	salir	saldr–	saldré
tener	tendr–	tendrá	haber	habr–	habría	querer	querr–	querría
saber	sabr–	sabrías	hacer	har–	haré			

Irregular Past Participles

Most Spanish past participles follow the *–ado/–ido* pattern. But several common verbs form irregular past participles:

- **abrir:** *abierto*—"open"
- **resolver:** *resuelto*—"resolved" (any *–solver* verb)
- **cubrir:** *cubierto*—"covered" (any *–cubrir* verb)
- **decir:** *dicho*—"said"
- **escribir:** *escrito*—"written" (any *–cribir* verb)
- **hacer:** *hecho*—"done"; "made" (and compounds)
- **morir:** *muerto*—"died"
- **poner:** *puesto*—"put" (and compounds)
- **romper:** *roto*—"broken" (not "*rompido*")
- **ver:** *visto*—"seen" (and compounds)
- **volver:** *vuelto*—"returned" (and compounds)

Many of these verbs can also be found as part of other compound verbs. The verb *volver* means "to come back." The verb *devolver* means "to give something back." It's a different verb, but as you can see, it has *volver* in it, so it acts like *volver*.

Common Irregular Present Subjunctives

Some common verbs have irregular forms in the subjunctive:

Irregular Verbs in the Subjunctive

Verb	Subjunctive Form	Verb	Subjunctive Form
dar	dé, des, dé, demos, deis, den	saber	sepa, sepas, sepa, sepamos, sepáis, sepan
estar	esté, estés, esté, estemos, estéis, estén	ser	sea, seas, sea, seamos, seáis, sean
haber	haya, hayas, haya, hayamos, hayáis, hayan	ver	vea, veas, vea, veamos, veáis, vean
ir	vaya, vayas, vaya, vayamos, vayáis, vayan		

The past subjunctives are built from the preterite form of the verb. If a verb is irregular in the preterite, it will also be irregular in the past subjunctive.

Publisher
Marie Butler-Knight

Product Manager
Phil Kitchel

Managing Editor
Cari Luna

Senior Acquisitions Editor
Renee Wilmeth

Development Editor
Alana J. Morgan

Production Editor
JoAnna Kremer

Copy Editor
Krista Hansing

Illustrator
Jody P. Schaeffer

Cover Designers
Mike Freeland
Kevin Spear

Book Designers
Scott Cook and Amy Adams of DesignLab

Indexer
Angie Bess

Layout/Proofreading
John Etchison
Bob LaRoche
Gloria Schurick

Contents at a Glance

Contents

Appendixes

Foreword

There is no question that a strong working knowledge of Spanish is becoming increasingly important in the United States and Canada for cultural, commercial, and political reasons alike. Many English speakers who have a basic knowledge of Spanish need a text that can serve as a bridge between that knowledge and any advanced material they may need to focus on, such as in the fields of medicine, law, business, or literature.

Steven R. Hawson's *The Complete Idiot's Guide to Intermediate Spanish* is just such a text, explaining grammar and syntax in an innovative way and continuing to provide benefits through repeated readings.

The Complete Idiot's Guide to Intermediate Spanish is an ideal text for students who have already studied the fundamentals and are eager to enhance their knowledge and skills.

—Prof. Carl Fehlandt, Graduate School of Translation and Interpretation, Monterey Institute of International Studies, Monterey, California

Introduction

Welcome to *The Complete Idiot's Guide to Intermediate Spanish*. But wait … isn't there already *The Complete Idiot's Guide to Spanish*? Well, yes, there is. *The Complete Idiot's Guide to Learning Spanish on Your Own,* by Gail Stein, has become an extremely popular textbook for beginning students of Spanish. Similar teach-yourself guides have also enjoyed great success in recent years. With so many "advanced beginners" out there, we realized that it was time to offer an intermediate resource to those students who are ready to progress to the next level. That's where *The Complete Idiot's Guide to Intermediate Spanish* comes in. This book has been specifically designed to take you beyond the basics and introduce you to many of the finer points of the Spanish language.

You don't have to have read *The Complete Idiot's Guide to Learning Spanish on Your Own* to use this book. This is not a "volume two." In fact, the only "requirement" is that somewhere along the line you have acquired a basic knowledge of Spanish (no matter how rudimentary or rusty your skills might be) and that you feel ready to learn more. If this sounds like you, you've come to the right place. Hang on to your *sombrero* and get ready for *The Complete Idiot's Guide to Intermediate Spanish*.

How This Book Is Organized

Studying a new language is always a challenge, even under the best of circumstances. To make the experience as pleasant as possible, I have tried to make this book fun and easy to read—without compromising its content. Yes, you'll find grammar, vocabulary lists, quizzes, and activities. But there will also be jokes, time-saving hints, and new perspectives about the language that you probably weren't exposed to when you were a beginner. I promise that it won't be all dry linguistic stuff.

The Complete Idiot's Guide to Intermediate Spanish is divided into five parts:

Part 1, "So You Want to Learn Intermediate Spanish: ¡Qué Bueno!" prepares you for the rigors of the book by reviewing in detail some of the nuts and bolts of the language, such as pronunciation, spelling, stress, and accent marks. You'll also find suggestions for getting the most out of your learning experience.

Part 2, "Getting to Know the Spanish-Speaking World," introduces you to your first Spanish texts. Each reading deals with some aspect of a country or region where Spanish is spoken. You'll also learn some basic facts about the various countries that make up *el mundo hispanohablante*. The grammar sections review nouns, verbs, adjectives, and other basics, but with a new perspective that I hope you will find refreshing.

Part 3, "*La Vida Cotidiana*," means "everyday life." The readings in these chapters relate to family, friends, religious customs, food, and *fiestas*. The grammar sections move away from verbs and nouns and discuss issues such as *por* vs. *para,* the use of prepositions, *tú* vs. *usted,* and so forth.

Part 4, "Arts and Leisure," includes texts relating to literature (*Don Quixote*), sports, the Prado Museum, and other such topics. Grammar sections introduce (or review, depending on your experience) the past subjunctive and show you how prefixes and suffixes can be used to build new Spanish words.

Part 5, "Money, Science, Politics, and Transportation," presents some of the most challenging readings in the book. We'll look at computers, business correspondence, a political document, and other complex texts. As for grammar, we'll check out homonyms, cognates, and polite expressions, and I'll give you my own perspective on reflexive verbs.

What You'll Find in Each Chapter

As previously mentioned, the chapters in Part 1 are devoted to fundamental issues about pronunciation, spelling, accentuation, and facts about the language. Thus, they seem to dance to the beat of their own *conga*. But the chapters in Parts 2 through 5 all follow the same basic format. After a few paragraphs of introduction about the subject at hand, you'll find the following subsections:

> ➤ *Lectura* (The Reading)
>
> All chapters include a Spanish text, known from now on as the *lectura*. Each *lectura* will be related in some way to the chapter's main theme. The *lecturas* vary in length, difficulty, and style, becoming generally more difficult as the book progresses. These *lecturas* are "real, live" Spanish texts; they were written for native Spanish-speakers.

> ➤ *Vocabulario Útil* (The Useful Vocabulary)
>
> From the *lectura*, a list of vocabulary words will be generated. Not all of these words will be directly related to the general topic, but they will be selected based upon my hunch that you might not know what they mean. If the English definition starts with "here, …," this means that the word or phrase might have another meaning in a different context. Feel free to add any additional words from the text that you didn't find here.

> ➤ *Análisis del Texto* (Text Analysis)
>
> In this section, I focus on some of the more interesting parts of the *lectura* and discuss what they have to teach us. Translations may be provided for the more difficult passages.

> ➤ *Gramática* (The Grammar)
>
> No book such as this could be complete without some discussion of grammar. But the good news is that many of the topics I'll be covering probably won't be entirely new to you. Intermediate Spanish grammar is really just beginning grammar explained in greater detail. I'll expand on your current knowledge, explain things in a new and more detailed way, and provide examples of how the rules of grammar can be applied. I'll do my best to make it as painless as possible.

➤ *Diálogo* (The Dialogue)

Some chapters contain one or more dialogues. These have been included to give you additional exposure to how the language is actually spoken. Most of the dialogues are followed by a translation.

➤ **The Idiot's Guide to Idioms**

The chapters in Part 5 include an "Idiot's Guide to Idioms." Soon you'll be able to amaze your friends with the Spanish equivalents of phrases such as "There's more than one way to skin a cat" and "A bird in the hand is worth two in the bush."

➤ *Risa del Día* (Laugh of the Day)

I'll be doing my best to ensure that the material in each chapter is interesting and upbeat. But just in case I get a little long-winded (as my wife will tell you that I often do), you'll have a chance to laugh off your frustrations with a section devoted to Spanish humor. It's amazing how much Spanish you can learn from reading jokes. That's why this section will also be followed by a *Vocabulario Útil* section. Of course, I can't promise that these jokes will be "good," but I'll do what I can.

➤ *El Cuiz* (The Quiz)

I will allow myself one word of "Spanglish" in this book: *El Cuiz*. This word is not really Spanish, but it is understood by many Spanish-speakers. Besides, I didn't have the heart to call this *el examen*. This quiz is essentially a review of the vocabulary from the *lectura*. There may be a few words from the *Risa del Día* as well. You can take *El Cuiz* as often as you like. Simply refer back to the vocab lists in the chapter to check your work.

➤ *Tareas* (Activities)

After *El Cuiz*, you'll find some suggested activities you might do to further practice the material in the chapter. You can approach these *tareas* however you wish. If the *tareas* don't suit your needs, feel free to modify them to suit your personal learning style.

Approaching the Material

The most important thing to keep in mind as you read this book is that you should not expect to understand everything the first time through. If you come across something that doesn't make sense, move on and come back to it later. Most of us go through a two steps forward, one step back process when learning a new language, so unless you have superhuman powers of memory retention, you'll find it impossible to master the contents of this book after only one sitting.

After you read the entire book, I strongly suggest that you go back and read all the *lecturas*, grammar sections, and jokes again. You'll be amazed how much easier everything is the second time around.

Extras

You'll find many interesting facts about grammar, word usage, Latin culture, and linguistic pitfalls set aside throughout the book in our famous sidebars. Web sites will also be listed as a resource for additional information about certain topics. Look for the following icons:

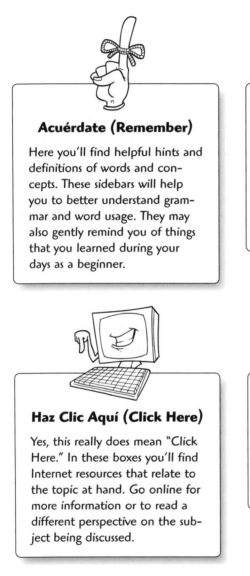

Acuérdate (Remember)

Here you'll find helpful hints and definitions of words and concepts. These sidebars will help you to better understand grammar and word usage. They may also gently remind you of things that you learned during your days as a beginner.

Ten Cuidado (Be Careful)

These boxes mention words to avoid and common grammar pitfalls. Read these to avoid making unnecessary mistakes or wasting time when you could be having fun.

Haz Clic Aquí (Click Here)

Yes, this really does mean "Click Here." In these boxes you'll find Internet resources that relate to the topic at hand. Go online for more information or to read a different perspective on the subject being discussed.

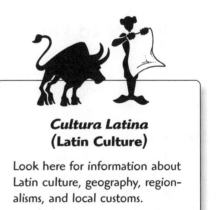

Cultura Latina (Latin Culture)

Look here for information about Latin culture, geography, regionalisms, and local customs.

Algo Nuevo (Something New)

This is a longer sidebar. Read these for lots of fascinating commentary about things that "I bet you didn't know."

Acknowledgments

I would like to thank the following individuals for their support and contributions during the writing of this book: Marga Vaquer (Spain), Lorena Martin (Panama), Norayda de Leon Jones (Cuba), Nataly Romero (Ecuador), Hermann Grunbaum (Colombia), Oscar Gioino (Argentina), Pedro Misner (Cuba), Tony Iglesias (Spain), and Jaime Lembach (Chile). I would also like to thank my agent, Andree Abecassis, whose hard work and guidance made this book possible. But most of all, my deepest gratitude goes to my wife, Kristin, for her input, ideas, help with the manuscript, and nearly unwavering patience during the writing process. *Muchísimas gracias* to everyone.

Special Thanks to the Technical Reviewer

The Complete Idiot's Guide to Intermediate Spanish was reviewed by an expert who double-checked the accuracy of what you'll learn here, to help us ensure that this book gives you everything you need to know about intermediate Spanish.

Trademarks

Part 1

So You Want to Learn Intermediate Spanish: ¡Qué Bueno!

¡Vámonos! *Let's begin the book with a review of the fundamentals. First we'll take a look at some statistics about the Spanish language, and then we'll move on to pronunciation, spelling, and accent marks. Now that you're at the intermediate level, I'll let you in on a few secrets about Spanish pronunciation and spelling that they probably didn't tell you when you were just starting out. I'll also suggest some creative ways for you to practice your* español *in addition to reading this* libro.

Chapter 1

Knowing Spanish: It's a Good Thing

In This Chapter

➤ Why learning Spanish is a good use of your *tiempo*

➤ Important statistics about Spanish and Spanish-speakers

➤ Are you ready for this book?

By now you probably don't need anyone to convince you that Spanish is important stuff. You have already invested valuable time studying the language, and you are about to take the next step by tackling an intermediate textbook. I congratulate you on your courage.

Why Spanish?

If you're still not completely convinced that it will be worthwhile to spend more of your valuable time studying *español*, I invite you to check out the following statistics:

➤ Spanish is one of the most important languages in the world. It is an official language of many international organizations, including the United Nations, the European Union, and the Organization of American States.

➤ More than 300 million people speak Spanish as their first language. Spanish is spoken in Spain; in North, Central, and South America; in parts of northwest Africa; in the Canary Islands; and in Equatorial Guinea. An old Spanish dialect is

Haz Clic Aquí

One of the best Web sites about Spanish and Latin culture in the United States is www. mundolatino.com. It's definitely worth a visit.

Cultura Latina

The Spanish–speaking world has produced great literature, film, and music. Both Spain and Latin America have been home to some of the world's finest painters, authors, musicians, actors, poets, and dancers.

Haz Clic Aquí

Check out www.puertorico.com for all the statistics on the lovely island nation of Puerto Rico. The site is mostly in English.

even spoken in a small Jewish community (Sephardim) in Istanbul, Turkey, and Spanish is still understood by some people in the Philippines.

➤ The United States is one of the largest Spanish-speaking countries in the world. Being able to speak Spanish is becoming a very important skill and can even increase your earning potential. The bilingual job market is expanding every year, and sometimes applicants are not being hired because they can't communicate in Spanish.

➤ Spanish-language radio, television, and advertising in the United States have combined to become a multibillion-dollar industry.

➤ The United States shares a 2,000-mile-long border with Mexico, the most populous Spanish-speaking country. Many Spanish-speaking communities are located along the border, as well as in cities such as New York, Miami, Chicago, Denver, Houston, Los Angeles, and Washington, D.C., among others. Spanish is even an official language of New Mexico (the Land of Enchantment).

➤ Hispanic voters counted for approximately 5 percent of the voter turnout in U.S. national elections in 1998. The political clout of Hispanic communities is increasing every year at all levels of government.

➤ The Commonwealth of Puerto Rico (population about 3 million) has a "Free Associated State" relationship with the United States. Puerto Ricans are U.S. citizens, but Spanish is the official language of the island. Puerto Ricans have the same rights as all U.S. citizens, but they do not vote in presidential elections (they do vote in the primaries) or pay federal income taxes while they live on the island. However, they may move to the U.S. mainland whenever they wish. Puerto Rico could someday become the 51st state.

➤ The possibilities for travel, personal development, and research in the Spanish-speaking world are practically endless. Whatever floats your boat—history, arts, music, archeology, architecture, philosophy, rain forests, wildlife, Native American cultures, international development, beaches, food … it's all there, somewhere in Latin America or Spain.

Are You Really Intermediate? Probably …

Do you find yourself saying things like "Yeah, yeah, I know this already" every time you browse through a Spanish textbook for beginners? If so, you have most likely progressed to the intermediate level.

But only you can decide whether you are an intermediate student. Learning a language is not a linear process, but rather a series of "three steps forward, two steps back" experiences. I would say, though, that if you feel relatively confident in the basics—even though you might find words or grammar that you have forgotten or never really understood—you are ready for *The Complete Idiot's Guide to Intermediate Spanish*.

This doesn't mean that you have mastered everything in basic Spanish. You always will need improvement or review in some areas. In fact, even advanced students have to go back and revisit the fundamentals now and then, just to see if they missed some minor detail along the way.

Before We Start …

In writing *The Complete Idiot's Guide to Intermediate Spanish*, I am forced to make certain assumptions about you and your level of Spanish proficiency at this point (yes, I know what they say about assuming things, but bear with me). Of course, because all readers will be at a different level, it will be impossible for me to tailor the material perfectly to everyone's individual needs. Nonetheless, I'm reasonably certain that I'll

Acuérdate

You'll get so much more out of your travels in Latin America and Spain if you can *conversar* with the locals. Whether you're in Argentina on business, in Madrid visiting the Prado, in the Yucatan assisting on an archeological dig, or in northeastern Peru exploring the rain forests, being able to communicate effectively in Spanish will help you at every turn.

Ten Cuidado

Take care when saying that something or someone is "Spanish." Technically, "Spanish" refers to Spain. If you say "I am talking to a Spanish person," that means that this person is from Spain. Just because you *speak* English doesn't mean that you *are* English. If you're not sure which country someone is from, say "Spanish-speaking" instead.

be on the right track if I assume that at least one of the following statements is true about you and your experiences with Spanish so far:

➤ You have read *The Complete Idiot's Guide to Learning Spanish on Your Own* or some other teach-yourself-Spanish book for beginners. You enjoyed what you read and are ready to continue where your beginning textbook left off.

➤ You have taken one or more introductory Spanish courses in high school or college and survived. Now you're ready to progress to a more advanced level.

➤ You have lived in a Spanish-speaking country at some point in your life and need to brush up on your skills. You know far too much already to consider yourself a beginner.

➤ You grew up in a bilingual home and want to build upon the Spanish you learned as a kid.

➤ You have picked up the basics over the years through contact with Spanish-speakers at your job or in your local community. Now it's time to fill in the missing pieces of your Spanish puzzle.

➤ You used to speak Spanish quite well—possibly even fluently—but over the years you've gotten a bit rusty and want to get back to where you once were with the language.

As I mentioned earlier, it isn't necessary for you to be an "expert" in beginning Spanish to use this book. In fact, your beginning Spanish may be quite rusty. That's okay. The only real requirement is that you feel ready to expand your *horizontes* (that's "horizons" in Spanish—get it?).

Algo Nuevo

Yes, you read right. The Spanish-speaking population of the United States is estimated at about 38 million (both legal and illegal immigrants) and could reach 50 million by the year 2005. This makes the United States one of the largest Spanish-speaking countries in the world. The number of Spanish-speakers in other English-speaking countries such as Canada, Australia, and the United Kingdom is also on the rise.

The Least You Need to Know

➤ There are many good reasons to learn Spanish—it can even help you professionally.

➤ Population-wise, the United States is one of the largest Spanish-speaking countries in the world.

➤ If you feel that you're an intermediate student, you probably are.

Chapter 2

A Closer Look

In This Chapter

➤ The similarities and differences between *español* and *inglés*

➤ Spanish from Spain—and elsewhere

➤ Regionalisms

➤ Making yourself understood on both sides of the Atlantic

➤ Culture: Is it important?

Now let's look at the Spanish language itself. This chapter begins by comparing and contrasting English and Spanish. You know that Spanish and English are very different—if they weren't, I'd be out of a job. But you may be surprised to learn that both languages also share some common ground.

After we examine the two languages, you'll see why all Spanish is not created equal, and learn what you can do to make sure that you'll be understood by everyone when you're *hablando español*.

Spanish vs. English

Sometimes it may seem as though Spanish and English are worlds apart. But believe it or not, the two languages actually have a few things in common:

➤ **Spanish and English are both Indo-European languages.** This means that many thousands of years ago, they both had a common linguistic ancestor.

Although much has obviously changed since then, you can at least take some comfort in knowing that Spanish and English are distant cousins.

➤ **Both Spanish and English use the same Roman alphabet.** Yes, I know that you already knew this. But you could have chosen to study Arabic, Chinese, Thai, or some other language that uses a vastly different writing system from the one you already know. So, count your blessings.

➤ **Spanish, being a Romance language, is made up mostly of words that started as Latin.** English also contains a huge number of Latin words. In fact, in almost every English sentence, you will find common words that were born in ancient Rome.

Of course, I must admit that the differences between Spanish and English greatly outweigh their similarities. The following section discusses how Spanish and English are not so similar:

➤ **Spanish pronunciation differs from English pronunciation.** Naturally, you will find yourself producing sounds in Spanish that you never make in English. But the good news is that Spanish is actually easier to pronounce than English (even though you might not think so at first). There are at least 11 distinct vowel sounds in standard English, whereas in Spanish there are only 6. Spelling rules in Spanish are logical and fixed, with virtually no exceptions. Once you know how to read and spell, you will always know how to pronounce a word. Wouldn't it be lovely if this were true in English as well?

➤ **Spanish nouns all have gender, while most English nouns do not.** In Spanish, all nouns are classified by gender. In English, unless we're talking about living things, nouns don't have a gender classification. But don't panic—although the concept of a gender for inanimate nouns may seem rather odd to you at first, it eventually will make perfect sense.

➤ **Spanish verbs change more than English verbs do.** Spanish expresses time and aspect ("do," "will do," "was going to do," "might do," "could do," "would do," "will have done," "did do, but my dog ate it") differently from English. While English tends to use other helping words before verbs such as *will, would, might,* and *could,* Spanish usually indicates these differences at the end of the verb with suffixes such as *–ó, –ía, –aba,* and *–ría.*

➤ **Verbs in Spanish don't have a "to" part at the beginning.** English verbs in the infinitive form need the word "to" at the beginning, as in "I want to go home." In Spanish, the "to" part of the verb is at the end of the word in the form of *–ar, –er,* and *–ir.*

➤ **In Spanish, you don't always have to use the words *I, he, she, we, they,* and so on, with the verb.** Unless you're sending a telegram, English sounds odd if you don't indicate who is doing what. We must say "*I* want to go" and "*They* like to play" and "*He'll* put out the cat tonight." If you leave out the *I, They,* and *He'll* parts ("want to go," "like to play," "will put out cat") you'll start sounding like Tarzan. But in Spanish, the verb by itself can indicate the person or thing that is doing the wanting or liking or putting by its ending, so the pronouns (*yo, tú, usted,* and so on) may often be omitted without sounding as though you were raised by wolves.

Acuérdate

Gender is not just some bizarre way of trying to see the universe in terms of masculine or feminine. This gender thing actually helps to hold Spanish sentences together. When dealing with inanimate nouns, don't think of them as "boys and girls," but rather as words with similar endings that belong to two different classes. You'll see later how gender will actually be very helpful to you.

➤ **Spanish words must "agree" with each other more often than English words.** Although Spanish-speakers themselves may vehemently disagree about many things, agreement within their language is mandatory. In English, we also have situations in which words must "agree." For example, according to the rules of standard English usage, it is grammatically incorrect to say "I wants" or "He know" or "We done" or "I is." In Spanish, though, the need for words to agree is much greater. Not only do the pronouns and verbs have to correspond, but the adjectives must also agree in gender and number with the things they describe. The word used for *it* must have the same gender as the thing it refers to. This isn't true in English because we don't classify our nouns by gender (except for living things, when we use *he* and *she*).

➤ **Word order in a Spanish sentence is usually different from that of an English sentence.** For example, in English we say, "I gave it to him," while in Spanish we say, "I to him it gave." Also, when something in Spanish is being described, we usually put the adjective after the noun rather than before it. Instead of "I see the blue car," we must say, "I see the car blue."

Ten Cuidado

Some people say that Castillian is the "real" or "pure" form of Spanish: "I don't speak Spanish," they say, "I speak Castillian," as if this should somehow impress us. Nonsense! There are only two ways to speak Spanish: You can speak it well, or you can speak it badly. Remember that not everyone in Spain speaks Castillian—some Spaniards speak Basque, Galician, or Catalán.

Ten Cuidado

Many people like to carry a pocket phrasebook while travelling. Although these books can indeed be useful, it's practically impossible to learn a language from a phrasebook alone. Although a good phrasebook would certainly make an excellent companion to this book, remember that most phrasebooks can't actually teach you the structure of the language.

Spanish: An International Language

Spanish, like English, is spoken by millions of people who live in many different places around the world. Just as folks in Mississippi speak differently from those in Manhattan—who in turn speak nothing like the good citizens of Manchester or Melbourne—it only stands to reason that the way Spanish is spoken varies greatly from place to place. Mexicans speak differently than Chileans. Spaniards don't sound at all like Guatemalans.

In fact, differences in pronunciation can exist even within the same country. People who live in the mountains speak differently from those living in the valleys or along the coast. The accents of some regions are so strong that people can immediately identify someone as being from a particular area from the very first word he or she utters.

Two principal varieties of Spanish exist: the Spanish of Spain (known as "Peninsular Spanish," or "Castillian Spanish") and the Spanish spoken in that country's former colonies.

With respect to Spanish pronunciation, we can make the following generalizations:

➤ **Castillian**—The chief distinguishing feature of Peninsular Spanish is the way the letters *c* and *z* are pronounced. Most people in Spain pronounce the letter *c* (when written before the letters *e* and *i*) and the letter *z* much like the *th* in our words *fifth* and *think*. Thus, *zapato* sounds like "*th*ah pah toh," and *ciudad* sounds like "*th*ee oo dahd." Another feature of the Spanish from Spain is the way in which most Spaniards pronounce the letter *s*. The *s* in Spain has a distinctive whistle to it, almost like the *sh* sound in *trash*. This sound is not found natively in Latin American Spanish.

➤ **Latin American Spanish**—The Spanish spoken in Latin America is so varied that one can't possibly say that there is one "Latin American" Spanish that includes all speakers. What we might call "New World Spanish" can really be identified only by contrasting it with Peninsular Spanish: The *c* and *z* are not pronounced as "th," and the *s* is not buzzy as it can be in Spain. I will include more information about variations in pronunciation in the following chapter.

Regionalisms

Pronunciation is not the only thing that varies from place to place. Quite often, certain words and phrases that are used in one country may be entirely unknown elsewhere (although television and film have changed this somewhat). Some words are perfectly acceptable in one country but have an entirely different meaning (or no meaning at all) in another. So, while a particular word may have worked just fine in Spain, it could provoke blank stares in Puerto Rico, unbridled laughter in Argentina, and righteous indignation in Mexico. Just think of all the different words and phrases used in Britain that are practically unknown in the United States.

Such issues are known as *regionalisms*. As a beginning student, you didn't have to be too concerned about this issue. However, now that you've progressed to the intermediate level, you should become more aware of regionalisms. I will be pointing out some of the more important regional issues throughout the book.

Cultura Latina

Not all Spaniards pronounce *c* and *z* like our *th*. Many people in southern Spain pronounce these letters the same way that Latin Americans do: *s*, as in *street* and *city*. Also, some Spaniards don't make the whistle-like *s*, either; it's a regional thing.

Acuérdate

The second person plural *vosotros* (y'all) form of address is used only in Spain. Except for religious ceremonies and old literature, you won't hear many Latin Americans saying *vosotros*. Depending on the materials you used when you were studying Spanish as a beginner, you might have skipped this form. You can continue to skip it, unless you plan to spend a lot of time in Spain.

What This Means to You

So, should you try to speak like a Spaniard or a Mexican? A Colombian or a Chilean? Well, that's entirely up to you. The way I see it, you basically have two choices. If you know that you'll be staying in a particular country for an extended period of time, then you might wish to fully adopt the Spanish pronunciation and usage of that country. When you return home, you will most likely feel a certain kinship with the people from that nation, and you probably will want to reflect that in the way you speak your Spanish. If you're in Spain, please learn Castillian. If you're in Mexico, learn Spanish the Mexican way. In Argentina? Learn to speak it like the natives do. Later, other Spanish-speakers will detect your regional accent, and you'll have a great way to break the ice at parties.

On the other hand, if you're one of those free-spirited individuals who hates being associated with one country in particular, then you probably would do best by adopting a Spanish that travels well and is place-neutral. I would *not* recommend that you adopt a Castillian accent if you plan to travel a lot through Latin America. A "standard" Latin American Spanish will be far more useful to you in the long run, and people in Spain will have no trouble understanding you.

Algo Nuevo

Once you feel comfortable with your Spanish, you can always change the way you speak it. In my own case, my Spanish tends to change depending on the situation. As a professional interpreter, I talk to Spanish-speaking people from just about everywhere. My solution? I speak Mexican Spanish with Mexicans, Caribbean Spanish with Puerto Ricans and Cubans, and Argentine Spanish with *Argentinos*. However, it would be equally valid for me to choose one way of speaking and stick to it all the time, no matter who my audience is. This is entirely a personal choice.

Being Understood Everywhere

The key to communicating effectively in Spanish is simple. No matter where you are—Mexico, Spain, South America, or even Equatorial Guinea—the rules are the same. Make sure that you always speak at a reasonable pace and enunciate your words clearly. Don't worry if you have a strong accent. People *will* understand you and will appreciate your efforts to speak their language.

What About Culture?

Edward Sapir, a noted linguist, wrote in 1928: "People who speak different languages live in different worlds, not the same world with different labels." He believed that language and culture were inseparable. More recently, other scholars have maintained that a language can be studied and understood without the need to take any cultural considerations into account. The truth, I am sure, lies somewhere between these two theories.

Unfortunately, speaking universally about "Spanish culture" is practically impossible; Spanish is spoken by many people who come from extremely diverse social, racial, and economic backgrounds. A *campesino* in Mexico has very little in common with the president of Argentina or a businessman from Spain—and yet they all speak essentially the same language.

Ten Cuidado

One example of a regionalism is the verb *coger.* Generally, it means "to get" and is quite common in Spain, the Caribbean, Colombia, and a few other areas: *Sonó el teléfono y María lo cogió* ("The telephone rang and Maria got it"). However, in much of Latin America, especially the Southern Cone, this seemingly innocuous little verb refers to the sex act and is quite vulgar. Avoid *coger* and use *agarrar* instead in most of Latin America.

Algo Nuevo

When I started studying Spanish in junior high school, our exposure to the language and culture of Spain and Latin America was limited to an ancient textbook, black-and-white filmstrips, and a few tattered Mexican *sombreros* dangling on the wall. Boring! Today, things are much different. The student of Spanish has access to so many resources that learning the language doesn't have to be as painfully dull as it used to be. Welcome to the twenty-first century.

Haz Clic Aquí

While you will find a lot of useful and interesting information about Latin culture in this book, you can research cultural issues in much greater depth at your local library and on the Internet. www.latino.com is a good place to start.

While it is true that understanding the people who speak a language will be much easier if you are familiar with their culture, the nuts and bolts of the language tend to remain consistent independent of cultural issues. Spanish-speakers might not always share a unified culture, but their language is basically consistent, in spite of the occasional differences in the way it is spoken from country to country.

The Least You Need to Know

➤ Linguistically speaking, Spanish and English actually share some common ground.

➤ Certain key structures in the two languages are, however, very different.

➤ Not everyone speaks the same Spanish; pronunciation and word choice can vary considerably.

➤ Culture is always a factor, but it can be considered as a separate issue from the basic nuts and bolts of the language.

Chapter 3

ABCs, etc.

In This Chapter

➤ An in-depth look at the sounds of Spanish

➤ What they never told you about Spanish pronunciation

➤ Capitalization

➤ Punctuation

Most introductory books and courses tend to simplify the sounds of Spanish in order to get you speaking as fast as possible. This is as it should be, because there is no need to overburden you with too many details at the beginning. But now that you've moved beyond the basics, it's time to talk about the sounds of Spanish in greater detail.

If you're at all uneasy about pronouncing your Spanish, you've come to the right place. You'll do just fine after you read this chapter.

The Sounds of Spanish

Spanish spelling is very logical; the way a word is written always indicates its pronunciation. Once you're comfortable with the sounds of the letters, you'll know how a word is pronounced. This certainly can't be said of English, where *daughter* rhymes with *water*, and *laughter* sounds like *after*.

Acuérdate

Knowing the names of the letters in Spanish can be very useful, especially if you have to spell something over the telephone such as your name or street address. If you need to review the names of the letters, consult Appendix A, "Basic Grammar Resource."

Ten Cuidado

Don't stress too much about pronouncing Spanish diphthongs (two vowels pronounced together as one syllable in words such as "boil"). Actually, diphthongs (and even triphthongs, three vowels together) are pretty easy. Just try to pronounce each vowel quickly but with its full value. The diphthongs will practically pronounce themselves. Don't make this harder than it needs to be. More about diphthongs in Chapter 4, "Accéntuating the Pósitive."

Los Vocales (Vowels)

Let's begin by clarifying the sounds of the Spanish vowels.

a

The letter *a* is always pronounced like its name, "ah," and never like the *a* in words such as "wait," "Amy," "able," "ant," "at," and "apple." The sound is actually closer to the *o* in "hot," as pronounced in Standard American English. Thus, the Spanish word *amar* (to love) sounds like "ah mahr," and "blah blah blah" is written as *bla bla bla* in Spanish and sounds exactly the same.

e

The letter *e* is generally pronounced like its name, "ay" (sounds like "day" and "way"): *le* ("lay"), *me* ("may"), *se* ("say"). However, *e* is pronounced like the *e* in "Edward" when it begins a word. Thus, *esto* is not "ay stoh," but "eh stoh"; *entonces* is not "ayn tohn sayss," but "ehn tohn sayss." It will also take this sound in the middle of a word if the word has more than two syllables: *excelente* = "ehk seh lehn tay." Only the last *e* sounds like "ay." You may find that the actual sound in such cases is somewhere between "ay" and "eh." When Spanish wants to make absolutely sure that the "ay" sound is made, the diphthong *ei* is written.

i

The Spanish *i* always sounds like the "ee" sound in "sleep" and "cheap," never as in "pin" or "pine."

o

The *o* always is long, as in "stone," never like "pop" or "too."

u

The *u* sounds like the "oo" sound in "to," "too," and "two." It's never short, as in "cut" or "put."

Los Consonantes (Consonants)

Now for the consonants. The following group of letters make the exact same sounds in Spanish as they do in English. No need to worry about these—just follow your instincts:

➤ f, k, l, m, n, p, t, "ch"

Now take a look at the following letters. While similar to English in many ways, a few words of explanation are needed for accuracy.

b and v

The sound of the Spanish *b* and *v* is distinctive. It is not the same sound as the English *b*, as in "boy," which sounds a bit like our *p* to Spanish-speakers. The correct sound lies somewhere between the English *b, v, w,* and *m*: for instance, *burro* = "vwooroh." If this is too confusing for you, try pronouncing both *b* and *v* like the English *v* in "Victoria" and "velvet"(as some Chileans do) until your ear becomes more attuned to the actual sound.

c

As in English, this letter can sound like *k*, as in *car*, and *s*, as in *city*. When the letter is written before *e* or *i*, it is pronounced like *s*. Thus, in Latin America, *ciudad* is "see oo dahd," and *césped* (lawn) is "say spehd." When *c* is written before *a, o,* or *u*, it is hard, like *k* as in *cantar* and *coco*.

As I mentioned in the last chapter, in Spain most people (but not all) pronounce *c* like the "th" in "think" and "fifth" when written before *e* and *i*. So, in Europe, *ciudad* is "thee oo dad." One advantage to pronouncing the *c* (and *z*) this way is that some spelling errors can be avoided. You may have to ask "Is that spelled with an *s*, a *z*, or a *c*?" In Latin America the verbs *casar* ("to marry") and *cazar* ("to hunt") sound exactly the same.

Cultura Latina

A common spelling error made by some Spanish-speakers is to confuse the letters *b* and *v*: "*se bende*" = *se vende*; "*vurro*" = *burro*. Technically, there is a slight difference in pronunciation between *b* and *v*, but it's only observed in some countries. So you see, even native Spanish-speakers sometimes are confused by their language.

Ten Cuidado

Unless you're going to be in Spain for a while, I suggest that you not adopt a Castillian pronunciation. Naturally, it is entirely up to you, but some people in Latin America may have difficulty understanding your Castillian, especially those living in rural areas. Because of the diversity in Spain, few people there will have difficulty understanding a Latin American accent.

Acuérdate

When the letter *g* is followed by the letter *e* or *i*, it makes the "h" sound, as in *gente*. When the letter *g* makes its hard *gato* ("gah toh") sound before *e* or *i*, Spanish places a silent *u* between the two letters: *gue* = "gay," *gui* = "ghee." You will pronounce the *u*, however, in the combinations *gua* and *guo* ("gwah," "gwoh"). But if the *u* has dots on it, it will also be pronounced as in *güero* ("gweh roh").

Acuérdate

You probably already know whether you are able to make the trilled "rrrr" sound. Try as they might, some people just can't make this sound. If this sounds like you, don't worry. Just pronounce the *r* and *rr* the same as you normally do in English, but with as much emphasis as you can. No, you may never sound like a native, but people *will* understand you.

d

The Spanish *d* sounds almost the same as in English, but it's softer and closer to the "th" in "that" and "these," as in *dado* ("thah thoh"). The hard English *d* in words such as "dandy" and "dime" sounds like *t* to Spanish-speakers. Try to soften your *d* in Spanish.

g

Like the letter *c*, *g* has two sounds. Before *a*, *o*, and *u*, it is hard, as in "gone," "gate," and "gun." But before *i* and *e* (and *y*), it is soft and sounds like a raspy *h* from the back of your throat. So, *gente* ("people") sounds like "hehn tay," but *gato* sounds like "gah toh." The letter *g* never makes the English *j* sound, as in "gentleman" or "Ginger Rodgers."

q

Spanish could have lived without this letter. It sounds exactly the same as the *k* in "kite" and is always followed by *u* (same as English). The letter *q* is not pronounced like "kw," as in "quick" and "quack." The word *queso* (cheese) is pronounced "kay soh," never "kway soh." Spanish uses the letters *qu* to indicate a hard *k* sound before the vowels *i* and *e*—that's its main job. The letter *q* is not written before other vowels. The letter *c* is used for that: *cuidado* = "kwee dah doh."

r

The Spanish *r* is trilled (rolled), as in Scotland—but not too much when the letter is by itself. Just a wee bit. At the beginning of a word, you can flutter your tongue more if you like, but be careful not to overdo it. Save that for the next sound.

rr

See the previous section (now you may overdo it).

s

In most of the Spanish-speaking world, the letter *s* sounds exactly as it does in English. In Spain, however, it has a bit of a whistle to it. If you're in Spain, try to imitate the locals. Otherwise, stick to the same old *s* sound that you use now (as in "silver" and "stress"), and you'll be fine. Spaniards will have no problem understanding you either way.

w

Used only in foreign words, the *w* usually maintains the same pronunciation as the original word. Thus, "Washington" and "William" have the same pronunciation in Spanish as they do in English. But "Wagner" (Richard) and "Wilhelm" (Schmidt) maintain the German *v* sound.

x

Knowing how to pronounce the *x* can be tricky because its sound can vary (as it can in English: "xylophone"). Basically, *x* usually sounds like the "ks" sound that we have in "excellent" and "axe." It almost never sounds like the *z* sound in "examine."

Until the letter *j* was invented, Spanish used *x* to represent the *h* sound. That's why we see *México* ("Meh hee koh") instead of *Méjico*. However, in Spain, you see the word spelled *Méjico*, which irritates the Mexicans to no end. This is also why the name *Javier* can sometimes be seen written as *Xavier*.

When the Spanish arrived in the New World, *x* was used to represent certain indigenous sounds (with varying degrees of success). For example, *x* sounds like *s* in *Xochimilco* ("Soh chee meel koh"), the water gardens in Mexico City. In Mayan regions, *x* sounds like our *sh* in "shell": *Uxmal* ("oosh mahl"). Elsewhere, ask the locals.

y

Pronounce this like the *y* you grew up with: "yes," "yellow." Be aware, however, that its pronunciation varies within the Spanish-speaking world. In Argentina and Uruguay especially, the letter *y* sounds like the "zh" sound in "trea*s*ure."

The letter *y* may also act as a vowel, as in *gymnasio*, where it sounds the same as its Latin cousin *i*. It also makes this sound when standing alone, at the end of a word, or in certain older spellings of words (mostly names)

Ten Cuidado

Some people don't practice their Spanish because they are worried that their pronunciation isn't perfect. But this is a bad idea. Don't be afraid if you simply cannot produce some Spanish sounds. Just do the best you can, and people will understand you.

Acuérdate

The combinations of letters *ll* and *ch* were once considered to be one letter, but now they are dealt with as two separate letters that make one sound. As a consequence, older dictionaries have a *ch* and an *ll* section. When breaking up a word into syllables (more on that in the next chapter), however, the *ch* and *ll* still stay together: *ma cho* and *va lle*.

Acuérdate

Both Latin and Greek gave Spanish a letter called *ee*. To differentiate between them, *y* was called the "Greek *I*". It's important to distinguish between *y* and *i*. If you just say *ee*, people will assume that you mean *i*, but some names can be spelled with either letter, so you should always say *Y griega* "ee gree ay gah" when you mean *y*.

when it comes at the beginning of a word and is followed by a consonant: *Ysleta* ("ees leh tah"), *Ybarra* ("ee bah rah").

z

The Spanish *z* sounds the same as *s*: *zapato* = "sah pah toh." Try not to pronounce it like the *z* in "zebra." In Spain, it sounds like the "th" in *these*. The letter *z* is rarely written before *i* and *e*; the letter *c* is used for that.

Letters That Don't Play Fair ...

Finally, here are the consonants that behave very differently from their English cousins:

➤ *h*—This letter is never, never, never pronounced. No sound. Zip, zilch, *nada*. If you really must make an *h* sound, please see *j*, *g*, or even *x*.

➤ *j*—This is pronounced like a raspy "hchhhh" (same as the soft *g*). Think "Loch" or even *"Achtung,"* in German.

Algo Nuevo

The raspy "hchhhh" sound of *j* is mainly heard in Spain. If you find it difficult to make this sound, you may pronounce both the *j* and the soft *g* just like the English *h* in "Hillary" and "help," and people will understand you. Many people in Central America and the Caribbean say it that way naturally, so you can, too. The letter *j* spends most of its time written before *a*, *o*, and *u*, while *g* (when sounding like an *h*) is found before *e* and *i*.

➤ *ll*—This combination is usually pronounced like the letter *y* in English: *llama* ("yah mah"). In some regions (Spain, Colombia, Paraguay, Bolivia, and among purists), this letter is pronounced like the *l* + *y* sound in "million" and "Will

you." You can pronounce it this way if you
like, but it's not necessary. In Argentina and
Uruguay especially, this letter sounds like the
"zh" sound in "trea*s*ure."

➤ *ñ*—Don't let this one throw you off. It's just
the Spanish way of writing the *n* + *y* together
in one letter, as in "onion," "canyon," and
"dominion." Remember *el Niño*.

Haz Clic Aquí

Check out www.eden.com/
~tomzap/sp_key.html for an online guide to pronouncing your
Spanish.

What They Didn't Tell You About Spanish Pronunciation When You Were a Beginner

Just as English is not always spoken perfectly, Spanish-speakers don't always follow
the pronunciation rules *al pie de la letra* ("to the letter"—there's a pun in there somewhere). In fact, the textbook pronunciation of Spanish can be quite different from the
way many people really pronounce the language. Here are some tips to help you understand people when they don't apply the rules:

La Sinalefa

When the last vowel of a word is followed by a word that begins with a vowel, a very
interesting phenomenon called *sinalefa* may occur. Take, for example, the following
sentence:

> *La casa de Eduardo Ortíz se va a vender a Ana Álvarez.*

> Eduardo Ortíz's house will be sold to Ana Álvarez.

In rapid speech, the *e*'s between *de* and *Eduardo,* the *o*'s between *Eduardo* and *Ortíz,*
and the *a*'s between *va* and *a, a* and *Ana,* and *Ana* and *Álvarez,* may be sinalefized
into one sound instead of two distinct sounds: *La casa deduardotriz se va vender anal-
varez.*

So, if someone in a store asks you "*¿Quiere destos?*" that person is not asking you if
you want any *destos,* but rather *de estos* (of these). It may take some time before your
ear gets used to separating these "welded" vowels.

The Swallowed s

In many regions of Latin America, as well as in southern Spain, people tend to drop
or "swallow" the letter *s,* especially at the end of words. This phenomenon is most

common in the Caribbean, Central America, coastal Ecuador, the Southern Cone (Argentina, Uruguay, and Chile), and in other coastal areas throughout the New World. In some speakers, a slight *h* sound can be detected where the *s* is supposed to be. This *h* sound can even find itself attached to the beginning of the next word.

Following are some examples of things that you might hear from a Spanish-speaker who comes from an area where the *s*'s are dropped.

Pronouncing the *s*

What They Say	What They Mean
uno, doh, treh	*uno, dos, tres*
tu tieneh seih zapatoh	*tú tienes seis zapatos*
loh tre hamigoh	*los tres amigos*
¿Cuál ehtu nombre?	*¿Cual es tu nombre?*
nohotroh habemoh	*nosotros sabemos*

You need to be aware of this "dropped *s*" phenomenon. Otherwise, you'll start seriously doubting your abilities to understand Spanish. Don't worry, it isn't you.

Cultura Latina

If your local broadcaster or cable TV company offers *Univisión*, try to watch *El Show de Cristina*. Her show is one of the most popular programs among Spanish-speakers in the United States (and elsewhere). You'll hear Cristina swallowing her *s*'s left and right. Sometimes it seems like the letter *s* never quite made it to Miami.

Dropped Initial *v, m, and s in Rural Mexico*

Some Mexicans, especially those who live in rural areas, may drop an initial *v, m,* or *s* from certain words. This isn't a major issue, but it can throw you off if you're not aware of it. Here are some of the most common examples:

➤ *"ámonos" = vámonos*

➤ *"irá" = mira*

➤ *"heñora" = señora*

➤ *"í" = sí*

ue → u

In rapid speech, some Spanish-speakers may not fully pronounce the diphthong *ue* in short words. This is not a major issue, but if you've never been exposed to it, you might waste a lot of time looking up words in your dictionary that don't exist. Take a look at the following sentences:

➤ **Mi hermano fu a la tienda a comprar pan:**
My brother went to the store to buy bread.
(The *fu* is really *fue*.)

➤ **Pos, yo no podo ir hasta mañana.** Well, I
can't go until tomorrow. (The *pos* is really
pues, and the *podo* is really *puedo*.)

Para → Pa'

As you know, the word *para* means "for." Many
Spanish-speakers often shorten *para* to *pa'*. Thus,
you may hear phrases such as *Esto es pa' ti,* for *Esto
es para ti.*

This *pa'* phenomenon gets even more interesting
because the *a* can now form a *sinalefa* with other
a's that begin the following words:

➤ *pal = para el (Es pal niño)*

➤ *pallá = para allá (Vamos pa'llá)*

➤ *patrás = para atrás* (means "back" as in
"send it back")

➤ *pa'ella = para ella* (not the Spanish dish)

Cultura Latina

In Puerto Rico, final *r*'s are often
pronounced as *l*'s. So you'll hear
"*hablal*" instead of *hablar*. Also,
at the beginning or in the middle of a word, the *rrr* sound may
be sounded in the back of the
throat. Therefore, some *puertorriqueños* pronounce words like
arroz as "*aggggggoz*."

Está → 'ta

You may hear *está* shortened to simply *'ta*, especially in the Caribbean and in
Uruguay:

➤ *Ta' bien* (should be *está*)

➤ *Los niños 'tan jugando* (should be *están*)

Lost d and –ado → ao

Some speakers swallow the *d* at the end of words or between final vowels especially in
rapid speech. So, you may hear "*usté*" for *usted,* and "*paré*" for *pared* (wall). You may
also hear the *d* drop out of the ending *–ado: ¿Ha hablao con Juan?* means *¿Ha hablado
con Juan?; To' ta' bien = Todo está bien.*

25

Punctuation

Generally, the punctuation marks in Spanish are the same as in English, but there *are* some differences. Let's take a quick look at the basics:

➤ Spanish places a ¿ before a question: *¿Muerde su perro?* ("Does your dog bite?")

➤ Commas can be used very much the same way that they can in English: *No, no muerde mi perro.* ("No, my dog does not bite.")

➤ In Spanish, the ¿ is rather handy, letting you know before you speak that what follows is a question. It can be placed before the interrogative part of a sentence, without having to start a new sentence: *Si no le importa, ¿puedo cariciar su perro?* ("If you don't mind, may I pet your dog?")

➤ The upside-down ¡ is placed before an interjection: *¡Ay! ¡Pensaba que no mordía su perro!* ("Ouch! I thought you said your dog didn't bite!")

➤ Both Spanish and English use the same period at the end of a statement. Spanish sometimes uses dashes to indicate dialogue (you'll see those later). However, when a word at the end of a sentence is enclosed by quotation marks, the period must be written outside of the quotation marks: *"Ése no es mi perro".* ("That's not my dog.")

Algo Nuevo

Even though you might not sound like a native speaker just yet, at this point you should be reasonably familiar with the sounds made by the Spanish alphabet. So, you won't need any more of those phonetic spellings like "ah bloh ehs pahn yohl." From now on, you'll be doing it *solo*. Review the information in this chapter as often as you need to.

Capitalization

Capitalization in Spanish is much less confusing than it is in English (as are most things). If a word starts a sentence or is the proper name of a person or place, it is capitalized. But months, days of the week, nationalities, languages, and many other nouns that we capitalize in English must begin with a lowercase letter in Spanish. Even professional titles start with a lowercase letter, unless they are written with the name of the person. So, *el Presidente Jorge Washington* is capitalized, but when there is no last name, it is not: *El presidente durmió aquí.* When in doubt, if the word isn't a proper name, don't capitalize it unless it is at the beginning of a sentence. You'll be right most of the time.

The Least You Need to Know

➤ The spelling of a Spanish word always indicates its pronunciation.

➤ Spanish-speakers don't always pronounce everything perfectly.

➤ Punctuation in Spanish is similar to English, except for ¿ and ¡.

➤ Far fewer words are capitalized in Spanish than in English.

Chapter 4

Ō-lah!

Accéntuating the Pósitive

In This Chapter

➤ The secrets of those darn áccent márks, revealed at last

➤ The Spanish syllable

➤ What happens when the rules are broken

➤ *Tildes* to distinguish similar words

Even the most advanced students of Spanish can have trouble understanding how to use those accent marks (from now on, called *tildes*). Even if you know what to do when you read one, many students are rarely sure when to write one, when not to write one, and why the silly thing needs to be written in the first place. Well, I'm gonna tell you so that you don't have to stress about them anymore (pun intended).

Truth be told, these little *tildes* (á, é, í, ó, ú, and ü) actually make sense if you know the rules. The problem is that many textbooks and Spanish teachers have traditionally been unable to adequately explain the logic behind why and when these marks are needed. I promise that I am about to establish a new tradition ....

Esteban's "No Stress" Method to Spanish Accentuation

I am now going to outline the rules of Spanish stress and accentuation. Skip this part at your own peril! I know that this stuff is pretty dry, but trust me—it'll be worth the effort.

What Is Accentuation?

Accentuation simply refers to the part of a word that's the loudest. We say that the stress or accent falls on this or that syllable. We do it in English all the time. Often, stress in English falls on the first syllable of a word:

➤ TELephone

➤ CANdle

➤ BAby

➤ CATegory

➤ ADequate

➤ COMfortable

➤ ELephant

➤ APple

Sometimes the stress falls on an internal syllable:

➤ comPUter

➤ reUNion

➤ hippoPOTamus

➤ inSTINCtive

➤ anthroPOLogy

Stress in English doesn't often fall on the last syllable, but it does happen:

➤ enDOW

➤ reMAIN

➤ reBOOT

➤ reVIEW

➤ acQUIRE

Okay, so far, so good. Now for some rules about stress in Spanish.

Acuérdate

The *tilde* in Spanish always goes the same way: *é*. That other accent mark that the French use, *è*, is never seen (except in French, of course).

Haz Clic Aquí

A great place to practice your Spanish syllables and pronunciation in general is at http://geocities.com/Athens/Ithaca/4224/sounds.html. The site is even better if your computer has *bocinas* (speakers).

The Spanish Syllable

First, let's define what constitutes a syllable in Spanish. A Spanish syllable is formed by the combination of a consonant (or consonant cluster) and a vowel (or diphthong). Here are a few examples of simple consonant + vowel Spanish syllables (I'll discuss diphthongs in a minute):

➤ ba

➤ pi

➤ chu

➤ que

➤ mo

➤ ño

➤ ra

➤ ru

➤ le

➤ te

➤ mi

Acuérdate

You know that Spanish and English share many cognates, or *amigos*. One thing to remember is that Spanish words rarely need a double consonant. Where you would see *nn, tt, ss, mm,* and other such combinations in English, you will almost always see only one of these letters in the Spanish word: communica-tion = *comunicación;* commit-tee = *comité.*

Consonant pairs (a.k.a. "clusters") such as *pr, pl, br, bl, fr, fl, tr, dr, cr, cl, gr,* and *gl* stick together and begin a single syllable:

➤ *primo = pri mo*

➤ *broma = bro ma*

➤ *clavo = cla vo*

➤ *gripe = gri pe*

➤ *fruta = fru ta*

➤ *extremo = ex tre mo*

➤ *tri go = tri go*

➤ *progreso = pro gre so*

But if the vowel or diphthong is followed by two consonants other than the clusters just mentioned, the first consonant will stick with the first syllable, and the second will latch on to the second:

➤ *pasta = pas ta*

➤ *diente = dien te*

➤ *presto = pres to*

➤ *glenda = glen da*

➤ *triste = tris te*

➤ *trampa = tram pa*

➤ *estrógeno = es tro ge no* (*s* and *t* separate; *tr* together)

If a vowel or vowel sound begins a word, it is usually considered a syllable by itself if followed by a single consonant, a cluster, or a consonant sound such as *ch* or *ll:*

➤ *amigo = a mi go*

➤ *achicar = a chi car*

➤ *allende = a llen de*

➤ *hugo = hu go* (watch that silent *h*)

➤ *hico = hi co*

➤ *atrever = a tre ver*

➤ *jugo = ju go*

➤ *ocampo = o cam po*

In one-syllable words, the syllable may end in a consonant:

➤ *dan*

➤ *sin*

➤ *mis*

➤ *pez*

➤ *mil*

➤ *sol*

➤ *pum*

➤ *tras*

Spanish Diphthongs

A diphthong consists of two vowels together, as in "soil." The following diphthongs in Spanish count as one syllable (unless you see a *tilde* written over one of them … more on those later): *ia, ai, ei, ue, ie, io, oi, iu, ua,* and *au.* All of these are one-syllable diphthong combinations.

This means that *pue, cie, fei, pia, troi,* and so on, count as one syllable, not two. In other words, with respect to accentuation, most diphthongs are treated as if they were a single vowel, not two distinct vowels. (Yes, I'll elaborate on the diphthongs that do not follow this rule momentarily.)

➤ *puente = puen te*

➤ *cielo = cie lo*

➤ *afeitar = a fei tar*

➤ *austral = aus tral*

➤ *farmacia = far ma cia*

➤ *coima = coi ma*

➤ *ausente = au sen te*

➤ *guano = gua no*

Great. Now, hold on to your *sombrero* ....

Doing What Comes Naturally

In Spanish, when the stress in a word is falling where it is supposed to, there is no need to write a *tilde*. It's only when the rules are broken that *tildes* need to be written. So, let's start with the rules.

In order for you to truly understand how this all works, you *must* come to believe the following rules with all your heart and soul.

Esteban's Rule No. 1

The stress in *every* Spanish word that ends in the following letters falls on the *penultimate* (that is to say, the second-to-last) syllable:

1. A vowel (or one of the one-syllable diphthongs listed previously)

2. The letters *n* or *s*

This is an important rule. It *does not* matter what kind of word it is, what form of a word it is, or how many syllables the word has. If the word has 10 syllables, this rule applies. If the word has two syllables, this rule still applies because the first syllable of a two-syllable word is *still* the second to the last syllable.

Acuérdate

Occasionally you will see dots written over *u*, as in *ü*. These dots allow the *u* to be pronounced after the letter *g* before *i* or *e* as in *bilingüe* ("bee ling gway") and *pingüino* ("peen gwee noh"). Otherwise, the *u* would be silent and these words would be "bee ling gay" and "peen gee noh."

Algo Nuevo

Notice that *n* and *s* are very special. They are the only two consonants that will never change the expected placement of the stress in a Spanish word. It is no accident that these two letters are also very common when conjugating verbs or when making nouns plural. If you need to add an *n* or *s* to the end of a word for grammatical reasons, it will not change the stress of that word.

In the following examples, the stress must always fall on the second-to-last syllable. Because the rules are being followed in these examples, you won't see any *tildes:*

➤ SApo

➤ CArro

➤ eSTAba

➤ eSTAban (the *–n* doesn't change anything)

➤ eSTEban

➤ eleFANte

➤ MUcho

➤ comPRENdo

➤ yo HAblo

➤ tú HAblas (the *–s* at the end makes no difference)

➤ ellos HAblan (the *–n* doesn't change anything)

➤ congreSISta

➤ presiDENte

➤ presiDENtes (the *–s* at the end makes no difference)

➤ mexiCAno

➤ mexiCAnos (the *–s* at the end makes no difference)

➤ intereSANtes (the *–s* at the end makes no difference)

Acuérdate

When adding an object pronoun or reflexive to an infinitive, there will be no need to write a *tilde* because no accentuation rules are broken: *hablarme, sentirla, quererse,* and so on. The stress falls on the penultimate syllable. However, you will need to write a *tilde* when two pronouns are added, as in *decírselo.* More on this later.

This takes care of words ending in a vowel, in a one-syllable diphthong, in *n*, or in *s*. But wait, there's more ….

Esteban's Rule No. 2

If a word ends in a consonant other than *–n* or *–s*, the stress *always* falls on the last syllable.

In the following list, no *tildes* are written because everything is happening just as it should:

➤ hablAR

➤ beBER

➤ conduCIR

➤ entretenER

➤ comuniDAD

➤ ciuDAD

➤ relOJ

➤ manTEL

➤ ParaGUAY

➤ riGOR

➤ fugAZ

➤ manzanAL

Very good. Now, keep holding on to your *sombrero* because here's where you need to stretch your brain a little ....

Exceptions to Esteban's Rules

Every time the pronunciation of a particular word does not follow Rules No. 1 or No. 2, a *tilde* will be required to show that the rules have been broken.

To illustrate the previous point, read on:

Ten Cuidado

If a *tilde* appears on the last syllable of a noun ending in a consonant (such as *–ón*), it will disappear when you add a plural *–es* ending. The syllable with the *tilde* has just become the penultimate (second to last) and thus no longer requires a special mark: *balcón → balcones*. The *–ón* now gets stressed automatically.

➤ Let's say that you know the Spanish word for "number" is *numero*. According to the rules of Spanish stress, this word ends in a vowel, so it should be pronounced "noo MEH roh," with the stress falling on the penultimate (second-to-last) syllable. However, let's say that you also know that the correct pronunciation for this word is "NOO meh roh," with the stress on a syllable other than the one on which it is supposed to fall. So, to indicate that the rules have been broken, a *tilde* must be written over the *u*. Thus, the word is written as *número*.

➤ The name of the country you're writing is *Peru*. If you check the rules, it ends in a vowel. So, this word, as it stands, would be "PEH roo" because the stress is obligated to fall on the second-to-last syllable (which, in *Peru's* case, also happens to be the first of the word). But you know that this country's name is really "peh ROO," and so the *tilde* must be written on the *u: Perú*.

➤ A person who studies human activities is called an anthropologist. This word in Spanish is *antropologo*. If we follow the rules, this word, which ends in a vowel, should be pronounced "ahn troh pohl OH goh" with the stress falling on the penultimate syllable. But that isn't how this word is pronounced. Our cherished rules have been broken. So, a *tilde* must be written to indicate this fact: *antropólogo*.

➤ The surname *Calderon* ends in an *n*. The letters *n* and *s* at the end of a word still require the stress to fall on the penultimate syllable: "Kahl DEH ron." But we know that this person's name is pronounced "Kahl deh ROHN," with the stress on the last syllable. So, we need to put an accent mark on the final *o: Calderón*.

Haz Clic Aquí

Another good Web site for learning about Spanish pronunciation and spelling rules is www2. msstate.edu/~krreddy/spanish/language/pronunciation.html. If you do a search for "Spanish orthography," you'll find even more great resources.

Cultura Latina

Even native speakers mess up a *tilde* now and then. Some e-mail programs don't send *tildes* very well, so many Spanish speakers leave them out on purpose when sending e-mails. I have done my best to make sure that the *tildes* in this book are correct, but even here you may find one missing or misplaced somewhere. But don't worry: If you forget the *tilde*, people will still understand what you've written.

➤ The word *alcazar* ("castle") ends in a consonant. We checked it out, and, no, it's not *n* or *s*. This means that the stress must fall on the last syllable, "ahl kah SAHR." But the word that we are trying to write is actually pronounced "ahl KAH sahr." Therefore, we must write a *tilde* over the middle *a* to show that the rules have been broken and the stress really falls in the middle: *alcázar*.

Back to Those Diphthongs

I told you not to stress over the diphthongs. But there's one final thing I need to mention before this all comes together: As it turns out, not all Spanish diphthongs are created equal. Here's why:

The vowels *i* and *u* (and occasionally *y*) are considered weak with respect to accentuation. The others (*o, a, and e*) are strong. Any combination of vowels that consists of a weak + weak (*iu, ui*) or a weak + strong (*au, ei,* and so on) will form a one-syllable diphthong, as you saw previously.

On the other hand, when both vowels are strong (*oa, ea, eo,* and so on), they must be dealt with as two separate syllables: *ae* = "ah eh"; *oe* = "oh eh"; *eo* = "eh oh"; *oa* = "oh ah."

When we want a diphthong that consists of two weak vowels (or of one weak vowel and one strong vowel) *not* to form a one-syllable diphthong (which is what it will *naturally* do), we must write a *tilde* on one of them to prevent this from happening. Usually it's the first vowel that gets the *tilde*. Take a look at the following examples:

1. As you know, the surname *García* is pronounced "Gahr SEE ah." Without the *tilde* over the *í*, this person's name would have only two syllables: GAHR syah.

2. The name *María* is pronounced "Mah REE ah." It would sound like "MAH rya" without the *tilde*.

3. The word *cortesía* ("courtesy") is pronounced "kohr teh SEE ah." Without the *tilde,* it would be "kohr TEH syah."

4. The word *baúl* ("box," "chest") needs that *tilde* over the *u;* otherwise, it would sound like a one-syllable "bahwl" instead of the correct two-syllable "bah OOL."

But remember that two strong vowels will be separated naturally into two distinct syllables:

➤ *maestro* = mah EH stroh

➤ *poema* = poh EH mah

➤ *paella* = pah EH yah

➤ *proa* = PROH ah

Acuérdate

If a final *n* or *s* is preceded by another consonant, that consonant is considered stronger; the word will be stressed on the final syllable, without the need to add a *tilde.* There are few such words; most are names: *Casals, Isacs, Isern.*

Algo Nuevo

Spanish calls words that are stressed on the penultimate syllable *palabras graves* (or *llanas*). Words with the stress on the last syllable are called *palabras agudas.* Words that are stressed on the third-to-last syllable are called *palabras estrújulas.* There are even *palabras sobresetrújulas,* which are stressed on the first syllable among four: *cómpreselo.* You don't need to memorize these terms to understand how this all works. But don't let anyone say that I never told you.

Tildes and Other Words

Occasionally a *tilde* must be written simply to distinguish one word from another word that looks exactly the same. These *tildes* have nothing to do with accentuation; they are simply a way for Spanish to tell two otherwise identical words apart.

Using Tildes

Word	No Tilde	With Tilde	Example
el	article	pronoun	*él es el hombre*
de	"of"	verb *dar*	*dé una caja de tres*
se	pronoun	verb *saber*	*se sabe que yo sé*
te	pronoun	a drink	*te gusta tomar té*
mi	"my"	pronoun	*mi taco es para mí*
si	"if"	"yes"	*si Juan dice que sí*
tu	pronoun	"your"	*tú quieres tu taco*
mas	but/plus	more	*tengo más, mas no te las vendo*

The Least You Need to Know

➤ Spanish follows very logical rules as to where the stress in a word is expected to fall.

➤ Whenever the rules are broken, a *tilde* must be written over the vowel.

➤ A few little words have *tildes* just to make them look different.

Chapter 5

Caminos Hacia el Español (Roads to Spanish)

In This Chapter

➤ Suggestions to help you learn

➤ About dictionaries

➤ Using the Internet as a learning tool

➤ Ideas for effective practice

Learning a new language is a bit like going to the doctor: It's always a good idea to get a second opinion. No book can teach you everything—not even this one—and the more information you have at your disposal, the better. Sometimes you just need to hear the same stuff explained in a different way before everything makes sense. This chapter will give you some ideas for further study so that you'll have as many second opinions as possible.

Gathering Your Tools

Even though *The Complete Idiot's Guide to Intermediate Spanish* will be your tool *número uno* right now, let's start by going over some additional resources that you should have at your disposal.

The Bilingual Dictionary

If nothing else, you must have a decent Spanish/English dictionary. *The Complete Idiot's Guide to Intermediate Spanish* is not designed to give you all the vocabulary or definitions that you'll ever need—that would be impossible. Every language student must feel comfortable using his or her dictionary.

To get the most out of your dictionary, make sure that it is relatively new (no more than 10 years old). This really *does* make a difference; if you have an older dictionary, I'd advise replacing it with something more up-to-date. There are currently many Spanish/English dictionaries on the market. Some are definitely better (and more expensive) than others. You don't have to spend a lot of money to get something decent, though; you can always buy that gold-plated $250 hardback dictionary with a CD-ROM and action figures later. I'll recommend some possibilities in Appendix B, "Other Books."

If you really don't want to buy a new dictionary, there are several "virtual dictionaries" on the Internet. Simply search for "Spanish Dictionary" and surf around until you find one that you like. Just make sure that you're accessing a general reference dictionary, not a technical glossary.

The Internet

Outside of actually living in a Spanish-speaking country, the World Wide Web is now the best place to find up-to-date Spanish. The Internet will allow you free access to an endless number of Spanish texts, chatlines, and tutorials. If your computer has audio and video capability, you can even watch and listen to programming in Spanish. Anything and everything you ever wanted to know about the Spanish language and Latin culture is as close as a click on your *ratón* (believe it or not, *el mouse* is also acceptable for your computer mouse). The number of Web sites in Spanish is enormous; bookmark the sites that strike your fancy, and visit them often.

Acuérdate

Not only will your dictionary help you to learn new words, it can also show you new ways to use words that you already know. For example, you know that *gato* means "cat." But this same word also can refer to the "jack" you use to lift up your car when you have a flat tire. With a good dictionary, you can indeed learn something new every day.

Ten Cuidado

Yes, your dictionary can be your best friend—but not always. Sometimes it will offer you little or no guidance when giving definitions, especially for cognates. You might look up a word such as *translimitación* and get "translimitation" as a definition, as if that really helps! My motto: Dictionaries are wonderful, but they are *guides*, not *gods*.

Books, Magazines, and Newspapers

In cities with large Spanish-speaking populations, you should have no trouble finding books or newspapers in Spanish. There may even be a *librería latina* in the area. Check your local telephone directory under the Bookstores heading.

In addition to many lesser-known Spanish language *revistas*, *Newsweek* and *Readers' Digest* have been publishing Spanish versions of their magazines for years (*Newsweek en Español* and *Selecciones de Readers' Digest*). Many other "mainstream" magazines such as *Cosmopolitan* and *People* also have begun to publish in Spanish. If you'd like to subscribe, contact the publishers to find out more.

Many university libraries stock Spanish-language newspapers as well. Ask the librarian if you can take home a few older editions that might otherwise be headed for the recycle bin. If you're interested in receiving newspapers by mail, you may be able to subscribe to a Spanish daily or weekly paper from a city with a large Hispanic population, such as Los Angeles, Miami, or New York.

Used bookstores offer another excellent (though unpredictable) resource for Spanish-language materials. You'll be amazed at what can turn up at a used bookstore, especially in a university town. I've found Spanish reference materials, teaching texts, and several volumes of Spanish and Latin American literature for a fraction of their original price. While there's no guarantee that you'll find what you need, it's always worth a try.

Cassettes and Videos

Most bookstores sell "teach-yourself" audio tapes and video courses for Spanish and other languages. The in-flight magazine of your favorite airline probably advertises similar products. You can also purchase these packages over the Internet.

Some of these courses are excellent; others are not. The problem is that it can be difficult to learn the language from cassettes or videos alone. Some programs merely throw a lot of words at you without

Acuérdate

While there is no doubt that the Internet is one of the best resources for learning Spanish, you shouldn't worry if you don't have Internet access yet. You can often find much of the same information at your local or school library. Many libraries have computers that you can use to surf the Web for free.

Ten Cuidado

Before you spend any more money on additional books or tapes, see what's available for free at the public library. You may find books and instructional tapes or videos in Spanish on the shelves. Libraries run by colleges and universities certainly will have books in Spanish.

any grammar or context. But cassettes still can be an excellent way to hear the language pronounced correctly. They can also help you to expand your vocabulary. Before you spend any money, see if your local library has Spanish instructional tapes or videos that you can check out for free.

Other Books About Spanish

In the spirit of my "get a second opinion" approach, you may find it useful to look at some other references about Spanish in addition to *The Complete Idiot's Guide to Intermediate Spanish*. Although I might like to think otherwise, there really isn't anything new under *el sol* when it comes to Spanish grammar. Still, you may find it helpful to hear the same material explained in a different way. Just remember to check out what's free before you spend money (of course, you can always buy as many copies of this book as you want).

Haz Clic Aquí

Visit Visual Education's Web site at www.vis-ed.com/lang.html. This site offers a full line of Spanish flashcards, including cards for grammar, vocabulary, verbs, and "think sets." All are designed to promote speaking ability and enhance understanding of the spoken and written language.

Flashcards

Instructional Spanish flashcards can be purchased at college bookstores and over the Internet. Of course, you can always make your own cards by writing the English word on one side and the Spanish word on the other. Go through a stack of 15 to 20 cards whenever you have a free moment. Practice Spanish to English first. Then go from English to Spanish. Once you have learned a word well enough to produce it in both languages, put the card in the "I-know-these" pile.

Practice Makes Perfect

The best way to practice your Spanish is to go to any country where Spanish is spoken and stay there for as long as you can. Of course, this is not a possibility for everyone. But even if you aren't able to travel at this point in your life, there's still a lot you can do for your Spanish. The following is a list of activities that can help you maintain and perfect your *español*—right from the comfort of your own home town.

Watch Spanish-Language TV and Films

Check to see what Spanish-language programming is offered in your area. In the United States, *Univisión, Telemundo, Galavisión,* and local Spanish-language broadcasters may already be on your TV. Most cable companies offer at least one of these stations as part of their expanded basic cable service. If you have a satellite dish, you definitely have Spanish TV at your disposal. If you're not sure, call your cable company or satellite provider.

Univisión, Telemundo, and *Galvisión* have quality news programs every evening. Or, you could start with something easier, such as PBS's *Plaza Sésamo,* the Spanish-language version of Sesame Street. For a more "mature" approach, try getting hooked on a Latin American soap opera (*telenovela*).

Your local video rental store or library should carry a few movies in Spanish. Although the selection might be limited, only the best foreign language films tend to make it to the mainstream English market. So, the Spanish-language movie you choose will probably be reasonably good (there are exceptions). Read the jacket to make sure that the movie is subtitled and not dubbed into English.

Having your own copy of at least one film in Spanish can be a great way to work on your language skills because it gives you the opportunity to watch the same movie over and over whenever you want. Each time you see it, you'll pick out and understand new words and phrases. Have your dictionary and notebook on hand, and keep your finger on the pause button to give yourself a moment to write things down.

Speak Spanish as Much as You Can

Hooking up with a native Spanish speaker can be very helpful to you. A native speaker can guide you in your pronunciation and vocabulary, and you'll feel encouraged each time this person understands something you've said in Spanish.

If you don't know any native Spanish-speakers who can help you with your studies, ask around to see if there is someone who speaks Spanish in your area. If this doesn't work, consider one of the following ideas:

1. Mexican restaurants are a good place to start (although I once came upon a Mexican restaurant that was owned by a Chinese family who didn't speak a word of Spanish—go figure).

Acuérdate

If you live on a remote Aleutian Island, you won't have quite the same opportunities for contact with a Hispanic community as someone who lives in Miami or El Paso. And if you're in college, you're obviously not going to be hosting a foreign exchange student in your dorm room (well, maybe, but that's not what I mean). You might have to modify some of these suggestions to fit your situation.

Cultura Latina

There's so much pressure in the world today to learn English that many Spanish-speakers deeply appreciate your efforts to learn their language. Even if you have a lot of trouble speaking it, most *hispanohablantes* are more than happy to help you with your Spanish. Just ask.

Haz Clic Aquí

A great Web site about Spain and Spanish is www.el-castellano.com. You could spend days exploring this site and still not see it all.

Ten Cuidado

You can get the addresses of many pen pal organizations over the Internet. Just search for "pen friends" or "pen pals." But be careful—some of these organizations are actually fronts for mail-order marriage services.

Haz Clic Aquí

If you don't like sitting in a classroom but want to take a course, there are several free courses offered over the Internet. One of the best is at www.studyspanish.com/tutorial.htm.

2. How about a retirement home? You may meet a Spanish-speaking senior citizen who would greatly appreciate your company.

3. Call the local Catholic church or diocese. They'll probably know if there are any Spanish-speakers in the area.

4. Put up posters on public bulletin boards and at colleges with a number where you can be reached: *Quiero practicar mi español con usted* ("I want to practice my Spanish with you"). You may get some good leads. Offer English lessons in exchange for help with your Spanish.

5. See if there are any charitable organizations working with Spanish-speakers that are looking for volunteers.

Still no luck? Well, desperate times may call for desperate measures. Open the phone book and look under last names such as García, González, Hernández, López, and Martínez, and start calling around. You may find that someone out there would love to help you with your Spanish. It's a bold step, but if you're really stuck, it's worth a try.

Write in Spanish

Hook up with a Spanish-speaking pen pal. For the last 13 years, I have maintained an active correspondence with a friend I met in Argentina. During that time, I have learned lots of Spanish simply by reading his letters.

If you prefer e-mail, you're in luck. Finding Spanish-speaking "e-pals" is easy. Visit www.mundolatino.org to start your search. Another possibility is www.latin-chat.com. America Online, CompuServe, and many Internet service providers are also good places to hook up with Spanish-speaking "virtual amigos."

Take Classes

Find out what Spanish classes are being offered at your local community college or adult learning center.

Tuition is usually pretty reasonable, and there may be both day and night classes to fit your schedule.

Listen to Spanish Radio

Spend a few minutes roaming through the FM and AM bands of your radio. Depending on your location, you may be able to find Spanish language programs on the radio. Many major U.S. cities, as well as Toronto and Vancouver, have at least one station that broadcasts in Spanish. Listening to the radio can be a great way to keep your Spanish active.

You can definitely hear Spanish language programming on any short-wave radio. Of the many programs you'll hear, *Voice of America* seems to come in the strongest. Unfortunately, the audio quality on short-wave radios usually isn't very good. But if you're unable to find any stations on the FM or AM frequencies, you can at least find something to listen to over the short-wave. Don't expect to hear anything during the day; night is always best for short-wave reception.

Use Your Computer!

Spanish instructional software is readily available at your local software or computer store and over the Internet. As with the audio tapes, software programs that simply throw words at you randomly, even if they do have those cute little pictures, may not actually teach you the language. Knowing a lot of words is great, but if you can't put them together in a sentence, you won't really be speaking Spanish.

More Things You Can Do

If you can't actually *be* an exchange student, you may be able to invite a Spanish-speaking student into your home. The International Rotary Club, American Field Service, and other exchange organizations place foreign students with host families. Contact AFS at www.afs.org/welcome.html and the Rotary Club at www.rotary.com.

Acuérdate

A great way to take advantage of the radio is to record an hour or so of a Spanish program that appeals to you. You should try to record some music, an announcer, and maybe even the news. Listen to the tape over and over until you practically have it memorized. I promise that it will do wonders for your Spanish.

If you're not in a position to actually have someone stay with you, contact your local high school or college to inquire about the possibility of arranging to speak with a Spanish-speaking exchange student attending classes in your area. Just make sure that your contact with any high school students is in an appropriate setting and is not too frequent.

Ten Cuidado

While some instructional software programs do seem reasonably priced, you must be careful. Far too many students have purchased a cheap "Teach Yourself Spanish" software package only to discover that it's practically useless because of its dull and uninspired format. Read the box carefully before you open your wallet, and make sure that the program's presentation really appeals to you.

Need even more ideas? Try talking to yourself. We all think about things. Sometimes we think too much. Ever have one of those days when your mind just won't shut up? Well, why not harness some of that energy and put it to good use by privately translating your thoughts into Spanish?

When you look at your watch, say the time to yourself in Spanish. If you suddenly remember that you need to take out the garbage and put out the cat, think *basura* and *gato*—even if you don't know how to say "to take out" or "to put out."

And, of course, you could always marry or date someone who speaks Spanish. There's no doubt about it, if you do form a romantic relationship with someone who speaks Spanish, you'll get lots of practice. Now, I'm not saying that falling in love with someone just because you can practice your Spanish with him or her is a strong foundation for a long-term relationship. But, hey, who am I to stand in the way of *el amor*? If you're already married, this option is definitely out. Sorry.

Algo Nuevo

Whenever I have trouble falling asleep, it's usually because my mind is working overtime reviewing the day's events, planning for the next day, or analyzing some childhood memory. If you find yourself doing too many mental gymnastics at night, try thinking your thoughts in Spanish instead of English. Even if your vocabulary is limited, you can still fill in Spanish here and there. At least this activity might put you to sleep a little faster.

The Least You Need to Know

➤ You must have a good bilingual dictionary.

➤ The Internet is a great place to find and learn about Spanish.

➤ You can do many things to improve your Spanish without ever having to leave your house.

Part 2

Getting to Know the Spanish-Speaking World

Get ready to learn about the various countries that make up el mundo latino. *This part introduces you to your first* lecturas. *Each* lectura *discusses some aspect of a country or region where Spanish is spoken. The grammar sections go into greater detail about the building blocks of Spanish, such as nouns, adjectives, and verbs. Even if you feel that you know this stuff, taking another look with a new perspective may help you to fill in any gaps.* ¡Adelante!

Chapter 6

España: Where It All Began

> **In This Chapter**
>
> ➤ Your first *lectura*
>
> ➤ Statistics about Spain
>
> ➤ The Spanish noun
>
> ➤ Your first *Risa del Día*

When it comes right down to it, it's really all Spain's fault. Even if your focus is strictly on Latin America, Spain is where it all started: No Spain, no *Complete Idiot's Guide to Intermediate Spanish*. And then where would we be?

Spain is as diverse culturally as it is geographically. Its topography ranges from the Pyrenees mountains in the north, to the dry Meseta plain, to a coastline that stretches from the Atlantic Ocean to the Mediterranean Sea. The Spanish economy relies on agriculture, heavy industry, and tourism. Each year, more than 50 million people visit the country that financed Christopher Columbus' first voyage to what would become the Americas and Spain's colonial empire.

So, get ready to sink your *dientes* into some real Spanish! This chapter begins with your first reading. You'll have a short vocabulary list, an analysis of the juicy parts of the text, and a grammar section about nouns. Not to worry—I'll keep it all as painless as possible.

Lectura: La Geografía de España

For your first *lectura*, read this brief geographic description of Spain. Go through it a few times if you need to, and don't get bogged down if you can't understand a particular word or phrase. If you don't understand something, skip it for now. Refer to the *Vocabulario Útil* section and your dictionary for any new words. *No te alarmes* ("Don't panic"); you'll do just fine. We'll analyze the passage in detail afterward.

Haz Clic Aquí

To find out more about Spain, visit one of the following Web sites: www.sispain.com, www.andalucia.com, or www.gae.unican.es. You can find hundreds of other great Web sites by doing a simple search for "Spain" or "*España*."

Cultura Latina

Spain shares the Iberian Pen-insula with Portugal. In Roman times, this region was called Iberia, hence the name we use today. *Castellano* comes from Castilla, one of Spain's most populous *autonomías*. But not everyone in Spain speaks *castel-lano*.

España está situada al suroeste de Europa, en la Península Ibérica. Comparte este territorio con Portugal, ocupando un 80 por ciento del mismo. Incluye también las islas Baleares (Ibiza, Mallorca, y Menorca), en el mar Mediterráneo, las Islas Canarias en el Océano Atlántico, al suroeste de la península, frente a la costa de Marruecos, y al norte de África cuenta con las ciudades de Ceuta y Melilla. Es el 3° país europeo en extensión y el 5° en población. Al norte limita con Francia y Andorra, encontrando su frontera natural en los Pirineos.

Geográficamente posee cinco grandes cadenas mon-tañosas que la atraviesan y casi un 40 por ciento de su territorio se asienta sobre mesetas. Sus costas están bañadas por el mar Mediterráneo, en el Este, desde los Pirineos hasta Gibraltar, por el Océano Atlántico en su costa Oeste, y en su costa Norte por el mar Cantábrico.

Great! You survived. Now, let's take a closer look at what you just read. First, some vocabulary:

Vocabulario Útil:

➤ **suroeste**: southwest

➤ **situar**: to be situated

➤ **compartir**: to share

➤ **incluir**: to include

➤ **frente a**: facing; in front of

➤ **limitar**: to share a border with

➤ **por ciento**: percent

➤ **atravesar**: to go across

➤ **asentarse**: to sit; to lie (in a topographical context)

➤ **meseta**: plateau

➤ **extensión**: size

➤ **contar con**: literally "to count on"; here, "to have"

➤ **los Pirineos**: the Pyrenees Mountains

➤ **Marruecos**: Morocco

➤ **frontera**: border

Análisis del Texto

Now let's take a closer look at the juicy parts of the text:

➤ *España está situada al suroeste de Europa.*

España is feminine. So, *está situada* is in the feminine. *Situada* is a past participle being used as an adjective, and the *a* ending tells us it's feminine.

Note also the use of *al* meaning "to the" southwest. When you want to state the cardinal direction (*norte, sur, este, oeste*) in which something is located, use *al* (*a + el*). North, south, east, and west are all masculine in Spanish.

➤ *Comparte este territorio …*

Compartir means "to share." Notice that *España* is understood to be the subject here, so there is no need to say *España comparte*. *Este* means "this" and is a demonstrative adjective (more on those later).

➤ *… ocupando un 80 por ciento del mismo.*

Ocupar is cognate with "to occupy." Here *ocupando* is in the present participle *–ing* form.

➤ *Es el 3° país europeo ….*

The little ° makes the number 3 into an ordinal number (first, second, third, and so on). It would be read as *tercero*. If the noun had been feminine rather than the masculine *país*, there would have been a little *a* there instead.

➤ *Sus costas están bañadas ….*

Literally, "Its coasts are bathed." Use your imagination.

Cultura Latina

About 800–1400 A.D., Spain was ruled by Arabic-speaking Moors. While the Arabic language had little influence on the grammatical structure of Spanish, it did introduce many new words and place names. For example, the name *Guadalajara* comes from the Arabic *Wadi al-hayara*, which means "River of Stones."

Vista Panorámica de España

Now learn a few more geographical and demographic statistics about Spain. There are many cognates in this section. If you read a word and can guess what it means by the way it sounds, you'll do fine. There's a lot of great vocabulary here:

Cultura Latina

People in Galicia, the northwestern part of Spain, speak *el gallego*. This dialect is actually closer to Portuguese than to *castellano*. But you won't have any trouble making yourself understood by speaking regular old Spanish in Galicia. In Barcelona, many people speak *el catalán*. Catalan shares some words and grammatical constructions with Spanish, but it is definitely a distinct language. Many Barcelonans, however, also speak or understand Spanish.

➤ **Nombre oficial**: *Reino* (kingdom) *de España*

➤ **Gobierno**: *Monarquía constitucional con 17 autonomías*

➤ **Capital**: Madrid

➤ **Ciudades principales (major cities)**:

    Madrid

    Barcelona

    Valencia

    Bilbao

    Sevilla

    Málaga

    Zaragoza

➤ **Tamaño (size)**: 504.783 *kilómetros cuadrados*

➤ **Población (population)**: *Aproximadamente 40 millones; 77 por ciento urbana, 23 por ciento rural*

➤ **Divisa (currency)**: *Peseta (Pta.)*

➤ **Forma adjetiva (adjectival form)**: *Español/ española*

➤ **Recursos naturales (natural resources)**: *Carbón, hierro* (iron), *uranio, mercurio, yeso* (lime), *cinc, plomo, tungsteno, cobre, energía hidroeléctrica, otros*

➤ **Industrias**: *Textiles, calzado* (footwear), *acero* (steel), *automóbiles, alimentos preparados* (prepared foods), *aparatos electrónicos* (electronic devices), *bienes de consumo* (consumer goods), *turismo, otras*

➤ **Productos agrícolas**: *Frutas (cítricas y uvas), granos, verduras, aceitunas, aceite de oliva, otros*

Gramática: Los Sustantivos (Nouns)

Now we'll begin to focus on fundamental grammar. Even though you may have studied much of this already, a quick review with a new perspective can't hurt (or can it?).

Boy Meets Girl? Not Exactly ...

You know that nouns are people, places, things, ideas, and beliefs. You also know that there are both abstract nouns (such as progress, freedom, and destiny) as well as concrete nouns (such as houses, dogs, trees, and, well, concrete).

Spanish nouns are classified as being either masculine or feminine. In general terms, Spanish nouns that end in *–a* are feminine, while those that end

Acuérdate

Remember that *el* is the masculine definite article and *la* is the feminine. These correspond to *the* in English. The indefinite articles are *un* and *una*; these correspond to *a* or *an*. The plurals are *los* and *las*. Don't you love it when people tell you things that you already know?

in *–o* are masculine. There is no neuter gender for Spanish nouns, so your "fixed" cat is still a *gato,* even though he may not be quite as *macho* as he once was.

Most living things have both a masculine and a feminine form. Usually, the final letter is the only difference between the two forms (see the following table).

Nouns and Their Genders

English	Masculine	Feminine
teacher	*maestro*	*maestra*
neighbor	*vecino*	*vecina*
child	*niño*	*niña*
friend	*amigo*	*amiga*
boyfriend/girlfriend	*novio*	*novia*
cat	*gato* (tomcat)	*gata* (female cat)
dog	*perro* ("tom" dog)	*perra* (female dog)

You probably have come to accept by now that Spanish indicates girls with *–a* and boys with *–o*. But the concept of masculine and feminine words still confounds many English-speakers. While we can accept the idea of gender when it comes to living things, inanimate nouns (money, patriotism, mud, doornails, and so on) are all obviously neither girls nor boys. So what's the deal?

Well, those words are also either masculine or feminine, and the *–a* and *–o* rules apply just the same. But try not to think of nonliving Spanish nouns as male or female, per se. If the masculine/feminine thing doesn't work for you, consider all inanimate Spanish nouns as belonging to one of two grammatical categories: A class words and O class words—sort of like blood types. Usually it's just the spelling of the word rather than any latent masculine or feminine qualities that determines the gender of inanimate nouns.

Unlike animates, nonliving nouns usually do not have an equivalent in the opposite gender. For example, the Spanish word for beer is *cerveza*. There is no such thing as *cervezo*. It doesn't matter if a man or a woman is drinking it—the word *cerveza* never changes. It ends in *–a*, so it's feminine (or A class, if you prefer).

Algo Nuevo

Yes, Spanish nouns are classified as either masculine or feminine. But before you start to criticize those silly Spaniards for their folly, you should know that centuries ago, English also had masculine and feminine nouns. It was only due to historical events that inanimate gendered nouns in English were discarded. Had Britain not been settled (invaded?) by so many different peoples over the centuries, each noun that we write today in English might well have been masculine, feminine, or even neuter.

Spanish uses all this gender stuff to help hold the language together once you start building sentences. Usually "maleness" and "femaleness" have nothing to do with it. For example, in the second sentence of the *lectura*, you read the following:

> *Comparte este territorio con Portugal, ocupando un 80 por ciento del mismo.*

This *del mismo* literally means "of the same" and is serving as a pronoun. But there's more here than meets the *ojo*. It refers back to *territorio*. How do I know this? Because *mismo* is displaying the same masculine gender of *territorio;* their gender is linking the two words together. We could have repeated the word *territorio* here as well ("It shares this territory … ocupying 80 percent of the same territory"), but to make the passage sound better, *mismo* functions as a pronoun for *territorio* to avoid repetition. We'll study more of this "gender-linking" in subsequent chapters.

Nouns with Other Endings

The bad news, of course, is that not all Spanish nouns end in *–a* or *–o*. But even so, there are many useful guidelines that can help you to know what the gender of a word is without having to look it up in your dictionary.

Nouns ending in consonants such as *r, l, s, z, j,* and *n* tend to be masculine, as do words that end in the vowels *i* and *u* (not too many of these). And words that end in an accented vowel (as in *el bongó*) also tend to be masculine. Those that end in *–e* can go either way (although *–ie* tends to be feminine).

Fortunately, you'll usually learn the gender of a new word when you hear or read it in a sentence. But if you come across a word by chance or out of context, it may be a good idea to check your dictionary just to be sure:

> ➤ **un reloj:** a watch
> ➤ **el árbol:** the tree
> ➤ **un balcón:** a balcony
> ➤ **el pañal:** the diaper
> ➤ **un imbésil:** an unintelligent male person
> ➤ **el francés:** French (language)
> ➤ **el alemán:** German (language)
> ➤ **un sofá:** a couch or divan
> ➤ **un hotel:** one hotel
> ➤ **el café:** coffee
> ➤ **el esquí:** the ski; skiing
> ➤ **el maní:** peanut (in South America)
> ➤ **un restaurante:** a place to eat
> ➤ **el bote:** small boat; tin can (in Mexico)
> ➤ **el Perú:** a South American country

But …

> ➤ **la flor:** the flower
> ➤ **la gente:** the people
> ➤ **una nube:** a cloud

Nouns ending in *–dad, –tad, –tud, –ción,* and *–sión* are abstract nouns and are all feminine. Always! No extra guesswork is required. Words ending in *–umbre* (*costumbre* =
habit) and *–ie* (*serie* = series) are nearly always feminine.

Algo Nuevo

Occasionally there can be two versions of the same inanimate word, one masculine and
one feminine. For example, both *cesto* and *cesta* mean "basket." There's also *bolsa* and
bolso, which both mean "bag." Don't let this trouble you. Such words usually have approximately the same meaning. Sometimes one is just larger than the other; the usage
may be simply a matter of personal or regional preference.

"Wrong-Ending" Words

Some words that end in *–a* are actually masculine. Most nouns that end in *–ama,
–ema, –ota,* and *–eta* are masculine:

➤ **el planeta:** the planet

➤ **un idiota:** a male idiot (for a female, use *la*)

➤ **un mapa:** a map

➤ **el programa:** the program

➤ **el problema:** the problem

➤ **el clima:** the climate

But not always …

➤ **la forma:** the form; the manner

➤ **la paleta:** the Popsicle (in Mexico)

Some nouns simply change the article to indicate male or female:

➤ **un/una estudiante:** male/female student

➤ **un/una paciente:** male/female patient

➤ **un/una joven:** male/female young person

➤ **un/una modelo:** male/female fashion model

Nouns that end with the suffix –*ista* (cognate with –*ist* in English) also fall into this category. When the word refers to a man, it's *el,* but it takes *la* when referring to a woman:

➤ **un socialista:** a socialist (a man)

➤ **el capitalista:** the capitalist

➤ **un sandinista:** a Nicaraguan left-wing party member

➤ **un turista:** a male tourist

But …

➤ **una capitalista:** a female capitalist

➤ **una turista:** a female tourist

A few nouns do not change, regardless of the gender of the person or people in question:

➤ **la persona:** the person (never becomes *el persona*)

➤ **la víctima:** the victim (never becomes *el víctima*)

➤ **la gente:** could be a group of men

The good news about all these irregular nouns is that after a while, even the exceptions seem to make sense and follow a logical pattern. You'll eventually see that such words aren't really exceptions at all, but are just following the beat of their own *conga.* With a little practice, you'll be able to guess the gender of a word from its ending (and be right about 95 percent of the time).

Plurals

In English, we put an –*s* on the end of a word to indicate plurality: one car, two cars; one telephone, two telephones; one house, two houses; one mouse, two mouses (okay, not always). Spanish also uses the –*s* at the end of a word to indicate "more than one."

Ten Cuidado

Words beginning with a stressed *a* (or *a* sound, as in *hacha*) take a masculine article in the singular, even though the words are really feminine and need feminine adjectives. The most common is *agua:* You must say *el agua.* The idea is that *la agua* would create an undesired *sinalefa* and be hard to say. *Las aguas* is fine. In the *lectura,* you saw the word *África,* which also works this way.

Pluralizing Nouns That End in a Vowel

English	Singular	Plural
the hat(s)	*el sombrero*	*los sombreros*
the shirt(s)	*la camisa*	*las camisas*

For words that end in a vowel (such as the previous examples), all we need to do is add an –*s* at the end. If the word ends in a consonant (including *y*), –*es* is added.

Pluralizing Nouns That End in a Consonant

English	Singular	Plural
the rumor(s)	*el rumor*	*los rumores*
the mouse (mice)	*el ratón*	*los ratones*
the diaper(s)	*el pañal*	*los pañales*
the session(s)	*la sesión*	*las sesiones*
the king(s)	*el rey*	*los reyes*

When a noun ends in –*z*, the *z* becomes *c* in the plural.

Pluralizing Nouns That End in –z

English	Singular	Plural
the voice(s)	*la voz*	*las voces*
the ostrich(es)	*el avestruz*	*los avestruces*

If a noun or family name already ends in –*es* or –*z* in the singular, there is no change in the plural, except for the article.

Pluralizing Nouns Ending in –es and Family Names Ending in –z

English	Singular	Plural
Monday	*el lunes*	*los lunes*
the Gonzalez family	*el González*	*los González*

You may add a number before the plural article to indicate a specific quantity:

➤ **los tres amigos:** the three friends

➤ **las cuatro hermanas:** the four sisters

➤ **los cuarenta ladrones:** the 40 thieves

➤ **las noventa y nueve botellas de cerveza:**
the 99 bottles of beer

In this construction, the indefinite articles are really acting like adjectives. *Un* and *una* may also take a plural: *unos* and *unas*. The concept of a "pluralized singular" may seem strange, but it's a good way to express the idea of "some," as in "there are some X's here":

➤ **unos amigos:** some friends

➤ **unas nubes:** some clouds

➤ **unos problemas:** a few problems

Ten Cuidado

Don't forget that gender does not change a cardinal number. So *cuatro* doesn't change to *cuatra* just because the noun is feminine. However, when the number is 1, you must use *un* or *una* according to the gender of the noun, and in the hundreds, *cientos* must change to *cientas* for feminine nouns.

Risa del Día

Let's get away from grammar for a moment. It's time for a joke—not a good joke, but a joke nonetheless.

Humor is one of the hardest things to translate from one language to another. In fact, many jokes simply cannot be translated because the punch line usually has some pun or play on words that just won't work in another language. For your first *Risa del Día*, I will keep it very simple:

> *¿Por qué cruzó el pollo la calle?*
>
> *Para llegar al otro lado.*

Vocabulario Útil:

➤ **cruzar:** to cross

➤ **pollo:** chicken

➤ **calle:** road

➤ **llegar a:** to get to

➤ **otro lado:** other side

Cultura Latina

What we would call a "dirty" or "off-color" joke in English is known as *un chiste verde* (green joke) or *un chiste colorado* (red joke) in Spanish. There is most certainly no shortage of *chistes verdes*. I find it interesting that such jokes are "off-color" in English, but full of color in Spanish. Go figure.

El Cuiz

Your first *cuiz* is mostly a vocabulary review from your *lectura*. You can test yourself on any additional vocabulary you found in this chapter any way you want. Please give the English equivalents for the following words. Cheating is perfectly acceptable:

1. frontera _____
2. limitar _____
3. situar _____
4. meseta _____
5. compartir _____
6. frente a _____
7. extensión _____
8. atravesar _____
9. asentarse _____
10. los Pirineos _____
11. Marruecos _____
12. contar con _____
13. suroeste _____

Haz Clic Aquí

The Web site www.vokabel.com is an excellent vocabulary-building resource. Vocabulary lists are divided into general and subject-specific areas. It's a great place to practice old words and learn new ones.

Tareas

1. Explain to someone how nouns work in Spanish. If there is no one around, write a few paragraphs on a sheet of paper detailing everything you know about Spanish nouns.

2. Now that you've gone through the chapter, reread the *lectura* to see if it's any easier this time around.

The Least You Need to Know

➤ Spain is where Spanish started.

➤ Spanish nouns are either masculine or feminine.

➤ Inanimate nouns are also masculine or feminine, but "maleness" and "female-ness" have nothing to do with it.

➤ Some nouns take an unexpected gender, but after a while, even these make sense.

➤ Plural endings are *–s* and *–es*.

Chapter 7

México: Pyramids, Politics, and *Playas*

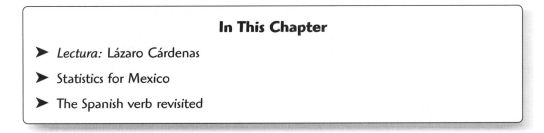

In This Chapter

➤ *Lectura:* Lázaro Cárdenas

➤ Statistics for Mexico

➤ The Spanish verb revisited

In Mexico, Aztec and Mayan ruins coexist with modern tourist resorts, untamed jungles, and vast desert landscapes. Mexico City competes with Tokyo as the most densely populated city in the world. The country is well known for its bright textiles, festivals, *picante* food, and liquor. Modern Mexico is also known for its volatile economy and politics.

Mexico has recently strengthened its economic ties with the United States and Canada with the enactment of the North American Free Trade Agreement (NAFTA, which, by the way, means "gasoline" in Argentina). It has the largest Spanish-speaking population in the world and is the Latin American country most visited by American and Canadian tourists. Sharing a 2,000 mile-long border with the United States, Mexico's history is greatly interwoven with that of its *vecino al norte*.

In this chapter, we'll read a *lectura* about Lázaro Cárdenas, check out some basic statistics about Mexico and, most importantly, take an in-depth look at the Spanish verb.

Cultura Latina

Mexico and the United States have not always been the good neighbors that they are today. The U.S. military has invaded Mexican territory on numerous occasions, and on March 9, 1916, Pancho Villa's men crossed the Mexican border and destroyed the American town of Columbus, New Mexico, killing several Americans. Of course, things have greatly improved since those days.

Lectura: Lázaro Cárdenas

Lázaro Cárdenas was one of Mexico's most popular presidents. This reading briefly discusses Cárdenas and the situation in Mexico during his presidency:

Lázaro Cárdenas llegó a la presidencia el 1° de diciembre de 1934. En su gobierno, se propuso cumplir algunas de las promesas de la Revolución. El problema de los campesinos fue el que más le preocupó y durante su régimen se expropiaron grandes latifundios para repartir esa tierra entre quienes la trabajaban; se fundaron ejidos y se dedicó más dinero para atender al campo. Cárdenas se preocupó por multiplicar las escuelas, sobre todo rurales, y por impulsar la enseñanza técnica. Amplió la red de carreteras y dio facilidades para que creciera la industria nacional.

Los años treinta fueron difíciles. Para mejorar la economía de México, el gobierno impulsó la formación de industrias. Se abrió un banco para prestar dinero a los campesinos y se fundó el Instituto Politécnico Nacional para mejorar la enseñanza técnica.

En España, la rebelión de una parte del ejército contra el gobierno de la república provocó la Guerra Civil (1936–1939) y obligó a miles de españoles a salir de su país. Muchos de ellos fueron recibidos por México y enriquecieron la vida del país, sobre todo en el terreno de la educación, la ciencia y las artes.

Vocabulario Útil:

➤ **ejercito:** army

➤ **enriquecer:** to enrich; to make richer

➤ **promesa:** promise; vow

➤ **terreno:** land; terrain

➤ **enseñanza:** education; teaching

➤ **campesinos:** country people; peasants

➤ **multiplicar:** to increase the number of; to multiply

➤ **prestar dinero:** to lend money

➤ **proponer:** to propose

➤ **régimen:** administration; government; regime

➤ **latifundios:** large landholdings

➤ **repartir:** to distribute

➤ **ejido:** communal land farmed by campesinos

➤ **campo:** rural land

➤ **red:** network (feminine)

➤ **carretera:** highway; roadway

➤ **provocar:** to provoke

Análisis del Texto

Now let's analyze some of the more interesting parts of the text:

➤ *llegó a la presidencia*

Literally, this means "arrived at the presidency." A better translation would be "came to the presidency" or even just "became president."

➤ *En su gobierno, se propuso cumplir ....*

Proponer means "to propose." It has *poner* in it, so it acts like *poner*. Notice the passive *se propuso*, literally "it was proposed to fulfill ...." This is seen again in *se expropiaron*.

➤ *El problema de los campesinos fue el que ....*

Notice the *fue el que*. This *el* is standing in for *el problema*. The masculine gender links *el* to *el problema*. The phrase literally translates as: "the problem of the rural peasants was the one that ...."

➤ *Cárdenas se preocupó por multiplicar ....*

The *se* here is reflexive: *preocuparse*, which in this context means "to be concerned about." Notice that *procuparse por* can be followed by an infinitive (*multiplicar*). In English, it would have been followed by an *–ing* form of the verb: "concerned about increasing." We'll review *por* and *para* later.

➤ *entre quienes*

This simply means "among the people who." It could also have been written *entre las personas que*.

Haz Clic Aquí

Learn more about Mexico by visiting the following Web sites: www.mexicool.com, www.mexweb.com, www.knowmexico. com, and http://style.mexicohost.com.mx.

You can also do a general search for "Mexico" and find hundreds of other great Web sites about art, history, culture, and tourism.

Ten Cuidado

I have included literal English translations of some Spanish phrases simply to explain certain constructions. If you're really trying to translate something, you'll want to stay away from a "word-for-word" translation because that rarely sounds natural. Instead of translating, try to understand the Spanish without thinking of the English equivalents.

➤ *los años treinta*

"The Thirties." When you want to talk about years in terms of a particular decade—the Roaring Twenties, the Warring Forties, the Boring Eighties—say *los años* + the corresponding decade.

➤ *obligó a miles de españoles a salir*

This could also have been expressed with a subjunctive construction: *obligó a que 'salieran' miles de españoles*. Certain verbs that by nature require a subjunctive (*obligar* = "to obligate") can sometimes take an infinite to express the same thing. More on the subjunctive in Chapter 12, "Los Estados Unidos de America."

Vista Panorámica de México

➤ **Nombre oficial:** Estados Unidos Mexicanos

➤ **Gobierno:** *República Federal de 31 estados y un Distrito Federal*

➤ **Capital:** *México, D.F. (con aprox. 22 millones de habitantes)*

➤ **Ciudades principales:**

México, Distrito Federal

Chihuahua

Tijuana

Monterrey

Mazatlán

Tampico

Veracruz

Guadalajara

Coatzacoalcos

Puebla

Ciudad Juárez

Acapulco

➤ **Tamaño:** 1.958.201 *kilómetros cuadrados*

➤ **Forma adjetiva:** *Mexicano/mexicana;* also *mejicano/mejicana*

➤ **Población:** *Aproximadamente 100 millones; 70 por ciento urbana, 30 por ciento rural*

➤ **Divisa:** *Nuevo peso mexicano*

➤ **Grupos étnicos:** *Mestizo* (mixed race), 60 por ciento; *indígena,* 25 por ciento, *blanco europeo,* 15 por ciento.

➤ **Recursos naturales:** *Petróleo, cobre, plata, oro, plomo, cinc, maderas*

➤ **Industrias:** *Petróleo y sus derivados, productos químicas, productos eléctricos, textiles, minería, hule* (rubber), *bebidas, turismo.*

➤ **Productos agrícolos:** *Maíz, frijol, café, algodón, azúcar, verduras y frutas tropicales*

➤ **Transportes:** *Buen sistema de carreteras, ferrocarriles, y 78 aeropuertos con servicio nacional e internacional*

Cultura Latina

Since the Revolution (1916), Mexico has been ruled by the *Partido Revolucionario Institucional,* or *PRI.* The PRI has lost some control in recent years to other parties such as the *Partido de Acción Nacional* (*PAN*) and the *Partido de la Revolución Democrática* (*PRD*). However, the PRI still retains considerable control over many of the political structures in the country.

Gramática: The Spanish Verb

Spanish verbs are listed in the dictionary in what is known as the *infinitive* form. As you already know, all verbs in this form end in *–ar, –er,* or *–ir.* Though these endings come at the end of the verb (as most endings do), the *–ar, –er,* and *–ir* parts roughly correspond to the "to" part of an English verb. So, while you could take it literally as "go to," "eat to," and so on, it really means this: "*to* go," "*to* eat," "*to* love," "*to* sleep," "*to* be" or "not *to* be," and so on:

➤ **hablar:**   "speak-to"   to speak

➤ **trabajar:**   "work-to"   to work

➤ **comer:**   "eat-to"   to eat

➤ **entender:**   "understand-to"   to understand

➤ **sentir:**   "feel-to"   to feel

There's not much you can do with an infinitive all by itself. Sometimes an infinitive can be used as a very insistent command, usually when you're trying to boss someone around. I wouldn't recommend using it, however, because it can be a bit harsh. When used as a command, the infinitive may be preceded by *a:*

➤ **¡A trabajar!:** Get to work!

➤ **¡A callarte!:** Be quiet!

➤ **¡Escribir!:** Write! (Start writing!)

Algo Nuevo

You'll hear the terms "regular verb" and "irregular verb" tossed about quite a bit. These descriptions may in fact be misnomers; even the irregular verbs are logical once you understand the patterns. When we say that a verb is "regular," this means that there are no surprises when it is conjugated and that everything follows the rules. An "irregular" verb simply belongs to a class of verbs that follows a different set of rules. Don't automatically assume that every "irregular" verb is an island unto itself.

As in English, an infinitive can be used as the object of another verb. For example, look at *Yo quiero* (I want). If you follow this phrase with an infinitive verb, you are saying that you "want to ...." Other similar verbs, such as *necesitar, preferir, poder,* and *desear* (just to mention a few) do the same thing. Just remember that the pronouns included in this list are optional:

➤ **Yo quiero bailar:** I want to dance.

➤ **Puedo cantar:** I can sing.

➤ **Prefiero comer aquí:** I prefer to eat here.

➤ **Yo no quiero trabajar:** I don't want to work.

➤ **Yo no necesito ir:** I don't need to go.

➤ **No quiero pagar:** I don't want to pay.

➤ **No quiero tener problemas:** I don't want to have (any) problems.

Cultura Latina

Few Iberian women came to America, and the mixing of races was common. By the end of the colonial period, *mestizos* (people of mixed Native American and European ancestry) made up the majority in many Latin American colonies. This mixture of races and cultures has contributed greatly to the diversity of the region.

Conjugation 101

Conjugating a verb means that you are changing the verb's form to indicate when, how long, and who or what does, did, or will do the action. By conjugating the verb, you are committing it to actually doing something, where before you just had an infinitive suggesting some general action. So, the English verb "to go" is not conjugated, whereas "John *goes*" or "John *went*" is.

Conjugating a Spanish verb usually means that you remove the *ar/er/ir* part of the infinitive and add some suffix. This suffix will indicate who is doing the action of the verb. When you remove the infinitive ending, the part left behind is called the stem. So, the stem of *hablar* is *habl–,* and the stem of *comer* is *com–.*

The English word *tense* comes from the Latin word *tempus,* which means "time." The tense of a verb tells you when something occurred and whether the action has been completed. The first tense that you learned was probably the present indicative: *Yo hablo.* It's used to express the idea of "now and in general, but not necessarily at this very minute."

Now, look at the following sentences. They are all examples of regularly conjugated verbs in the present indicative tense:

➤ **Yo hablo el inglés:** I speak English.

➤ **¿Es usted mexicano?:** Are you Mexican?

➤ **¿Habláis con Hector cada semana?:** Do you all speak with Hector every week?

➤ **Tú hablas un poco del español:** You speak a little Spanish.

➤ **Ella canta, pero él no:** She sings, but he doesn't.

➤ **Nosotros vamos cada día a la tienda:** Every day we go to the store.

➤ **Ellos tocan música mexicana:** They play Mexican music.

➤ **¿Viajan ustedes en avión cada año a Mazatlán?:** Do you all travel to Mazatlán by airplane every year?

➤ **Mi esposo come muchas tortillas de maíz:** My husband eats a lot of corn tortillas.

➤ **El niño sabe muchas cosas:** The child knows a lot of things.

Acuérdate

Quick reminder: *yo, tú, él, ella, usted, nosotros/nosotras, vosotros/ vosotras* (in Spain), *ellos, ellas, ustedes.* Present indicative conjugation is part of basic Spanish grammar. If you feel a bit rusty, you may wish to review your basic books. You'll also find a few verb tables in Appendix A, "Basic Grammar Resource." There's never a bad time to go back to the fundamentals.

Acuérdate

The present indicative can also be used colloquially to indicate what someone is willing to do or intends to do in the near future. In this case, a future time must be specified or implied: *Lo hago mañana* = "I'll do it tomorrow."

Algo Nuevo

When asking a question, you should place the pronoun after the conjugated verb: *¿Habla usted el español?* But you'll also find that some Spanish-speakers don't always follow this pattern. Often, a rising tone is all that's required to indicate a question. Thus, you may hear *¿Usted habla el español?* In the Caribbean, especially in Puerto Rico, you may be asked "*¿De dónde tú eres?*" instead of the more usual "*¿De dónde eres tú?*"

Stem-Changing Verbs

Now that you've reviewed some regular verbs, let's look at some not-so-regular verbs. The most common irregularity occurs in stem-changing verbs, where there is an actual change within the stem when the verbs are conjugated. You may have heard of these verbs referred to affectionately as "shoe verbs." If this helps you, great. Personally, I've never quite bought into the idea of these verbs having anything to do with shoes, but whatever floats your *barco* ....

These are the various changes that can occur in the stem of a stem-changing verb:

Infinitive	Present Tense (First Person)	What Happens
contar	*cuento*	o → ue
poder	*puedo*	o → ue
jugar	*juego*	u → ue
querer	*quiero*	e → ie
pensar	*pienso*	e → ie
pedir	*pido*	e → i

The Stem Just Can't Take the Pressure

Rather than shoes, I like to think of stem-changing verbs as weak verbs with vowels in their stems that can't handle the added stress that lands on them when conjugated. If you will recall the rules for accentuation from Chapter 4, " Accéntuating the Pósitive," infinitive verbs are all stressed naturally on the last syllable (*haBLAR, coMER, peDIR*) because they end in a consonant other than *n* or *s*. However, conjugation shifts the stress back to the penultimate syllable, and sometimes the vowel in that syllable is "too weak" to handle all that stress by itself. So, it turns into a diphthong or a more stable vowel.

Let's look at the verb *poder* ("to be able"):

➤ **(Yo) puedo:** I can.

➤ **(Tú) puedes:** You can.

➤ **(Él) puede:** He can.

The verb *poder* has an *o* in its stem. When conjugated in the present indicative tense, the stress shifts from the final syllable of the infinitive (*poDER*) back to the penultimate *o: POdo*. But this little *o* is too weak to carry all that stress, so it changes into a more stable diphthong: *ue*.

In the *nosotros/nosotras* form, however, the syllable with the *o* is no longer the penultimate syllable and is off the hook here. Now the *e* of the *–emos* ending is sitting in the penultimate spot (same for *–amos* and *–imos* endings in other verbs). For *vosotros/vosotras,* the stress is on the last syllable, and the *o* still gets a break:

➤ **nosotros/nosotras:** pod*e*mos

➤ **vosotros/vosotras:** pod*é*is

In the second and third person plural (*ellos/ustedes*) the stress falls back on the poor *o:*

➤ **pueden:** They can.

The Verb **Haber** *and the Past Participle*

The verb *haber* means "to have." But its role in Spanish is mostly confined to that of a helping verb. It does the same thing as the "have" in the following sentence: "I have written this book and you have bought it." You probably remember the present indicative of *haber* from your beginning text: *he, has, ha, hemos, habéis, han.*

Acuérdate

Some relatively common verbs end in *–go* in the first person singular: *hacer = hago; poner = pongo.* Some of these guys are also stem-changing verbs (from *tú* onward): *tener = tengo, tienes, tiene.* Others are regular in all other aspects except for the *–go* part. You can find a list of more such verbs in Appendix A.

Acuérdate

Your dictionary should indicate stem-changing verbs with a $(o \rightarrow ue)$ or $(e \rightarrow ie)$ or $(e \rightarrow i)$ after the verb. It may also refer to another common verb that is conjugated in the exact same way as the verb you're looking up. Check your dictionary to see how it indicates verbs that are stem-changing. If it doesn't, consider buying a better dictionary.

And just what is a past participle? Well, participles are made from verbs, but they are not conjugated. In fact, they are actually used as adjectives. For example, English words such as *opened, closed, finished,* and *defeated* are all participles because they are adjectives formed from verbs. Most English past participles are formed by adding *–ed* or *–en* to the verb.

Ten Cuidado

When a stem ends in a vowel, add a *tilde* on the *nosotros/ nosotras* ending to prevent the formation of a diphthong. For example, with the verb *sonreir* ("to smile"), the stem is *sonre–*. When you add the *–imos* ending, you get *sonreimos*. But the *ei* combo would form a one-syllable diphthong and sound like sohn RAY mohs. You must add the *tilde* to prevent that from happening: *sonreímos* (sohn ray EE mos).

Ten Cuidado

Don't use *haber* for "to own." That's where *tener* comes in.

Formation and Use of the Past Participle

With most verbs, just drop the ending and add the past participle ending. For *–ar* verbs, add *–ado*. For verbs ending in *–er* and *–ir*, add *–ido*. It doesn't matter whether the verb is stem-changing in the present indicative—it's the same deal.

The tense formed by *haber* + past participle is known as the present perfect tense. It tells of an action that occurred at an indefinite time in the past, but which may still be ongoing or having an influence on the present.

➤ **Yo he cantado la canción:** I have sung the song.

➤ **Hemos comprado los boletos:** We have bought the tickets.

➤ **Ustedes han aprendido muy bien el español:** You all have learned Spanish very well.

➤ **Quiero haber terminado el trabajo:** I want to have the work finished.

➤ **No hemos estado en Puerto Vallarta todavía:** We haven't been to Puerto Vallarta yet.

Later, we'll see other uses of *haber* + past participle.

The Verb Ir

You should already know this verb (*voy, vas, va,* and so on). It's pronounced like those things on the side of your head that you hear with.

Take a look at the following sentences. They demonstrate some of the principal uses of this versatile little verb. You may wish to consult your dictionary under *ir* for even more examples:

➤ **Voy a la playa:** I'm going to the beach.

➤ **Vamos al centro a ver el desfile:** We're going (Let's go) downtown to see the parade.

➤ **El camino va por la costa:** The road goes along the coast.

➤ **La cerveza no va bien con el helado:** Beer and ice cream don't go well together.

➤ **Los turistas van en autobús a las ruinas:** The tourists go to the ruins by bus.

➤ **Me gusta el ir y venir de la gente por la calle:** I like the comings and goings of the people on the street.

➤ **A eso voy:** I am getting to that (issue).

➤ **Esta vez, va en serio:** This time, he (she) means business (is serious).

➤ **Voy a ir de payaso a la fiesta:** I'm going to the party (dressed) as a clown.

Acuérdate

There are also a number of irregular past participles, such as *escrito, hecho,* and *puesto.* You should have seen them in your beginning textbook. If you need to review, you'll find a list of irregular past participles on the reference card at the beginning of this book.

Algo Nuevo

Although technically a present-tense construction, the present perfect is a great way to express a past tense aspect for actions that have been completed. It should be fairly easy for you, given its similarities with the English "I have done it" construction. In fact, if you don't feel comfortable with the preterite tense yet, you should consider this as your past tense until the preterite flows more naturally for you.

The Ir + a + *Infinitive Future Tense*

If you put an infinitive verb after the *a*, you can express a future tense—very much like the English "I'm going to ...." This form of the future tense is very common in daily speech and should come somewhat naturally to you because it follows the same pattern as English:

Ten Cuidado

When used with forms of *haber*, the past participle is always left in the masculine form. Don't change words such as *abierto* to *abierta* when used with *haber*, even if you or the person doing the action is female, or the object of the action is a feminine noun. You'll see *abierta* in other constructions with *estar*, rather than *haber*.

Acuérdate

The verbs *ser*, *estar*, *ir*, and *dar* ("to give") have an *–oy* ending in the first person singular: *Yo soy, estoy, voy, doy*. Because these verbs are so short, it was probably a good idea to give them a slightly longer ending in the *yo* form. Otherwise they would have been "*so, esto, vo,*" and "*do.*"

➤ **Voy a viajar a Veracruz en barco:** I'm going to travel to Veracruz by boat.

➤ **Vamos a ver:** Let's see. (We'll see.)

➤ **¿Vas a poder pagar la cuenta o no?:** Are you going to be able to pay the bill or not?

➤ **No van a querer pelear conmigo:** They aren't going to want to fight with me.

➤ **Vamos a tratar de llegar temprano a la re- unión:** We are going to try to arrive at the meeting early.

➤ **Vais a tener que comprar un nuevo coche:** You all are going to have to buy a new car. (Spain)

➤ **Y ahora, La Sra. Esperanza Cano va a hablar con ustedes:** And now, Mrs. Esperanza Cano will talk with (to) you.

When *ir + a + infinitive* itself is the object of a verb (more on objects later), it translates as "in order to":

➤ **Quiero ir a jugar al tenis ahora:** I want to go and play tennis now.

➤ **Piensan ir a conocer las ruinas aztecas:** They are thinking of going and getting to know the Aztec ruins.

➤ **No puedo ir a ver los mariachis hoy:** I can't go and see the mariachis today.

Passive Constructions with Se

The most common way in Spanish to form a passive (something "is done," "is said," "is known," and so on) is to use *se* in combination with the third-person conjugation of the verb. The subject of these constructions may be a nonspecific *it*, as in "It is spoken" and "It is done here."

The trick to recognizing these passive constructions is to look for a verb in the third-person singular or plural conjugation next to *se*. You will never see phrases such as *se hablas* or *se sabemos."* Study the following examples:

➤ **Se habla español:** Spanish is spoken.

➤ **Se vende este terreno:** This land is for sale ("is being sold").

➤ **El español no se entiende en Brazil:** Spanish is not understood in Brazil.

➤ **¿Cómo se dice eso en el inglés?:** How do you say that in English? (How is that said?)

➤ **No se sabe si lo van a cambiar o no:** It isn't known whether they will change it or not.

➤ **¿Aquí se compran libros usados?:** Do you buy used books here?

➤ **Sí, se compran:** Yes, we do. (They are bought.)

Acuérdate

If you want to say "I'm on my way" or "I'm coming" when someone calls for you, say *Voy.* Literally, *voy* does mean "I'm going," but in the context of telling someone that you are on your way (to answer the door, going to a meeting, and so on), it means "I'm headed in that direction."

Algo Nuevo

The pronouns *usted* and *ustedes* are often abbreviated as *Ud., Vd.,* and *Uds.* in writing. However, the trend these days is to write them out in full. You must learn to recognize *Ud.* and *Vd.* as standing for *usted,* but you should probably get used to writing out the word in full. *Usted* is never capitalized unless, as here, it comes at the beginning of a sentence.

Risa del Día

Too much grammar? I agree. Here's your second joke. At least it's a step up from the chicken joke you got in the previous chapter:

> Doctor, ¡me he fracturado el brazo en varios lugares!

> Bueno, entonces no regrese a esos lugares.

Vocabulario Útil:

- ➤ **fracturar:** to fracture; to break
- ➤ **brazo:** arm
- ➤ **varios:** various; several
- ➤ **lugares:** places
- ➤ **bueno:** "Well …"
- ➤ **entonces:** then; so
- ➤ **regresar:** return
- ➤ **esos:** those (masculine plural)

El Cuiz

Give the English translation for the following words. Cheating isn't cool, but hey, it's your choice:

1. enseñanza _____
2. ejercito _____
3. enriquecer _____
4. proponer _____
5. terreno _____
6. provocar _____
7. promesa _____
8. campesino _____
9. multiplicar _____
10. prestar dinero _____
11. repartir _____
12. régimen _____
13. latifundios _____
14. carreteras _____
15. red _____

Tareas

1. Explain to someone how verbs work in Spanish. If there is no one around, write a few paragraphs on a sheet of paper detailing everything you know about Spanish verbs.

2. Learn more about Mexico on the Internet or by researching the topic at your local library.

The Least You Need to Know

➤ Population-wise, Mexico is the largest Spanish-speaking country.

➤ Verbs in Spanish conjugate to show time, aspect, and subject.

➤ You don't always need to say *yo, tú, él,* and similar pronouns.

➤ Some verbs also change in the stem when conjugated.

El Cono Sur: South America's Southern Cone

Chile, Argentina, Uruguay, and Paraguay are known collectively as *el Cono Sur,* or South America's Southern Cone. I suppose that the area is rather cone-shaped. Let's take a quick look at the diverse countries that make up this region.

Chile

Chile is unique for its very long (2,650 miles) and comparatively narrow (maximum 250 miles) shape, and for the great variety of its natural features. The country's northern region near the Peruvian border is one of the driest areas in the world, while Chile's southern regions are among the wettest in South America. The country shares the Andean mountains (known by the locals as *la cordillera*) with its eastern neighbor, Argentina.

Chilean democracy is still recovering from the dictatorship of General Augusto Pinochet, who came to power in 1973 after a military coup (*golpe de estado*). However, in its economy and public services, Chile is one of the most developed countries in Latin America and is often mentioned as a potential partner in the North American Free Trade Agreement.

Argentina

Although Argentina declared its independence from Spain in 1816, the culture in South America's largest Spanish-speaking country is still greatly influenced by Europe. Much of the national identity centers on its sophisticated capital, Buenos Aires. Argentina was home to legendary first lady Eva Peron, who was the inspiration for the musical *Evita*. Decades of military control, which included a lengthy "Dirty War" against leftists that left thousands dead, ended in 1983. Since then, Argentina has enjoyed a modest economic recovery by privatizing many government-owned industries and by checking the hyper-inflation it endured during the 1990s. Currently, the Argentine peso has official parity with the U.S. dollar (1 peso argentino = 1 dollar).

Paraguay

Ninety-five percent of Paraguayans are of mixed Spanish and Guarani Indian descent. Between 1865 and 1870, more than half of Paraguay's population died in the brutal War of the Triple Alliance, which Paraguay waged against neighboring Brazil, Argentina, and Uruguay. In the years that followed, Paraguay suffered a series of short-lived and often oppressive governments. A new constitution established in 1992 has helped the country move toward democracy. Paraguay held free elections in 1993.

Cultura Latina

Buenos Aires and Montevideo are both located on the *Río de la Plata,* or River Plate. People from Buenos Aires are known as *porteños,* which means "people from the port." The Spanish spoken in both Montevideo and Buenos Aires has been greatly influenced by Italian immigrants. Argentines are often referred to as *ché,* which means "hey," because they are known to say "ché" a lot.

Uruguay

The first inhabitants of what we now call Uruguay were a small tribe of Native Americans know as the *Charruas,* a nickname used for Uruguayans to this day. These *Charruas* were a tough bunch. When Spanish explorer Juan Diaz de Solís landed in 1516, he was promptly dispatched (that is, killed). Their stubborn resistance, combined with the lack of valuable natural resources in the area, kept European settlers out until 1624.

Today, Uruguay is one of the most urbanized countries in the world, with 44.5 percent of the population living in its capital, Montevideo. Known as the "Switzerland of South America," the country has had a long history of democracy. The political climate took a downturn in the 1970s and 1980s, however, after a military takeover. With the return of democratic elections, though, Uruguay's future looks brighter than ever.

Lectura: El Festival Nacional de la Tonada

The *tonada* is an Argentine form of folk ballad. Each year, a music festival in celebration of *la tonada* is held near Mendoza, the largest city in Argentina's Andean region. Here are some details:

> En el departamento de Tunuyán, ubicado a 80 kilómetros al sur de la Ciudad de Mendoza, se realiza todos los años, en los primeros días del mes de febrero, el acontecimiento de la música popular más importante de la Argentina: "El Festival Nacional de la Tonada".

> Músicos consagrados de todas las latitudes del territorio argentino y del Mercosur no quieren perderse este megaevento que, en la XVIII edición, en febrero de 1999, convocó en el Anfiteatro Ciudad de Tunuyán a más de 200 mil personas en cuatro jornadas. El Festival Nacional de la Tonada es una fiesta popular y a los analistas del género folklórico les resulta difícil comprender cómo en un departamento de sólo 38 mil habitantes no haya noche tonadera con asistencia inferior a los 50 mil espectadores.

> El festival será transmitido por Internet los días 3, 4, 5 y 6 de febrero del 2001.

Vocabulario Útil:

➤ **realizarse:** to happen; to take place; to make real

➤ **ubicar:** to be located

➤ **acontecimiento:** event; occurrence

➤ **consagrado:** sacred; well respected

➤ **latitudes:** latitudes; places; parts

➤ **Mercosur:** trade agreement among South American countries

➤ **perderse:** to miss

➤ **megaevento:** big event

➤ **convocar:** to convoke; to call together

➤ **jornada:** 24-hour period; day

➤ **género:** kind; type

➤ **resultar:** to be (after some effort); to turn out

➤ **tonadera:** time to play a lot of *tonadas*

➤ **inferior:** less than; inferior

➤ **asistencia:** attendance (false cognate)

➤ **espectador:** spectator

Cultura Latina

Both Argentina and Uruguay have a long history of cattle raising. Cattle are called *ganado*, and cowboys in Argentina and Uruguay are called *gauchos*. To say that someone is *muy gaucho* is a compliment, implying honesty, courteousness, and strength of character. In Chile, the word for a cowboy is *huaso*. Both words are originally from the Quechua language.

Análisis del Texto

Now let's take a closer look at the more interesting parts of the text:

➤ *se realiza todos los años*

The *se* makes this a passive construction. The verb *realizar* is almost a false cognate because it doesn't mean "to realize" in the sense of "I just realized that someone has stolen my wallet." Rather, it means "to make real" or "to make happen." It is, however, a cognate with the word *realize* in "to realize your dreams."

➤ *de todas las latitudes del territorio argentino*

Try not to let this sort of thing throw you off. This is just an elegant way of saying "from every part of Argentina."

➤ *Mercosur*

The countries of the Southern Cone (including Brazil) have a trade agreement called *Mercosur*. The author is just trying to be clever and save himself some time by not mentioning all of the countries in the region by name.

Algo Nuevo

In written Spanish, you often will come across a literary device known as "elegant variation." We also use this device in English. For example: The President of the United States; the Leader of the Free World; the Commander-in-Chief; the Resident of the White House. All of these refer to the same person. In a Spanish text, it is not uncommon to find the same subject referred to in a multitude of ways. Don't let this confuse you.

➤ *en la XVIII edición*

Edición here means "the 18th time they've held the festival." It's not an edition like a book. Sometimes you need to stretch your imagination to understand what is being talked about.

➤ *a los analistas del género folklórico les resulta difícil comprender*

The *a* ("to") at the beginning of this phrase lets us know that there is an object around somewhere. Later we find *les*, which points us back to *analistas del género*. So now we know who the object is. The verb *resultar* is just an elegant way of saying "is," as in *A mí me resulta difícil hablar* = "It is hard for me to speak." So this phrase means "It is difficult for the analysts of the genre to understand ...."

Cultura Latina

Spanish is the official language of Paraguay, but many people also speak *Guaraní*. While most official business is conducted in Spanish, *Guaraní* can be heard spoken on the street. To learn more about this fascinating language, visit http://merece. uthscsa.edu/gram/guarani/ facts-eng.html.

Vista Panorámica del Cono Sur

➤ **Nombres oficiales de los países:** *República Argentina; República Oriental del Uruguay; República del Paraguay; República de Chile*

➤ **Gobiernos:** *Argentina: República de 22 provincias; Uruguay: República de 19 departamentos; Paraguay: República de 19 departamentos; Chile: República de 12 regiones*

➤ **Capitales:**

  ➤ Buenos Aires (Argentina)

  ➤ Montevideo (Uruguay)

  ➤ Asunción (Paraguay)

  ➤ Santiago (Chile)

➤ **Tamaños:** *Argentina: 2.780.399 kilómetros cuadrados; Uruguay: 176.215 kilómetros cuadrados; Paraguay: 406.752 kilómetros cuadrados; Chile: 756.626 kilómetros cuadrados*

➤ **Poblaciónes:** *Argentina: 36 millones; Uruguay: 3 millones; Paraguay: 5 millones; Chile: 15 millones*

➤ **Divisas:** *Argentina: peso (con paridad con el dólar de EE.UU.); Uruguay: nuevo peso uruguayo; Paraguay: el guaraní; Chile: peso chileno*

➤ **Formas adjetivas:** *argentino; uruguayo; paraguayo; chileno*

➤ **Recursos naturales de la region:** *Tierras fértiles, petróleo, gas natural, mineral de hierro, uranio, plata, cinc, plomo, bosque, potencia hidroeléctica, otros*

➤ **Industrias:** *Carne, lana, pieles, productos de cuero, metales, textiles, comida, cemento, vinos, azúcar, madera, productos químicos, maquinaria*

➤ **Productos agrícolos:** *Carne de res, granos, semillas oleaginosas* (oil seeds), *caña de azúcar, trigo, remolacha, citrus, arroz, uva, maíz, soja, algodón, otros*

Gramática: Los Adjetivos

Adjectives modify or describe nouns: *tall* tree, *big* mistake, *heavy* load, *red* brick, *angry* bear, *annoying* insect, and so on. Yes, you knew this already.

You also know that in Spanish, adjectives *must* agree in number and gender with the nouns they modify. This means that if the noun is feminine, the adjective modifying it also takes a feminine ending. If it's masculine, you need a masculine ending. And if the noun is plural, the adjective must be pluralized:

➤ **hombre viejo**: old man

➤ **mujer alta**: tall woman

➤ **hombres viejos**: old men

➤ **mujeres altas**: tall women

In Spanish, descriptive adjectives are usually placed *after* the noun they modify. This is the opposite of what you are used to in English:

➤ **gato bueno**: Literally means "cat good" = good cat

➤ **perro malo**: Literally means "dog bad" = bad dog

Adjectives with Other Endings

Not all adjectives end in *–o* or *–a*. In fact, many adjectives end in *–e* or in a consonant such as *–l, –r, –s* or *–z*. But the good news is that this actually makes things easier. Most adjectives that end in a letter other than *–o* or *–a* are said to be "invariable" (do not change) with respect to gender. So, you can use the same form of the adjective with both masculine and feminine nouns:

➤ **un hombre inteligente**: an intelligent man

➤ **una mujer inteligente**: an intelligent woman

➤ **un vaso grande**: a large glass (for drinking)

➤ **las fiestas grandes**: the big parties

➤ **una reunión urgente**: an urgent meeting

Haz Clic Aquí

For more information about the countries of the Southern Cone, visit the following Web sites: www.uruguay.com, www.paraguay.com, www.chile-online.com, and www.argentina-guia.com.ar. You can also do a general search and find many more great Web sites.

Acuérdate

Remember all the grief you suffered as a kid when you used a double negative such as "I don't got nothing"? Well, Spanish is your lucky language. Double negatives are a must in Spanish: *Él no hace nada* is the correct way to say "He doesn't do anything." Yes, the argument can be made that "if he doesn't do nothing, then he must be doing something." But not in Spanish! Get used to double negatives.

➤ **un caso urgente:** an urgent case

➤ **los muchachos felices:** the happy boys

➤ **la muchacha feliz:** the happy girl

However, even though there may be no change for gender, all adjectives must add *–s* (or *–es*, when they end in a consonant) if they modify plural nouns: *ocho mujeres inteligentes* = "eight intelligent women."

There is an exception to the previously stated rule: Adjectives referring to nationality or geographical division will take an *–a* if they end in a consonant (such as *–n*, *–s*, and *–l*):

➤ **un turista alemán:** a male German tourist

➤ **una turista alemana:** a female German tourist

➤ **un señor español:** a Spanish gentleman

➤ **las canciones españolas:** the Spanish songs

➤ **el pan francés:** the French bread

➤ **la sopa francesa:** the French soup

Remember that *de* can also help you construct an adjectival relationship:

➤ **la camisa de algodón:** the cotton shirt

➤ **el monitor de computadora:** the computer monitor

➤ **la puerta de madera:** the wooden door

➤ **el viaje de placer:** the pleasure trip

➤ **el boleto de avión:** the airplane ticket

Acuérdate

For gender-conforming adjectives, the dictionary usually gives you the masculine form only. Unless the feminine form is unexpected, it probably won't be listed. But that's okay because you'll know how to make the adjectives feminine all by yourself.

Ten Cuidado

Don't be thrown off if the noun ends in a letter other than *–o* or *–a*; the adjective must match the *gender* of the noun *only*. Use the article as your guide. The ending of the noun and adjective may be different: *balcón alto* (not *balcón altón*).

Dumb, Dumber, Dumbest: Comparisons and Superlatives

We often use adjectives to draw comparisons between two or more things. This is known as (get ready for this one …) a *comparative:* "I run *faster* than he does." And if we want to indicate which noun (or nouns) among several possesses the most or least of a specific quality, we call that a *superlative:* "I'm the *fastest* runner in the world."

In English, many adjectives follow the "fast, faster, fastest" pattern. But Spanish follows the "difficult, more difficult, most difficult" pattern.

Ten Cuidado

When adding letters to the end of words, *tildes* may appear or disappear. An added plural suffix will cause the stress to fall naturally on the expected syllable: *balón* → *balones*. Thus, no tilde is required. In other cases, the addition of a suffix or pronoun may take the stress away from the expected syllable, thus requiring a *tilde* to preserve correct stress: *deja* → *déjaselo*.

Acuérdate

When *de* comes before the definite article *el*, the contraction *del* is formed. This contraction is not optional. However, you should use *de el* if the *el* is part of a proper name, or if the *él* refers to a masculine living thing: *la ciudad de El Paso, Texas; el libro de él.*

Comparatives

Let's start with some basic comparisons:

➤ **un hombre alto:** a tall man

➤ **un hombre más alto:** a man more tall (taller)

➤ **una mujer menos alta:** a woman less tall (shorter)

To indicate what's being compared to what, *que* is needed:

➤ **hombre más alto que ...:** taller man than ...

➤ **Marco es más inteligente que José:** Marco is more intelligent that José.

➤ **José es menos inteligente que Marco:** José is less intelligent than Marco.

Superlatives

To say "the most" or "the least," or "the best" or "the worst" of something, we need to introduce the definite article *el, la, los, las* back into the picture:

➤ **el hombre más rico:** the richest (most rich) man

➤ **los más caros de la tienda:** the most expensive (ones) in the store

➤ **el turista menos inteligente del mundo:** the least intelligent tourist in the world

The little word *de* works with superlatives to indicate the group from which the subject is the most/least of the quality indicated:

➤ **Yo soy la menos rica del pueblo:** I'm the least rich (woman) in town (of the town).

➤ **Yo no soy el autor más famoso del mundo:** I'm not the most famous author in the world.

➤ **El edificio es el más alto de la ciudad:** The building is the city's tallest (tallest of the city).

Algo Nuevo

Adjectives can easily be changed into nouns simply by adding an article: *un chileno* = "a male Chilean person"; *una argentina* = "a female Argentine person"; *los uruguayos no, pero los paraguayos sí* = "the Uruguayans don't, but the Paraguayans do." By using the definite article (*el, la, los, las*) with the adjective, we can express the idea of "the X one," as in *No quiero el rojo, sino el amarillo* ("I don't want the red one, but rather the yellow one.") Also, *Quiero los nuevos* = "I want the new ones."

Adjectives That Don't Follow the Rules

A small group of common adjectives does not use *más* when making a comparative or superlative. They are invariable for gender.

Adjectives That Don't Follow the Rules

Adjective	Comparison:	Superlative:
bueno	*mejor* (never *más bueno*)	*el/la mejor*
malo	*peor* (never *más malo*)	*el/la peor*
grande	*mayor* ("older")	*el/la mayor* (referring to age only)

Here are a few examples of the adjectives in the previous table and how they would be used:

➤ **La comida del restaurante es la peor del mundo:** The restaurant's food is the worst in the world.

➤ **Pedro es el mejor estudiante de la clase:** Pedro is the best student in the class.

➤ **Soy el mayor de la familia:** I'm the biggest (oldest) in the family.

Ten Cuidado

The plurals of the irregular comparatives are logical: *las mejores, los peores, los mayores,* and so on.

Bueno, Malo, Grande

A small group of adjectives have a shorter form that must be used before any masculine *singular* noun. *Grande* becomes *gran* before any singular noun—masculine or feminine. Some of these you have seen before, while others may be new.

Adjectives and Singular Nouns

Adjective	with Singular Noun	Means ...
bueno (good)	*buen hombre*	good man
malo (bad)	*mal hombre*	bad man
alguno (some)	*algún hombre*	some man
ninguno (no, none)	*ningún hombre*	no man
primero (first)	*primer hombre*	first man
tercero (third)	*tercer hombre*	third man
uno (one)	*un hombre*	a man
santo (holy, saint)	San Pablo	Saint Paul
grande (big, great)	*un gran día*	a great day
	una gran idea	a great idea

The Last Word on the Placement of Adjectives

By now you have accepted the idea that adjectives are placed after the nouns they modify. However, some adjectives have a different meaning depending on whether they are placed in front of the noun or after it.

Adjectives Before and After

Adjective	Before Noun	After Noun
antiguo	ancient	former
cierto	some	definite
diferente	unlike	various
nuevo	another	new
grande	great; "grand"	large
pobre	pitiable	not rich
varios	several	varied; different
viejo	long-standing	old (age)

Here are a few examples:

➤ **una casa nueva:** a new house (built recently)

➤ **una nueva casa:** a new house (a different one)

➤ **un amigo viejo:** an old friend (in age)

➤ **un viejo amigo:** an old friend (of long standing)

➤ **un hombre grande:** a large man

➤ **un gran hombre:** a great man (not necessarily big)

➤ **el papá pobre:** the destitute father (no money)

➤ **mi pobre papá:** my poor dad (I pity him)

Acuérdate

Colors are usually adjectives, but sometimes they are used as nouns. When this is the case, colors take a masculine article: *el blanco de los ojos* = "the white of the eyes."

While adjectives in Spanish do spend most of their time after the nouns they modify, descriptive adjectives may also be placed in front of a noun to emphasize the quality of the characteristic being described. This is extremely common in writing:

➤ **los malos sueños de Tomás:** Tomás' bad dreams

➤ **los bellos ojos de Marta:** Marta's beautiful eyes

➤ **las verdes plantas de la selva:** the green plants of the jungle

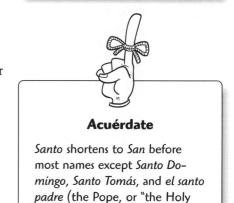

Acuérdate

Santo shortens to *San* before most names except *Santo Domingo*, *Santo Tomás*, and *el santo padre* (the Pope, or "the Holy Father").

Pointing Words: Este, Ese, Esta, Esa, Aquel, and So On

Spanish recognizes three levels of proximity. First we have the things that are really close to us. For these we use *este, esta, estos,* and *estas.* Then there are the things that are not so close, but are not necessarily out of reach. For those we need *ese, esa, esos,* and *esas.* Finally, we have the things that are quite far away. For those you'll use *aquel, aquella, aquellos,* and *aquellas.* You probably knew this already. But let's take a quick look at these pointing words one more time.

Demonstrative Adjectives

The demonstrative adjectives always appear together with the nouns they modify. There are no *tildes* on these. They must match gender and number of the thing(s) they are pointing or referring to. Study these examples:

➤ **Queremos compar estas cosas:** We want to buy these things.

➤ **¿Cuánto cuestan estos juguetes cada uno?:** How much do these toys cost each?

➤ **Aquellos tres turistas ya no tienen dinero:** Those three tourists over there don't have any money left.

➤ **Aquel hombre es vendedor de recuerdos típicos:** That man over there is a seller of typical souvenirs.

➤ **Este regalo será para mi abuelo. Ese regalo será para Juan:** This present is (will be) for my grandfather. That present is for Juan.

Demonstrative Pronouns

These are the same words that you just learned—only now they're written with *tildes*. Demonstrative adjectives modify nouns, but the demonstrative pronouns actually stand in for nouns (the added responsibility means that they get to wear the *tilde*).

The gender and number of the demonstrative pronoun will link it to the noun or nouns in question, so there is no need to mention the nouns specifically. You can often translate these as "this one," "that one," and even "these ones."

Study the following examples to see how they differ in usage from the demonstrative adjectives. Again, the noun or nouns being referenced won't actually be mentioned. The pronouns are here to give the real nouns a break:

➤ **Queremos compar éstas:** We want to buy these (feminine things).

➤ **Éste cuesta dos mil pesos, y ése cuesta mil cuatro cientos:** This one costs 2,000 pesos, and that one costs 1,400 (pesos).

➤ **Aquéllos no son baratos:** Those over there aren't cheap.

➤ **¿Cuál es el precio de éste?:** What is the price of this one?

➤ **Éste será para mi abuelo, y ése será para Juan:** This one is for my grandfather, and that one is for Juan.

Neuter Demonstrative Pronouns: Esto, Eso, Aquello

Yes, both the demonstrative adjectives and pronouns must match the gender and number of the nouns being modified or substituted. But there are other times when the "this" or "that" you are referring to is not a specific or quantifiable noun, but rather an idea, an event, a series of things, or something you don't know the name of yet.

When you say "This is great" or "That's a shame," you're referring to an idea or situation in general. And if you ask "What is that?" you won't know the gender of the noun because you don't know what the thing *is*. That's why you asked.

In such situations, the neuter demonstrative pronouns *eso, esto,* and *aquello* can save the day. If you don't know the name (much less the gender) of the thing you're referring to, these are the words for you.

Haz Clic Aquí

One of the best Spanish tutorials on the Web is www.studyspanish. com. You can access verb tables, take quizzes, improve your vocabulary, and check out travel opportunities, courses, and tapes. Everything is designed to help you learn more Spanish. It's definitely worth a visit.

Acuérdate

Don't stress too much over the *ese* vs. *aquel* issue. Many native speakers use *ese, esa,* and *eso* for "that" when technically *aquel, aquella,* or *aquello* should be used.

Read the following examples to see the neuter demonstratives in action:

➤ **¿Qué es esto?:** What is this? (This could be an unknown noun or a situation.)

➤ **¿Cómo se llama esto?:** What do you call this?

➤ **Esto no es justo.:** This isn't fair.

➤ **No queremos comprar esto, queremos comprar eso:** We don't want to buy this, we want to buy that.

➤ **Aquello es otro tema:** That's another issue.

➤ **Eso es una buena idea:** That's a good idea.

Risa del Día

A popular form for humor in Spanish is the *Jaimito* or *Pepito* joke. *Jaimito* is a mischievous little kid who is always in trouble at school or saying crazy things to his parents. Many of the words that come out of his mouth are not fit for chaste ears. The following joke is rather tame. See if you get it:

Jaimito vuelve de la escuela:

—Papá, papá, ¡hoy casi me saqué un 10!

—¡Bárbaro! … pero ¿por qué "casi"?

—Porque se lo pusieron al nene del banco de al lado.

Vocabulario Útil:

➤ **volver:** to return

➤ **casi:** almost

➤ **sacar:** to get; to come out with

➤ **un 10:** a perfect score; an "A"

➤ **¡bárbaro!:** wonderful!; great!

➤ **se lo:** "to him it" (it = *un 10*)

➤ **pusieron:** preterite form of *poner*

➤ **nene:** kid; boy

➤ **de al lado:** at the side; next to (me)

El Cuiz

Give the English equivalent of the following words. Cheating is all right, but don't get too used to it:

1. espectador _____
2. realizarse _____
3. género _____
4. consagrado _____
5. acontecimiento _____
6. resultar _____
7. Mercosur _____
8. perderse _____
9. convocar _____
10. jornada _____
11. inferior _____
12. asistencia _____
13. ubicar _____

Tareas

1. Explain to someone how adjectives work in Spanish. If there is no one around, write a few paragraphs on a sheet of paper detailing everything you know about Spanish adjectives.

2. Explain to someone how demonstrative pronouns and adjectives work in Spanish. If there is no one around, write a few paragraphs on a sheet of paper detailing everything you know about Spanish demonstratives.

The Least You Need to Know

➤ The *–o* and *–a* endings work with adjectives, too.

➤ Most adjectives must match the gender of the noun.

➤ All adjectives must match the singular and plural form of the noun they modify.

➤ Demonstrative pronouns take a *tilde;* the adjectives and neuters don't.

Chapter 9

Los Países Andinos: The Land of the Incas

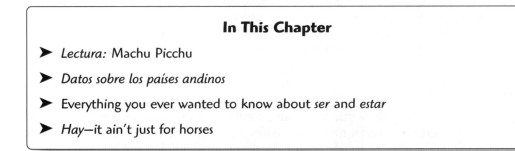

In This Chapter

➤ *Lectura:* Machu Picchu

➤ *Datos sobre los países andinos*

➤ Everything you ever wanted to know about *ser* and *estar*

➤ *Hay*—it ain't just for horses

The northern Andes was once the cradle of an advanced and powerful indigenous civilization: the Incas. Today, the descendents of this great nation, together with immigrants from many parts of the world, live in one of the most culturally rich areas in Latin America.

El Perú

Peru, the largest of the Andean countries, was the focus of Spanish colonial domination for well over 200 years. What remains of pre-Columbian America with regard to people, culture, and settlements is perhaps better represented in Peru than in any other nation. Thus, it is no surprise that the country has seen a dramatic increase in tourism over the last few decades. Unfortunately, political insurgency has plagued Peru for many years, and the government has spent countless resources fighting rebel groups such as Tupac Amaru and the Shining Path.

Bolivia

Bolivia, the only landlocked Andean country, also has a largely indigenous Indian population that has preserved its native languages and much of its traditional way of life. It is South America's least-developed country, and nearly two-thirds of its people live in poverty. In recent years, however, improvements in the Bolivian economy have been made due to the government's austere economic reform measures. Most Bolivians live in the thin air of the Altiplano, a plateau along the western edge of the country that is 11,550 feet above sea level.

El Ecuador

As its name suggests, Ecuador extends over both sides of the equator. It is the smallest of the Andean countries, but has the highest average population density in South America. Interestingly, Ecuador's two largest cities share few things in common. Quito, the capital, is situated high in the Andes. Guayaquil, the country's largest city, is at sea level and is a major port on the Pacific. The Galapagos Islands form Ecuador's Colón province. Charles Darwin visited the islands in 1830, where he conducted the major portion of his observations that led to his theories on evolution. Scientists continue to carry out research on the islands, and the Galapagos have become a popular destination for eco-tourists.

Colombia

Colombia is the only South American country with ports on both the Atlantic and Pacific oceans. People living on the coasts share more in common with the neighboring Caribbean countries than with their Andean neighbors. However, much of the mountainous interior of the country is definitely Andean in culture and climate.

Colombia's main exports include oil and coffee, but the country is equally renowned as the world's largest producer of cocaine. Regional drug cartels also deal in heroin and marijuana. Colombia has had a violent history, including bloody civil wars at the beginning of the twentieth century and again in the 1940s and 1950s. Drug-related killings plagued the country in the 1980s but have declined since the death of Medellin cartel leader Pablo Escobar in 1993.

Haz Clic Aquí

Here are some great Web sites about the countries of the northern Andes: www.boliviaweb.com, www.colombiaemb.org, www.ecuador.com, and http://peruonline.com.

Lectura: Machu Picchu

This text describes Peru's most popular archeological attraction. It's a little longer than some of the previous *lecturas*. Don't worry if you need to read the passage more than once.

Descubierta en 1911 por Hiram Bingham (profesor de la Universidad de Yale, EE.UU.), Machu Picchu viene a ser el atractivo arqueológico más importante de América del Sur.

Se podría decir que con el tiempo, este lugar se ha ido convirtiendo en el símbolo de todo lo que fue la vida y el esplendor prehispánico de los Andes. Su ubicación geográfica y el entorno físico hacen de Machu Picchu un espacio de ensueño y de rara belleza comparable a los más bellos paisajes creados por la naturaleza y adornados por la vida del hombre.

No se sabe a ciencia cierta cuándo fueron construidos los edificios prehispánicos. Afirman las más recientes investigaciones que las primeras construcciones pueden ser atribuidas al famoso Inca Pachacuti, el organizador del Imperio.

Debido a la gran cantidad de esqueletos de mujeres encontrados, se piensa que fue un lugar donde vivían las mujeres del Inca o un refugio de mujeres durante la época de la conquista. De lo que si no hay duda es que Machu Picchu representa un extraordinario ejemplo de arquitectura e ingeniería.

Por lo general un tour a Machu Picchu dura un día entero. Empezando temprano por la mañana se toma el tren en Cuzco.

Después de 3 horas se llega a Aguas Calientes (la ciudadela de Machu Picchu se encuentra en la cima de una montaña a la cual se llega mediante pequeños autobuses). Una vez en las ruinas empieza el recorrido guiado, finalizando con un almuerzo en el hotel. Después del almuerzo hay tiempo para sacar fotos o hacer un breve recorrido por su cuenta.

Cultura Latina

The music of the Andean countries has become very popular recently. The panpipes played by Andean musicians are known as *quenas*. Andean musicians also play a small mandolin-like instrument called a *charrango*, which is usually made from the body of an armadillo. Many music stores have Andean music tapes and CDs. You also can find Andean music online by searching for "Traditional Andean Music."

Cultura Latina

Two main native languages are spoken in this region: Quechua and Amarayá. Quechua-speakers can be found from Peru to southern Colombia. Amarayá is spoken mainly in Bolivia and along Peru's southern border. The two languages are not mutually intelligible. If you want to learn more about these languages, a simple Internet search should do the trick.

Vocabulario Útil:

➤ **descubrir:** to discover

➤ **debido a:** due to

➤ **atractivo:** attraction

➤ **convertirse:** to become; to convert

➤ **esplendor:** splendor

➤ **ubicación:** location

➤ **edificio:** building

➤ **espacio de ensueño:** place of dreams; fairy-tale land

➤ **entorno:** environment

➤ **raro:** rare (adjective before noun)

➤ **afirmar:** to confirm; to substantiate

➤ **imperio:** empire

➤ **esqueleto:** skeleton

➤ **refugio:** refuge

➤ **duda:** doubt

➤ **ingeniería:** engineering

➤ **durar:** to last

➤ **entero:** whole; entire; complete

➤ **ciudadela:** village

➤ **cima:** top

➤ **recorrido:** a trip; a round

➤ **por su cuenta:** on your own; by yourself

➤ **belleza:** beauty

➤ **paisaje:** landscape; "view"

➤ **adornado:** decorated; adorned

➤ **sacar fotos:** to take pictures

➤ **arqueológico:** archeological

Análisis del Texto

This text has a lot of goodies to teach us. Let's take a closer look:

➤ *viene a ser*

Venir a ser really just means "to be" here, with the idea that Machu Picchu is "coming to be" the most important archeological site in South America. *Venir* has many idiomatic uses apart from its basic meaning of "to come." For example, we can use *venir* to say that something *ha venido a menos* which loosely translated means "it isn't what it used to be." Check your dictionary for more uses of this versatile little verb.

➤ *este lugar se ha ido convirtiendo*

This is a tough one. The subject is *este lugar* ("this place"), which is really just standing in for Machu Picchu. The *se* is a third person reflexive and actually goes with *convirtiendo,* the present progressive *–ing* form of *convertirse* (to convert, to change oneself into, to become). *Ha,* naturally, is from *haber* and means "has," and *ido* is the irregular past participle of *ir* and means "gone." So, literally, we have "this place itself has gone becoming." Of course, this makes no sense. A better translation might be "Machu Picchu has, over a period of time, been in the process of becoming ...."

➤ *los más bellos paisajes creados por la naturaleza*

Notice that the adjective *bellos* is placed before the modified noun *paisajes*. This adjective might also have come after the noun, as most adjectives in Spanish tend to do: *Los paisajes más bellos* .... But there is a difference between the two placements, albeit a subtle one. With the adjective coming before the noun, the beauty of the landscapes is emphasized ("the most beautiful landscapes"). With the adjective after the noun (*paisajes bellos*), the emphasis is more on the landscapes ("the landscapes that happen to be beautiful"), suggesting that there might also be a lot of ugly landscapes around that aren't being considered.

Algo Nuevo

Take another look at this phrase from the reading: *Afirman las más recientes investigaciones que* .... Notice the word order here. A literal translation would be "They substantiate the most recent investigations that ...." In Spanish, because the verb indicates the subject by its conjugated form, there is more flexibility in terms of subject placement. So, I can say either *Juan lo compró* ("John bought it") or *Lo compró Juan* ("Bought it John"). It makes no difference. Don't let this throw you off.

Haz Clic Aquí

A great site for information about Machu Picchu is www. ifip.com/Machupijchu1.htm. Visit this Web site to see great pictures of the ruins and learn about its history in greater detail. Other sites include great information, too—just search under "Machu Picchu" and surf around.

➤ *a ciencia cierta*

Literally "by certain science," this idiomatic phrase just means "with certainty."

➤ *se piensa que*

The *se* makes it passive: "it is thought that." There are several passive *se* constructions in this text.

➤ *De lo que sí no hay duda es que Machu Picchu*

This construction would normally be a lot simpler: *No hay duda que Machu Picchu ...*. However, because the previous sentence casts some doubt as to what Machu Picchu was used for, this sentence, as a contrast to the uncertainty of the previous statement, starts off by telling the reader what we really do know for a fact. The *de lo que* literally means "of that which." The *sí* is an intensifier for what is being said. So, a better translation: "What there really is no doubt about is that ...."

➤ *la cima de una montaña a la cual se llega mediante pequeños autobuses*

The *a la cual* means "to which." The *la* refers to *cima* because both words are feminine. Literal translation: "The top of a mountain to which (feminine) it is arrived by way of small buses." Better translation: "You get to the top of the mountain on small buses."

➤ *por su cuenta*

Literally, "by your account." A better translation: "on your own."

Vista Panorámica de los Países Andinos

➤ **Países de la región:** *República de Bolivia; República del Perú; República del Ecuador; República de Colombia*

➤ **Gobiernos:** *Bolivia: República de 9 departamentos; el Perú: República de 23 departamentos y una provincia; el Ecuador: República de 20 provincias; Colombia: República de 23 departamentos, tres intendencias, y cinco comisarías*

➤ **Capitales:** *Bolivia: La Paz (administrativo), Sucre: (constitucional); Perú: Lima; Ecuador: Quito; Colombia: Santa Fé de Bogotá*

➤ **Tamaños:** *Bolivia: 1.098.581 km. cuadrados; Perú: 1.285.000 km. cuadrados; Ecuador: 269.178 km. cuadrados; Colombia: 1.141.748 km. cuadrados*

➤ **Poblaciones:** *Bolivia: 9 millones; Perú: 28 millones; Ecuador: 13 millones; Colombia: 35 millones*

➤ **Divisas:** *Bolivia: boliviano; Perú: nuevo peso peruano; Ecuador: el sucre; Colombia: peso colombiano*

➤ **Formas adjetivas:** *Boliviano; peruano; ecuatoriano; colombiano*

➤ **Recursos naturales:** *Carbón, petróleo, gas natural, esmeraldas (emeralds), hierro, plomo, oro, piedra, madera, metales, minerales, pesca, estaño (tin), plata, arroz, tungsteno, cinc, otros*

➤ **Industrias:** *Comida y bebidas, minería, textiles, productos químicos, procesamiento de minerales, harina de pescado, ensamblaje de autos, productos farmacéuticos, cemento, plásticos, otras*

➤ **Productos agrícolos:** *Café, bananas, flores, algodón, azúcar, tabaco, papas, soja, sorgo (sorgum), maíz, cacao, mariscos, ganadería, lana, trigo, otros*

Cultura Latina

Studies have proven that people living on the high Altiplano actually have slightly larger hearts and are able to better utilize oxygen than lowlanders. I've been to the Altiplano, and believe me, I was gasping for air for a few days. People in the Andes call altitude sickness *soroche*. If you feel dizzy, nauseated, tired, and have a splitting headache, you've got *soroche*.

Gramática: *Ser* vs. *Estar*

As you know, two Spanish verbs translate as "to be" in English: *ser* and *estar*. Each has its own special uses. This phenomenon often causes confusion among students of Spanish. This section tries to better explain the differences in usage of these two verbs.

Acuérdate

If you need to review the conjugations of *ser* and *estar*, please consult your beginning textbook.

Ser *and* Estar *with Nouns*

Ser is used to indicate where nouns come from, their relationship to one another, and the groups to which they belong. *Ser* describes who owns a noun or what it's made of. *Ser* usually speaks to a quality that is unchanging, static, and at least semipermanent.

Algo Nuevo

If you're into memory tricks, you might want to learn "PONMORR." It may help you recall the following situations in which *ser* is most often used: Profession, Origin, Nationality, Material, Ownership, Relationship, and Religion.

➤ **Profession:** *Mi tío es médico.* My uncle is a doctor.

➤ **Origin:** *Soy de Lima.* I am from Lima.

➤ **Nationality:** *Mi abuela es colombiana.* My grandmother is Colombian.

➤ **Material:** *La casa es de madera y ladrillo.* The house is made from wood and brick.

➤ **Ownership:** *El libro es de Oscar.* The book is Oscar's.

➤ **Relationship:** *Esta llama no es mía.* This llama is not mine.

➤ **Religion:** *Cecilia es católica.* Cecilia is Catholic.

When used with nouns, the verb *estar* refers to location and position:

➤ **Location:** *Mi esposo siempre está en el trabajo.* My husband is always at work.

➤ **Position:** *El baño está al lado de la puerta.* The bathroom is next to the door.

Ten Cuidado

Although you'll almost always use *estar* to indicate where someone or something is located, you must use *ser* for the location of an event: *¿Dónde es la fiesta?* = "Where's the party?"

Ser *and* Estar *with Adjectives*

Ser is used to express characteristics that are not expected to change any time soon. Use *ser* when you wish to be objective about the state or appearance of something. *Ser* is used to define things at their core.

Estar, on the other hand, is used to indicate more temporary characteristics or situations (how things are at the present time). Use *estar* when you want to express a more subjective opinion about something. *Estar* is used more for descriptions than for definitions. Read the following examples carefully:

➤ **Soy guapo:** I am good looking. (I always have been.)

➤ **Estoy guapo:** I am "looking" good. (Usually I look terrible, but *today* I look great!)

➤ **Juana es loca:** Juana is crazy. (She suffers from a mental disorder and may need psychiatric treatment).

➤ **Juana está loca:** Juana is "acting" crazy. (She's behaving odd or silly at this moment, but usually she's got both feet on the ground.)

➤ **Antonio es gordo:** Anthony is fat. (Anthony is a large man. He has always been that way and is expected to remain so.)

➤ **Antonio está gordo:** Anthony is (looking) fat. (He has been eating too much lately and has developed a paunch. He'll probably go back to normal after the holidays.)

Take another look at the last two examples. Let's say that Antonio is tired of everyone saying "*Es gordo.*" So he goes on a diet. Once he is visibly thinner, people will start saying "*Antonio está delgado*" ("Anthony is 'looking' thin"). This means that although he usually isn't thin, he appears so now. He could gain the weight back at any time. But if he remains thinner for an extended period, sooner or later people will start saying "*Antonio es delgado*" ("Anthony is a thin man"). The change from *estar* to *ser* indicates that people are no longer thinking of him as *gordo*.

Ten Cuidado

Now and then you'll come across an expression that doesn't quite follow the rules. For example, *Ramón está muerto* means "Ramón is dead," even though most people would consider his death to be rather permanent. Sometimes both *ser* and *estar* can be used to express the same concept. For example, to say that you are married, you can say *Estoy casado/a* or *Soy casado/a*. It makes no difference.

Ser *and* Estar *with the Past Participle*

For *ser*, the same rules apply to past participles as for all other adjectives. You can use *ser* if the past participle describes some permanent characteristic. You probably won't find yourself using *ser* with past participles very often when speaking the language. It's use is more common in the written language:

➤ **Julio es un hombre muy bien conocido:** Julio is a very well-known man.

➤ **Es comprado por los turistas:** It is bought by tourists.

➤ **Es sabido por todos:** It is known by everyone.

➤ **Marcelo es una persona muy fría:** Marcelo is a cold (unfeeling) individual.

However, unlike *ser*, you'll be using *estar* with past participles all the time. Use *estar* + a past participle to describe the condition of a noun without considering who made it that way: *La tienda está cerrada* = "The store is closed." Here are some excellent examples:

➤ **El mercado está abierto, pero las tiendas están cerradas:** The market is open, but the stores are closed.

➤ **Estoy perdido:** I'm lost.

➤ **Estás equivocado:** You're wrong.

➤ **Estamos perdidos:** We're lost.

➤ **El agua está hervida:** The water has boiled. (Remember: *agua* is feminine but takes *el*.)

➤ **Ellas están muy preocupadas:** They (women) are very worried.

Hay—Not Just for Caballos

You know that the word *hay* (rhymes with the English *pie* and *sky*) means "there is" or "there are." Technically, it's a verb form derived from *haber;* but unlike all other verbs, it doesn't change with respect to singular or plural. Use *hay* when you want to state that (or ask if) something (or things) exists:

➤ **Hay mucha gente en el mundo:** There are a lot of people in the world.

➤ **Señor, disculpe. ¿Hay agua? ¿Hay comida?** Excuse me, sir. Is there (do you have) any water? Food?

➤ **Hay muchos problemas aquí:** There are a lot of problems here.

➤ **Sí, no hay bananas:** Yes, we have no bananas.

Hay also works with *que* + infinitive to say "we need to" or "one must" or "you gotta." *Hay que* is more general and less specific to a single person or persons than *tener que*.

➤ **¿Hay que pagar antes o después?:** Do I/we have to pay before or after? (in general)

➤ **Hay que comer para vivir:** One must eat to live. ("Ya gotta eat to live.")

➤ **Hay que tener paciencia:** We need to be patient. ("Ya gotta have patience.")

➤ **Hay que trabajar para ganar dinero:** People need to work to earn money. ("Ya gotta work ....")

Algo Nuevo

The preterite (simple past) form of *hay* is *hubo: Ayer hubo una manifestación en el centro* = "There was a political demonstration downtown yesterday." Use *hubo* whenever you wish to say *hay* in the past. You can pretty much ignore the other preterite forms of *haber*. Even writers tend to shy away from them. You'll learn more about preterites in Chapter 11, "Centroamérica."

A Word About Adverbs

And now for something completely different .... Adverbs modify verbs, adjectives, or other adverbs. English words that end in *–ly* such as *quickly, happily,* and *unfortunately* are adverbs. Other adverbs are shorter, such as *right* and *well.*

Spanish adverbs work in a similar way. Some are formed by adding an ending to an adjective, while many of the more common adjectives are simply short little words with no special ending. Unlike adjectives, Spanish adverbs do not take *–a* or *–o* as endings, and are never affected by gender, even when they modify an adjective that is gender-specific.

The equivalent ending for *–ly* in Spanish is *–mente.* Spanish adverbs can be formed by adding *–mente* to the feminine form of the adjective. If the adjective is invariable and ends in *–e* or with a consonant, *–mente* may still be added:

Acuérdate

You can use *Sí hay* and *No hay* to respond to *¿Hay "X"?* questions: *¿Hay pan? Sí, hay. ¿Hay tiempo? No, no hay.* I suppose my previous "Yes, we have no bananas" should really have been *No, no hay bananas* (but that wouldn't have been as funny).

Adjectives to Adverbs

Masculine Adjective	Feminine Adjective	Adverb	English
rápido	*rápida*	*rápidamente*	quickly
honesto	*honesta*	*honestamente*	honestly
básico	*básica*	*básicamente*	basically

continues

Adjectives to Adverbs (continued)

Masculine Adjective	Feminine Adjective	Adverb	English
natural	(no change)	*naturalmente*	naturally
urgente	(no change)	*urgentemente*	urgently

Ten Cuidado

A few *–mente* adverbs are false cognates:

Últimamente means "recently," not "ultimately."

Casualmente means "by chance," not "casually."

Eventualmente means "possibly," not "eventually."

Absolutamente should be used negatively, as in "absolutely not."

Acuérdate

Some adjectives can't take the *–mente* ending. Adjectives denoting physical appearance, origin, nationality, and religion usually do not take *–mente* to make adverbs, although there are a few exceptions.

Here are a few examples:

➤ **Los colombianos me han tratado muy cordialmente:** The Colombians have treated me very cordially.

➤ **Están casados felizmente:** They are happily married.

➤ **Probablemente, no sabe Juan cómo se llega a Arequipa:** Probably, Juan doesn't know how to get to Arequipa.

Although it's good to know how to use the *–mente* ending, you'll find that most of the more common adverbs you'll use on a daily basis won't need *–mente*.

Here are some common "non *–mente*" adverbs. A few are also adjectives:

➤ **bien** (well); **hablar bien** (to speak well)

➤ **más** (more); **más fácil** (easier)

➤ **menos** (less); **menos fácil** (less easy)

➤ **mejor** (better); **hablar mejor** (to speak better)

➤ **peor** (worse); **cantar peor** (to sing worse)

➤ **mal** (poorly); **hablar mal** (to speak poorly)

➤ **jamás** (never ever); **hablar jamás** (to never speak)

➤ **nunca** (never); **nunca cantar** (to never sing)

➤ **casi** (almost); **casi hecho** (almost done)

➤ **muy** (very); **muy fácil** (very easy)

➤ **siempre** (always); **siempre habla** (always talks)

➤ **también** (also); **también canta** (sings, too)

➤ **tampoco** ("either"); **tampoco baila** (doesn't dance, either)

➤ **todavía** (still); **todavía está** (is still here)

➤ **ya** (already, now); **ya está aquí** (it's already here)

Just a few examples should do the trick:

➤ **Es muy difícil leer el chino:** It is very difficult to read Chinese.

➤ **Tampoco no es fácil pronunciar el chino:** It's not easy to pronounce Chinese, either.

➤ **Mi suegra todavía está aquí con nosotros:** My mother-in-law is still here with us.

➤ **El bebé siempre llora:** The baby always cries.

➤ **El rey es tan rico:** The king is so rich.

➤ **Las montañas son tan grandes:** The mountains are so big.

The con + Noun Adverb Construction

You can also use nouns as adverbs by putting the word *con* in front of the noun. I sometimes think of this as the "Night Before Xmas" construction, as in: "The stockings were hung by the chimney *with care*." Observe:

➤ **El maestro siempre lee el diario con cuidado:** The teacher always reads the newspaper with care (same as "carefully").

➤ **Vamos a esperar con paciencia:** We are going to wait patiently (with patience).

➤ **Alejandro habla de su madre con mucho amor:** Alejandro speaks lovingly of his mother (with love).

Risa del Día

I think that this joke is rather international:

En la oficina:

—¡Sr. Perez! ¿No sabe usted que está prohibido beber durante las horas de trabajo?

—No se preocupe jefe, ¡no estoy trabajando!

Acuérdate

The adverb *tampoco* is the negative form of *también*. Because *también* means "also," *tampoco* means "not also" or "either," as in *No hablo el holandés, y tampoco no hablo el alemán* = "I don't speak Dutch, and I don't speak German, either." Be careful not to say *"también no." Ya* means "already." It can also mean "now." When used with "no," it means "anymore" = *Ya no toco la guitarra* = "I don't play the guitar anymore."

Vocabulario Útil:

- ➤ **estar prohibido:** to be prohibited
- ➤ **beber:** to drink (here, something with alcohol)
- ➤ **horas de trabajo:** working hours
- ➤ **preocuparse:** to worry
- ➤ **trabajando:** present participle: "working"

El Cuiz

Give the English equivalents for the following words. Cheat only if you absolutely have to:

1. imperio _____
2. convertir _____
3. esqueleto _____
4. belleza _____
5. debido _____
6. atractivo _____
7. cima _____
8. edificios _____
9. entero _____
10. duda _____
11. entorno _____
12. durar _____
13. adornados _____
14. ciudadela _____
15. recorrido _____
16. por su cuenta _____
17. ubicación _____
18. arqueológico _____

Tareas

1. Create sentences using *ser* and *estar*. Use the examples in this chapter as your guide. Substitute new nouns and adjectives for the words given in the examples: *Mi amigo es ecuatoriano; El gato está en el la casa;* and so on.

2. Make a list of 10 verbs. Change the verbs into past participles. Now, create sentences using *estar* + past participle to describe the state of things: *La puerta está abierta.* Then add any appropriate adverbs to modify the verbs: *La puerta está muy abierta.*

3. Create sentences using *hay* to tell people what's there and what isn't there. Use *hay que + infinitive* to say what you "gotta do."

The Least You Need to Know

➤ Both *ser* and *estar* mean "to be" but have very different uses.

➤ *Ser* is generally for permanent situations; *estar* is generally for things that may change.

➤ *Hay* means both "there is" and "there are"; singular and plural don't matter.

➤ The Spanish adverbial ending is *–mente,* but many shorter adverbs won't need this ending.

Chapter 10

Los Países del Caribe

In This Chapter

➤ *Lectura:* La República Dominicana

➤ *Datos sobre los países caribeños*

➤ Objects and object pronouns

When Cristóbal Colón (a.k.a. Christopher Columbus) discovered the Americas, it was to the islands of the Caribbean that he first came. So it's no wonder that he (and many other Europeans after him) kept coming back. When I think of a tropical paradise, this is the place. If it weren't for the political instabilities of the region, as well as the occasional hurricane, the Caribbean would indeed be a heaven on earth.

Come to the Islands

Santo Domingo, the capital of the Dominican Republic, was the first Spanish settlement in the Americas, founded in 1496, four years after Columbus first landed. The Dominican Republic has had a turbulent political history. The country was occupied twice by Haiti in the 1800s and by the U.S. Marines from 1916 to 1924. President Johnson sent the Marines back in 1965 to prevent a civil war. Since then, the political climate has settled down, making the country a popular spot for beachgoers, retirees, and eco-tourists.

Cultura Latina

Okay, so Venezuela isn't an is-land. But because the bulk of the country's population lives along the Caribbean Coast, the culture, speech, and lifestyle of most Venezuelans are similar to those of the other Spanish-speaking island nations in the region. That is why I have included the country in this chapter.

What we now call Puerto Rico was once called *Borinquen* by the Taíno Indians who originally inhabited the island. Today, Puerto Ricans often refer to themselves and their language as *boricua*. The United States took possession of Puerto Rico at the end of the Spanish-American War. The Commonwealth of Puerto Rico has a "Free Associated State" relationship with the United States. Puerto Ricans have the same rights as all U.S. citizens, and many Puerto Ricans have left the island to live "on the continent," especially in the state of New Jersey and in New York City.

Venezuela is home to both the world's highest water-fall, the 3,212-foot Angel Falls, and the anaconda, the world's longest snake. The two seem unrelated, how-ever. Venezuelans revere nineteenth-century hero Simón Bolivar, who led a decade-long revolution to oust the Spanish from much of South America. The country's currency bears his name. This oil-dependent country has held democratic elections since 1958, but in recent years Venezuela has struggled with economic decline and natural disasters. Indian languages are spoken by about 200,000 Amerindians in the remote interior of the country.

The birthplace of the *rumba, mambo,* and the *cha cha,* Cuba is the largest island in the Caribbean. It endures as one of the last bastions of communism. The country is ruled by Fidel Castro, who took power in 1959 with popular support. Cuba suffered an economic blow in 1989 when its European Communist trading partners began falling apart. Since Castro's revolution, many Cubans have left the island for political and economic reasons. From 1959 through the 1990s, almost one million Cubans immigrated to the United States, many of whom now live in Miami, Florida. Cuba also has a rich literary tradition.

Lectura: La República Dominicana

This *lectura* discusses some important facts about the Dominican Republic.

La República Dominicana, con una extensión de 48.442 km², ocupa las dos terceras partes de la superficie de la Zona Este. El lado Oeste lo ocupa la República de Haití.

Clima:

El clima que impera en la zona costera es cálido, como propio del trópico. En la región central, las temperaturas son más frescas. La temperatura promedio a lo largo del año es de 29 grados centígrados (84 grados F). En la zona montañosa, y principalmente en invierno, se registran muy bajas temperaturas, en ocasiones a menos de 0 grados C (32 grados F), principalmente en Valle Nuevo, Constanza y el Pico Duarte. El mes de

114

agosto es el más caluroso del año y enero el más fresco. La mayor temporada de lluvias se produce entre mayo y agosto y la menor en los meses de noviembre y diciembre.

Divisa:

La moneda nacional es el peso. El valor real del peso dominicano fluctúa frente al dólar americano y su valor está sujeto a las leyes de la oferta y la demanda. El peso está dividido en cien unidades.

Religión:

La mayoría de los dominicanos y de las dominicanas profesan la religión católica, apostólica y romana.

Tránsito:

En Santo Domingo se conduce a la derecha. Los visitantes con licencia de conducir vigente pueden usarla durante un período máximo de 90 días, sin necesidad de ningún trámite adicional. El máximo de velocidad permitida en las autopistas es de 80 kilómetros por hora; en zonas suburbanas, 60 kilómetros y 40 kilómetros por hora en las ciudades, salvo que haya señalización específica.

Vocabulario Útil:

- ➤ **superficie:** surface
- ➤ **ocupar:** to occupy
- ➤ **velocidad:** speed
- ➤ **autopista:** highway
- ➤ **imperar:** to prevail
- ➤ **promedio:** average
- ➤ **trámite:** procedure; paperwork
- ➤ **principalmente:** principally
- ➤ **temporada:** season; time of year
- ➤ **profesar:** to profess
- ➤ **fluctuar:** to fluctuate; to vary
- ➤ **estar sujeto a:** to be subject to
- ➤ **fresco:** cool
- ➤ **costero:** coastal
- ➤ **cálido:** hot and humid
- ➤ **caluroso:** warm

Acuérdate

The words for certain foods often change significantly from place to place. In the Caribbean, the word for banana is *guineo*. *Los plátanos* are the larger plantains that are fried. But in Mexico, a *plátano* is your regular old banana.

➤ **vigente:** valid; in force

➤ **unidad:** unit; measurement

➤ **señalización:** signs; signage

➤ **específico:** specific

Análisis del Texto

Now let's study some words and phrases from the text:

➤ 48.442 km^2

Read this number as *cuarenta y ocho mil, cuatro cientos cuarenta y dos kilómetros cuadrados.* In English: "square kilometers."

➤ *las dos terceras partes*

This means "two thirds"; literally, "the two thirds parts."

➤ *como propio del trópico*

You may have learned *propio* as meaning "own," as in *Quiero tener me propia casa* = "I want to have my own house." In the previous phrase, *propio de* has another meaning and translates as "usual for" or "characteristic of."

Algo Nuevo

Many common words sometimes have secondary meanings that you may not be aware of. Take, for example, the word *bajo*. Depending on the context, this little word can mean "low," "vulgar," "short," "under," "during," "the first floor of a building," "the hem of a dress," "the cuff of a shirt," "the underside of a vehicle," "a bass (instrument)," and more. If you come across a word that you are already familiar with, but in a context that doesn't make sense, you may need to look up the word again to see if it has any secondary meanings.

➤ *La mayor temporada de lluvias se produce*

Producir does indeed mean "to produce," and *se produce* could be translated as "are produced." But that really wouldn't sound right for this phrase: "The greatest season of rains is produced ...." In reality, *se produce* is just being used as an alternative to the verb "to happen" or "to occur" in order to make the text sound more interesting.

➤ *y la menor en los meses de*

Do you see what is happening here? The *la* is standing in for *temporada,* which was mentioned in the earlier part of the sentence. We know this because *la* is feminine and *temporada* is also feminine; the two words are linked by gender.

➤ *las leyes de la oferta y la demanda*

This phrase means "the laws of supply and demand."

➤ *salvo que haya señalización específica*

Haya is the subjunctive form of *hay.* We need subjunctive because *salvo que,* which means "unless," always requires a subjunctive.

Cultura Latina

Known as Little Havana, the Cuban section of Miami is a center for thousands of Cuban immigrants, offering them a place for hot debates over how to oust Castro and return to their beloved *isla* ... so close but yet so far.

Vista Panorámica de los Países Caribeños

➤ **Países de la región:** *República de Cuba; República de Venezuela; Estado Libre Asociado de Puerto Rico; República Dominicana.*

➤ **Gobiernos:** *Cuba: República socialista de catorce provincias; Venezuela: República federal de veinte estados, un distrito federal y dos territorios nacionales; Puerto Rico: Estado libre asociado de los EE.UU., con dos cámaras legislativas, un gobernador elegido. Tiene representantes en el Congreso de los EE.UU., pero no pueden votar; República Dominicana: República democrática de treinta provincias.*

➤ **Capitales:** *Cuba: la Habana; República Domincana: Santo Domingo; Venezuela: Caracas; Puerto Rico: San Juan.*

➤ **Tamaños:** *Cuba: 110.860 km cuadrados; República Domincana: 48.442 km. cuadrados; Venezuela: 912.050 km. cuadrados; Puerto Rico: 9.104 km. cuadrados.*

➤ **Población:** *Cuba: 11 millones, sin incluir a los cubanos que viven en los EE.UU.; República Domincana: 7.5 millones; Venezuela: 24 millones; Puerto Rico: 3 millones, sin incluir a los puertorriqueños que viven en los EE.UU.*

➤ **Divisas:** *Cuba: peso cubano; República Dominicana: peso dominicano; Venezuela: bo-livar; Puerto Rico: dólar estadounidense.*

➤ **Recursos naturales de la región:** *Níquel, oro, plata, madera, cobalto, hierro, cobre, manganeso, sal, pesca, petróleo, azufre, gas natural, carbón, dia-mantes, turismo.*

➤ **Industrias de la región:** *Industria petrolero (Venezuela), cemento, industria tabacalera (to-bacco), refinamiento de azúcar, textiles, minería de piedra, arena, grava (gravel), café.*

➤ **Productos agrícolos de la región:** *café, cacao, azúcar de caña, piñas, naranjas, guineos (ba-nanas), flores, leche, vegetales, tabacos, aves de corral, otros.*

Haz Clic Aquí

You can find some great Web sites about the countries of the Caribbean. Learn more about each country at http://venezuela. mit.edu, www.caribbeansupersite. com/domrep/index.htm, www. caribbeansupersite.com/cuba/ index.htm, and www.puertorico. com. For other sites. just search under the name of the country that most interests you.

Gramática: Direct and Indirect Object Pronouns

To speak Spanish with any level of fluency, you must dominate, control, manipulate, and otherwise have complete hegemony over the object pronouns. There's no way around them.

Your beginning Spanish text probably covered the object pronouns. But many students of Spanish seem to have trouble using them, so I think it would be wise to review these guys and give you my own perspective on how this all works.

Transitive and Intransitive Verbs

Basically, there are two kinds of verbs: those that pass on their action to something else and those that seem to just sit there. For example, in the sentence "I throw a stone," the verb "to throw" requires that I throw *something*. The stone is the object of my throwing. This kind of verb is called a transitive verb. So, the stone, as the thing being thrown, is the "direct object" of this verb.

Here are a few more examples of direct objects with transitive verbs. The direct objects are in italics:

➤ I see *Juan*.

➤ Elvira is learning *Spanish*.

➤ Alejandro answered *the telephone*.

➤ Juana sent *an e-mail.*

➤ The dog bit *the man.*

➤ The man bit *the dog.*

In each of the previous sentences, we could substitute the word *what* or *it* for the direct object, and the sentence would still make sense: "Juana sent it."

Verbs that don't or can't take a direct object are called "intransitive." They pretty much just "are":

➤ The telephone *rang.*

➤ Problems *exist.*

➤ The story *evolved.*

➤ I *think,* therefore I *am.* (Descartes)

Many verbs can be used both transitively and intransitively, depending on whether they are taking an object:

➤ Cindy eats every two hours. (intransitive)

➤ Cindy eats *cake* every two hours. (transitive)

➤ Our baby weighs 20 pounds. (intransitive)

➤ The butcher weighs *meat* on a scale. (transitive)

Acuérdate

Sometimes the direct object of a transitive verb is not actually in the sentence but is merely understood. In the sentence "He threw from the infield," the object of his throwing is still a baseball, even though the baseball is not mentioned. So, the verb is still transitive. However, "He throws with his left arm" is intransitive, because there is no direct object.

The Direct Object Pronouns (DOPs)

The object pronouns are not the same as the subject pronouns you learned for conjugating verbs (*yo, tú, él, ella,* and so on). But they do perform a similar function because they also stand in for nouns so that you don't have to repeat the noun. To use the direct object pronouns—DOP, for short—the noun for which the pronoun is substituting must be the direct object of a transitive verb. In other words, to avoid always having to restate the object of the verb ("I see the ball; I want to buy the ball; I like the ball; Give me the ball"), we use the DOP ("I see *it;* I want to buy *it*").

In English, we use *me, you, it, him, her, us,* and *them.* Look at these:

➤ He hit *me.*

➤ I love *you* and *them.*

➤ We eat *it.*

➤ The dog bit *him, her,* and *us.*

119

Naturally, you'll need to do the same kinds of substitutions in Spanish. You probably learned these before:

Spanish DOP	English DOP
me	me
te	you
lo/la	him/her/you (must match gender)
nos	us
os	you all (Spain)
los/las	them/you all (must match gender)

Ten Cuidado

When you are going to use a third-person DOP (*he/she/it/ they*), remember that the noun must already have been stated or at least be understood. Otherwise, no one will know what the DOP stands for.

Placement of the DOP

The direct object (I mean the *real* noun, not the pronoun) of a transitive Spanish verb usually ends up in the same place that it does in an English sentence: *Yo compro leche* = "I buy milk."

However, when a Spanish direct object *pronoun* is used with a *conjugated* transitive verb, it must come before the verb, not after it. This can be tricky for English-speakers because the structure is very different from what we are used to. In English, we say "I see you." In Spanish, it's "I *you* see."

Let's look at the *Yo compro leche* sentence again. To substitute a pronoun for *leche*, I need to put the DOP that means "it" before the conjugated verb: *Yo* la *compro* ("I it buy") = "I buy it." The *la* stands in for *leche*. We need *la* (and not *lo*) because *leche* is feminine.

Once again, gender is linking words and concepts together. Take a look at these examples:

➤ **Question:** *¿Habla usted el español?*

Answer: *Sí, lo hablo.* (Yes, I it speak.)

➤ **Question:** *¿Quién tiene los zapatos?*

Answer: *Yo los tengo.* (I them have.)

➤ **Question:** *¿Ves las montañas?*

Answer: *No, no las veo.* ("No, I don't them see.")

➤ **Question:** *¿Sabe usted la letra del himno nacional?*

Answer: *No, en realidad, no la sé.* (No, actually, I don't.)

The DOP, when used in a phrase containing an infinitive, may be affixed to the end of the infinitive verb. The DOP also may be placed before the conjugated verb. There's no change in meaning between these two forms. Only the placement of the DOP has changed:

Moving the DOP Doesn't Change Meaning

This ...	Or This ...	Still Means This ...
Puedo verte.	*Te puedo ver.*	I can see you.
¿Quieres verme?	*¿Me quieres ver?*	Do you want to see me?
Necesitamos pagarlo.	*Lo necesitamos pagar.*	We need to pay it.
Ella quiere llamarnos.	*Ella nos quiere llamar.*	She wants to call us.
Vamos a hacerlo mañana.	*Lo vamos a hacer mañana.*	We'll do it tomorrow.
No puedo entenderla.	*No la puedo entender.*	I can't understand her.
Tienes que decirlos ahora.	*Los tienes que decir.*	You must say them now.
¿No vas a besarme?	*¿No me vas a besar?*	Aren't you going to kiss me?
No van a poder oírnos.	*No nos van a poder oír.*	They aren't going to be able to hear us.

The Indirect Object Pronouns (INDOPs)

The indirect object of a sentence is the final destination of a transitive verb's direct object. In other words, this is where the direct object ultimately ends up. It isn't *what* is given, but *who* gets it: "to whom." For example, in the sentence "I gave Julio my bicycle," the object is *bicycle* and *Julio* is the indirect object because he was the recipient of my giving. In the sentence "I throw stones at my neighbor's house," the object is *stones*, and the indirect object is *my neighbor's house*.

The best way to explain indirect objects is by example. The indirect objects in the following sentences are italicized:

➤ I gave the ball *to Jorge*.

➤ I gave *Jorge* the ball.

Acuérdate

Remember that *lo/la* and *los/las* are gender-specific; the others aren't. For the third person (*he/she/it/they/those*, and so on), you must match the gender of the pronoun to the gender of the person or thing for which you are substituting. This is where gender helps link things together. Simply by matching the DOP with the gender of the word you have in mind, you can avoid repeating the noun again and again.

➤ He told *Alberto* the story.

➤ The police gave *Roberto* a hard time.

➤ We sold *Esteban* some Arizona beachfront property.

Notice that the placement of the indirect object in English can vary from sentence to sentence. If it's at the end, we need to put a *to* there to indicate that what follows is the indirect object: "to Jorge."

The Spanish indirect object pronouns, or INDOPs, look pretty much the same as the DOPs. In fact, the only difference between them is in the third person. The good news is that these guys are not gender-specific—only *person*-specific.

Indirect Object Pronoun Table

Spanish INDOP	English INDOP
me	to me
te	to you
le	to him/her (and *usted*)
nos	to us
os	to you all (Spain)
les	to them (and *ustedes*)

Study the following Spanish examples:

➤ **María nunca le dice la verdad:** Maria never tells him (her, *usted*) the truth.

➤ **¡Háblame!:** Talk to me! (Commands always put DOPS and INDOPS at end.)

➤ **Te doy mi número de teléfono:** I'll give you my phone number.

➤ **¿Me vas a dar un beso o no?:** Are you going to give me a kiss or not? (*Vas a darme …*)

➤ **Os van a llamaros a las cinco.** They are going to call you all at five. (Spain; *Van a llamaros …*)

➤ **Ellos no pueden darles mucha información:** They can't give them (or *ustedes*) a lot of information. (*No les pueden dar …*)

Getting the DOP and the INDOP Together

Except for third person combinations, getting the DOP and the INDOP together is no sweat. The INDOP always comes first. And, as before, you have some choices. If there is an infinitive, you may stick the two together at the end. If there is a conjugated verb only, the INDOP and the DOP must go first.

When placed before a conjugated verb, the INDOP and the DOP are written separately: *te lo*, *me los*, and so on. But if they are stuck to the end of an infinitive, they are written together. Watch for *tildes*—they may be needed to preserve correct stress:

➤ **Me los dan:** They give them to me.

➤ **Te lo digo:** I'll tell it to you.

➤ **Te las envío mañana:** I'll send them to you tomorrow.

➤ **Me lo van a dar el lunes:** They're going to give it to me on Monday. (*Van a dármelo …*)

➤ **Puede decírtelos:** He/She can tell you them. (also, *Te los puede decir …*)

➤ **Voy a comprártela el jueves:** I'm going to buy it (feminine noun) for you on Thursday. (or, *Te la voy a comprar …*)

As you can see from the examples, the INDOP comes first, followed by the DOP. When attached to an infinitive, the INDOP and DOP are stuck together, and *tildes* will appear to maintain correct stress.

Acuérdate

Note that the INDOP can also indicate "for someone," not just "to someone." In the sentence *¿Me puedes hacer un favor?* the idea is more "Can you do a favor *for* me?" rather than "Can you do a favor *to* me?"

Acuérdate

Remember that it's the verb that indicates "who" is doing, "what" they're doing, and "when" they are doing it (by virtue of the tense). The DOP indicates the "object" of their doing, and the INDOP indicates "who" or "what" is receiving the object or action.

Third-Person DOP Meets Third-Person INDOP

You may be thinking that if you put the third-person DOP and the third-person INDOP together, you'd get *lelo*, *lela*, *leslo*, *lesla*, *leslos*. And you're also no doubt thinking that the following examples should be entirely correct: *dárlelo*, *decírlela*, *comprárlesla*, *comprarlelos*, *le los compro* ("I buy them for him/her/you"), *les las doy* ("I give them to them"), and so on. Seems logical to me, too. Unfortunately, all of these examples are *wrong*.

Whenever a third-person DOP and a third-person INDOP are put together in a sentence, no matter if the objects are singular or plural, the INDOP always turns into *se*. For example, when you want to say "give it to him" = *dar* + *le* (or *les*) + *lo* (or *la, los, las*), the *le* or *les* needs to be replaced by *se*.

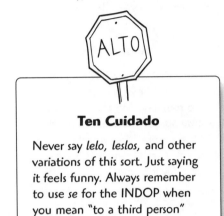

Ten Cuidado

Never say *lelo, leslos,* and other variations of this sort. Just saying it feels funny. Always remember to use *se* for the INDOP when you mean "to a third person" whenever a DOP is present. If there's no DOP, *le* and *les* don't change. Both singular and plural INDOPs change to *se* in combination with a DOP.

In other words, take the sentence *Se lo doy*. Here the little word *se* is standing in for *le*, which is standing in for "to a person we know." The *lo* indicates that the thing given is a singular masculine noun, and the *doy* indicates "I give." If the *lo* weren't there, the *le* wouldn't have to change to *se*.

Here are some more examples:

➤ **Se las mando:** I'll send them to him (her/*usted*)

➤ **Se los van a enviar mañana:** They're going to send them to him (her/*usted*) tomorrow. (*Van a dárselos …*)

➤ **Voy a comprársela mañana.** I'm going to buy it for them (or *ustedes*) tomorrow. (*Se las voy a comprar …*)

➤ **Se lo va a dar algún día:** He's (She's) going to give it to him/her/*usted* someday.

Avoiding Confusion

In most cases, you'll find that the context makes things pretty clear which noun a DOP is referring to. The gender also is a clue because it always links the DOP to the object being substituted.

However, the third-person INDOP can be a little tricky because *le* can mean "to him," "to her," "to it," or "to *usted*," and *les* can mean "to them" or "to *ustedes*." And when DOPs and third-person INDOPs get together, confusion may arise because the *se* can be singular or plural, and can refer to a man, a woman, both, or to one or more inanimate nouns.

Whenever the possibility for confusion exists, or when you wish to emphasize just who is actually involved, you can clarify the indirect object (and sometimes the object, if no indirect object is present) by adding *a* plus the person, persons, or things:

➤ **a él:** to him

➤ **a ella:** to her

➤ **a Juan:** to Juan

➤ **a María:** to María

➤ **a usted:** to you, Sir/Madam

➤ **a ellos:** to them

➤ **a ellas:** to them (women)

➤ **a los hombres:** to the men

➤ **a ustedes:** to "you all"

➤ **al señor:** to the gentleman

➤ **a las organizaciones:** to the organizations

And so on …

➤ **Se lo voy a decir a él:** I'm going to tell it to him.

➤ **Ya se lo he dado a Juan:** I've already given it to Juan.

➤ **Le voy a dar un peso a María:** I am going to give Maria a peso.

➤ **María nunca le dice la verdad a Hector:** Maria never tells Hector the truth.

Acuérdate

The *a* in phrases such as *a él* and *a ella* looks like the personal *a* I mentioned before. This *a* is actually called the "dative *a*." You don't need to worry about its name, but I'm trying to give you as much information as I can.

Risa del Día

Here's another *Jaimito/Pepito* joke. As with many of these, this one takes place at school. I hope you get it:

> *En una escuelita rural, todos los alumnos llegan tarde a clase. La maestra les pregunta:*
>
> *—A ver Jorgito, ¿por que llegaste tarde?*
>
> *—Y, porque cuando venía mi burro se tropezó con una piedra y se cayó y tuve que venir caminando.*
>
> *—¿Y tú, Pedrito?*
>
> *—Y, yo venía en el burro y apareció una piedra y …*
>
> *—¿Y tú Miguelito?*
>
> *—Lo mismo, señorita.*
>
> *—¿Y tú, Pepito?, y no me digas esa historia del burro porque yo sé que tú no tienes burro.*
>
> *—No, señorita, a mí me trajo mi papá en auto, pero con tantos burros tirados por el camino ….*

Ten Cuidado

Remember that when adding both DOPs and INDOPs to an infinitive, a *tilde* will appear over the last syllable of the infinitive to preserve the stress: *dárselo, decírselos,* and so on. Otherwise, it would be *darSElo* and *decirSElos*.

Haz Clic Aquí

Speaking of humor, you can see more Spanish jokes at www.chistes.com. This site has some of the more tasteful jokes on the Web. You can learn a lot of Spanish from reading these *chistes*.

Vocabulario Útil:

➤ **escuelita:** little school

➤ **a ver:** let's see; "Tell me."

➤ **tropezarse:** to trip

➤ **caerse:** to fall down

➤ **traer (trajo):** to bring (brought)

➤ **historia:** story

➤ **tirar:** to throw; "thrown all over"

El Cuiz

Provide the Spanish equivalents for the following words. Cheating is fine:

1. warm _____
2. procedures; paperwork _____
3. surface _____
4. speed _____
5. highways _____
6. to prevail _____
7. average _____
8. to fluctuate; to vary _____
9. principally _____
10. season; time of year _____
11. to occupy _____
12. coastal _____
13. to be subject to _____
14. cool _____
15. valid; in force _____
16. hot and humid _____
17. units _____
18. specific _____

Tareas

1. Create 15 statements or questions using a transitive verb + a direct object: *Tengo un gato; ¿Quiere pagar la cuenta?;* and so on. Then, using the examples in this chapter as your guide, substitute the DOP for the noun: *Lo tengo; ¿Quiere pagarla?* or *¿La quiere pagar?*

2. Choose a subject, a transitive verb, an object, and an indirect object to receive the object: Somebody + verb + indirect object + direct object, or somebody + verb + direct object + "to" + indirect object: "I give Eduardo the money" or "I give the money to Walter." Translate these into Spanish. Use the chapter's examples as your guide.

3. Create sentences that will help you to practice the third-person INDOP + the third-person DOP: *Se lo dije* = "I told it to him/her/*usted*/*ustedes*/them"; *Vamos a contárselo* = "Let's tell it to him/her/*usted*/*ustedes*/them." Remember to use *se*, not *le* or *les*. Use the previous examples as your guide. Add *a él, a ellas,* and so on, as needed for clarity.

The Least You Need to Know

➤ Direct objects receive the action of a verb.

➤ Indirect objects receive the direct objects.

➤ The Spanish third-person DOPs must match gender and number of the direct object.

➤ Never say *lelo* or *lesla,* or similar combos. Use *se* to replace *le* and *les* with a third-person INDOP + DOP.

➤ Use *a él, a Juan, a ustedes,* and so on for clarification when *se* leaves room for doubt.

Centroamérica

Central America is a land of volcanoes, rain forests, exotic wildlife, and ancient cultures. The Central American isthmus forms a bridge between North and South America, and is among the most diverse ecological areas in the world. For example, there are three distinct temperature zones in the region. The hot country, or *tierra caliente*, extends from sea level to about 900 meters (about 3000 feet) and has average yearly temperatures of 24° C (75° F) or more. The temperate country, known as *la tierra templada,* begins at about 900 meters and extends to 1800 meters (about 3000 to 6000 feet). Here the average temperatures range from 18° to 24° C (65° to 75° F). Finally, there's the *tierra fría* (yes, it can get cold in Central America), from about 1800 meters to 3050 meters (about 6000 to 10,000 feet). In this region the average yearly temperatures range between 13° to 18° C (55° to 65° F).

Los Países de Centroamérica

There are six Central American countries, five of which are Spanish-speaking.

El Salvador

The smallest country of the five, El Salvador, is also the region's most densely populated. Named after "the Savior," El Salvador has been plagued by civil war since it gained independence from Spain in 1821. Political turmoil dominated the country until 1992, when El Salvador finally resolved its 12-year civil war with the signing of a U.S.-sponsored peace agreement. In recent years, there has been a great deal of investment in the country by Salvadorians living in the United States. However, crime has also risen in the capital, and 260,000 weapons still remain in civilian hands. El Salvador's economy hinges almost entirely on its coffee crop.

Nicaragua

Nicaragua is Central America's largest country. Like El Salvador, for centuries Nicaragua has been plagued by internal power struggles and foreign invasions. In 1979, the rebel Sandinistas seized power and formed the country's first leftist government, only to be undermined by U.S.-backed Contras. Political instabilities have only recently begun to subside after a free election system was established in 1990.

Guatemala

Guatemala is Central America's most populous country. More than 50 percent of Guatemalans are direct descendants of the Mayans, and the country has retained many Native American traditions in its small fishing and agricultural villages. Guatemala has suffered greatly during three decades of civil war. In 1996, President Alvaro Arzú brokered a peace treaty with all parties involved in the conflict, formally ending the war. But sporadic incidents of violence, some aimed at tourists, continue in several regions of the country, including the capital, Guatemala City, where crime has risen steadily over the last several years.

Honduras

Honduras has also endured its share of uprisings, civil wars, and unpopular changes in government. Until the middle of the twentieth century, U.S. companies virtually controlled the economy through ownership of banana plantations along the northern coast. The military ceded formal power in 1981, and its role in the country has shrunk in recent years.

Costa Rica

Costa Rica's heavily European culture is unique in Central America. Anticipating vast mineral wealth, Spanish settlers in the early 1500s named this country "rich coast." But Costa Rica's riches are found above ground in its fertile landscape, lush with rain forests and dotted with volcanoes. After a civil war in the 1940s, Costa Rica adopted a new constitution that prohibits the country from maintaining an armed force. Today, eco-tourism is fast becoming one of the country's principal industries.

El Panamá

Panama was once a province of Colombia. The country is bisected by the 51-mile-long Panama Canal, built by U.S. military engineers between 1904 and 1914. The project was actually begun by the French, but abandoned due to a malaria epidemic. The canal provides strategic passage between the Atlantic and Pacific oceans, and generates nearly half of the country's income. Control of the canal recently reverted back to Panama.

Lectura: Reunión Militar

Your *lecturas* have been getting progressively longer. This time I'm giving you a break. This short reading is a news flash about a meeting in Guatemala. The style of writing is typical for news headlines and communiqués. So, although the reading is short, it's still pretty challenging:

> *Los ministros de defensa y comandantes de las fuerzas armadas de El Salvador, Guatemala, Honduras, y Nicaragua se reunieron el 9 de junio, en Guatemala para profundizar la integración de los ejércitos de la zona. Los jefes militares pasaron revista a las nuevas amenazas comunes que conforman su nueva agenda de seguridad, relacionadas con la nueva época de paz, narcotráfico, robo de vehículos, tráfico de ilegales, contrabando y otros ilíticos que están bajo el control de mafias organizadas del área.*

Cultura Latina

Central Americans actually have nicknames for each other: Guatemalans are known as *chapines*, El Salvadorians are known as *guanacos*, Hondurans are *catrachos*, Nicaraguans are *nicas*, and Costa Ricans are *ticos*. No offense is meant or taken when using these nicknames.

Cultura Latina

Many Guatemalans do not speak Spanish. Approximately 30 different Indian languages are spoken in the country, and the principal dialect is known as Quiché. You won't have any difficulties traveling in Guatemala, however, with your Spanish. Even in the most remote villages, there will always be someone who understands some Spanish.

Vocabulario Útil:

➤ **ministro:** minister (not religious)

➤ **defensa:** defense

➤ **comandante:** commander

➤ **fuerzas armadas:** armed forces

➤ **reunirse:** to meet; to get together

➤ **ejército:** army

➤ **profundizar:** to deepen; to go into depth

➤ **integración:** integration

➤ **jefe:** leader; "boss"

➤ **pasar revista a:** to review; to look over

➤ **amenaza:** threat

➤ **común:** common

➤ **conformar:** to constitute; to make up

➤ **seguridad:** security

➤ **narcotráfico:** drug trafficking

➤ **época:** period; time (not as grand as "epoch")

➤ **ilegales:** illegals (probably people)

➤ **ilícitos:** illegal activities

➤ **relacionado:** related to

Haz Clic Aquí

Here are some great Web sites for information on the countries of Central America: www.guatemalaweb.com, www.nortropic.com/el_salvador/index.html; www.hondurasinfo.hn, www.nicaragua.com, www.tourism-costarica.com, and www.iaehv.nl/users/grimaldo/panama.html.

Análisis del Texto

All right. Let's see what this little *lectura* has to offer:

➤ *se reunieron el 9 de junio*

Notice that there is no need for any additional preposition, such as *en* for "on." This would still be translated as "met on June 9," even though the "on" isn't needed in the Spanish. When discussing a date on which something occurred, it's usually not necessary to add any prepositions. If it's in the future, you may use *para,* but it is often optional.

➤ *jefes militares pasaron revista*

Pasar revista is a compound verbal phrase. Many such compounds use a common helping verb, such as *hacer, tener, pasar,* or *dar.* The verb *revisar* also could have been used here.

➤ *relacionadas con la nueva época de paz*

The participle *relacionadas* is linked to *amenazas* because it shares the feminine gender. Need I say more?

➤ *del área*

The word *área* is feminine but takes a masculine article in the singular because of the stressed *a* sound at the beginning.

Acuérdate

Remember that your dictionary can also tell you more about words that you already know. Look up some common verbs, such as *hacer, tener, dar,* and *pasar,* and study the examples that your dictionary gives you. If there aren't any, consider buying a better dictionary.

Vista Panorámica de Centroamérica

➤ **Nombres oficiales:** *República de Guatemala; República de El Salvador; República de Honduras; República de Nicaragua; República de Costa Rica; República del Panamá.*

➤ **Gobiernos:** *Guatemala: República de 22 departamentos; El Salvador: República de 14 departamentos; Honduras: República de 18 departamentos; Nicaragua: República federal de 16 departamentos; Costa Rica: República democrática de 7 provincias; Panamá: República centralizada en la que el presidente tiene el poder ejecutivo.*

➤ **Capitales:** *Guatemala: Ciudad Guatemala; El Salvador: San Salvador; Honduras: Tegucigalpa; Nicaragua: Managua; Costa Rica: San José; Panamá: Ciudad de Panamá.*

➤ **Tamaños:** *Guatemala: 108.780 km. cuadrados; El Salvador: 21.476 km. cuadrados; Honduras: 112.088 km. cuadrados; Nicaragua: 148.100 km. cuadrados; Costa Rica: 50.900 km. cuadrados; Panamá: 78.046 km. cuadrados.*

➤ **Poblaciones:** *Guatemala: 11 millones; El Salvador: 6 millones; Honduras: 6 millones; Nicaragua: 5 millones; Costa Rica: 3.5 millones; Panamá: 2.5 millones.*

➤ **Forma Adjetiva:** *Guatemalteco; salvadoreño; hondureño; nicaragüense; costaricense; panameño.*

➤ **Divisas:** *Guatemala: el quezal; El Salvador: el colón; Honduras: el lempira; Nicaragua: el nuevo córdoba; Costa Rica: el colón; Panamá: el balboa (dólar de EE.UU.).*

➤ **Recursos naturales de la región:** *Agricultura, bosque, pesca, energía hidroeléctrica, oro, lugar geográfico estratégico, cobre, otros.*

133

Cultura Latina

The U.S. dollar is legal tender in Panama. Panama does not print a paper currency of its own, but it does have coins. The coins all have Vasco Núñez de Balboa on the face and are inscribed *diez centésimos de balboa, un cuarto de balboa,* and *medio balboa.* These coins are used very commonly and are interchangeable with the American-equivalent coins, which are also used in Panama.

Cultura Latina

In parts of Argentina and Uruguay, people avoid the present perfect in favor of the preterite. In Spain, many people use the present perfect (*Yo he hablado*) when they should be using the preterite (*Yo hablé*). So, if you accidentally use the wrong past tense, people will still understand what you mean.

➤ **Industrias:** *Comida procesada, bebidas, textiles, maquinaria, materiales para construcción, procesamiento del café y del cacao, fertilizantes, calzado, productos químicos y petrolíferos, cigarros, llantas (tires), turismo, otras.*

➤ **Productos agrícolos:** *Frutas tropicales, azúcar, arroz, frijol, maíz, algodón, ganado, café, otros.*

Gramática: The Other Tenses

You are now officially ready to revisit the rest of the verb tenses. Once again, if this is all review for you, that's great. But I would still encourage you to carefully read this section, just to see if anything new comes your way.

The Preterite: I Did It, and It's Over

The preterite past tense is used to indicate a past action or occurrence that both began in the past and finished in the past. Concepts expressed with the preterite are not thought of as having a strong influence on the present—they are over and done with. Usually, the preterite tells of something that occurred only once. It may also express a past action or series of actions that occurred several times if they are considered to be related and finished as a group.

If you need to review the formation of the preterite tense, consult your beginning Spanish text book or look in Appendix A, "Basic Grammar Resource."

Now, here are some examples to help you better understand the uses of the preterite tense:

➤ **Mario fue al mercado de Chichicastenango a comprar regalos:** Mario went to the Chichicastenago market to buy gifts.

➤ **Hablé con el guía sobre la ruta a Petén:** I spoke to the guide about the route to Peten.

➤ **Anoche no pude dormir:** I couldn't sleep last night.

➤ **Compró una nueva mochila:** He/She bought a new backpack.

➤ **Me gustaron todas las obras de Orozco y Rivera:** I liked all of the works by Orozco and Rivera.

➤ **Los indígenas de aquella época abandonaron el uso de esa técnica:** The indigenous people of that period abandoned the use of that technique.

➤ **María tuvo que comprar una tarjeta postal:** Maria had to buy a postcard.

➤ **Cristóbal Colón descubrió las Américas:** Christopher Columbus discovered the Americas.

➤ **Ayer estuve bien, pero hoy estoy mal:** Yesterday I was fine, but today I'm not well.

Acuérdate

In regular *–ar* verbs, the *nosotros* form of the preterite is the same as the *nosotros* form in the present indicative. Thus, *hablamos* can mean "we talk" or "we talked." The context usually indicates whether the statement is in the past or present. If necessary, you may indicate "when" with words such as *ahora, ayer,* or *el año pasado* to avoid misunderstandings.

The Imperfect Tense: I Used to Do It Often

The other past tense is called the imperfect tense. But there's absolutely nothing wrong with it. These are the *–aba, –abas, –aba* and *–ía, –ías, –ía* endings. If you need a review, consult your beginning text or Appendix A, "Basic Grammar Resource."

The difference between the preterite and the imperfect is that the imperfect is used to express or describe past actions or events that occurred over an extended period of time, while the preterite tells of events which only occurred once (or are thought of as having occurred as a unit). Use the imperfect to describe conditions in the past or to tell of actions done often or habitually.

Ten Cuidado

The preterite forms for *ir* and *ser* are the same: *fui, fuiste, fue, fuimos, fuisteis, fueron.* But don't worry; confusion between the two is practically impossible. The context will make it clear whether the verb is "to be" or "to go."

You may have noticed that the first-person and third-person singular forms look the same. The context usually makes it clear what's going on, but pronouns and names may also be added for clarity.

Luckily, only three common verbs take an irregular imperfect form: *ser, ir,* and *ver* ("to see"). You'll need these right away, though, so you should learn them now.

The Three Verbs That Are Irregular in the Imperfect

Verb	Conjugation
ser	*era, eras, era, éramos, erais, eran*
ir	*iba, ibas, iba, íbamos, ibais, iban*
ver	*veía, veías, veía, veíamos, veíais, veían*

Here are some examples to help you to better understand the uses of the imperfect tense:

Acuérdate

Express a recent past action by using *acabar + de + infinitive*: *Acabo de salir de la biblioteca* = "I just left the library"; *Acaban de ver la película* = "They just saw the movie." *Acabar* can also be used in the imperfect tense: *Juan acababa de estudiar el retrato cuando cerraron el museo* = "Juan had just studied the painting when they closed the museum."

➤ Description:

> ➤ **Era la mañana y llovía bastante:** It was morning, and it was raining a lot.

> ➤ **La casa estaba pintada de un color gris:** The house was painted a gray color.

> ➤ **Desde el techo se veía el mar:** From the roof one could see the sea.

> ➤ **Los pintores del siglo veinte eran todos muy extraños:** The painters of the twentieth century were all very strange.

➤ Habitual action:

> ➤ **El pintor asistía a la escuela de arte cuando era niño:** The painter attended art school when he was a child.

> ➤ **Íbamos al mercado cada día cuando vivíamos en Managua:** We used to go the market every day when we lived in Managua.

> ➤ **Mi papá compraba muchos coches:** My dad used to buy a lot of cars. *(When and how many are not important)*

The imperfect and preterite can often be used in the same sentence. This is a good way to tell of an action that was occurring when something else interrupted it. The imperfect says what was going on when something happened (preterite):

➤ **Yo estaba leyendo *Don Quixote* cuando sonó el teléfono:** I was reading *Don Quixote* when the phone rang.

➤ **Estábamos conduciendo hacia el volcán cuando se nos descompuso el coche:** We were driving toward the volcano when the car broke down on us.

➤ **Me dijeron que Julio estaba hablando contigo cuando sucedió:** They told me that Julio was talking with (to) you when it happened.

Algo Nuevo

In the sentence *Compré diez coches el año pasado* = "I bought 10 automobiles last year," the preterite form of *comprar* must be used, even though the transactions may have taken place at different times during the course of the year. There are no implications that this action will impact this year or next. The purchase of the vehicles is over and done with. Because these actions are being considered collectively as a group, the preterite is required here. An imperfect *Compraba muchos coches* would change the focus to "I used to buy a lot of cars," making the listener wonder what might have changed since then ("Well, are you still buying a lot of cars or not?").

Remember that perfect tense from before? Well, *haber* can also be used in the imperfect (yes, an "imperfect perfect tense"). This tense, called the past perfect, corresponds to the English "had done," "had been," "had seen," and so on. It tells of a condition that existed prior to a later past occurrence or action. Observe:

➤ **No fue la primera vez. Lo había hecho el año pasado:** It wasn't the first time. I had done it last year.

➤ **Se había casado tres veces ya cuando conoció a su cuarta esposa:** He had already been married three times when he met his fourth wife.

Acuérdate

The verb *querer* in the past has two different meanings in the negative: *No quiso* means "refused to do," while *no quería* means "didn't want to." So, *querer* in the imperfect is not as forceful.

➤ **Ya se había renovado el edificio cuando se convertió en museo:** The building had already been renovated when it was converted into a museum.

The Future Tense

The future tense in Spanish is similar to the "shall" future tense in English. It isn't as common in daily conversation as the *ir + a + infinitive* model that you reviewed a few chapters ago. However, when you do use it, it's as clear as a *campana*.

Acuérdate

You've already learned that *con* means "with" (*chile con carne* = "chile with meat"). There's nothing really special about *con*, except that when it's used with "me" and "you," it takes a special form: *con + yo = conmigo* "with me"; *con + tú = contigo* "with you."

Algo Nuevo

There is a third form of these "sigos": *consigo*. It means "with himself/herself" and is a combination of *con + se*. *Está muy enojado consigo mismo* = "He's very angry with himself"; *Llevaba consigo dos pistolas grandes* = "He was carrying (with himself) two large pistols."

For most verbs, all you need to do is add the corresponding future tense ending right on the infinitive. You can review the formation of the future tense in Appendix A if you need to. Otherwise, read on:

➤ **Hablaré con el agente de viajes mañana:** I will speak with the travel agent tomorrow.

➤ **¿Bailaremos?:** Shall we dance?

➤ **Estaremos en San José por un mes:** We will be in San Jose for a month.

➤ **No irás nunca jamás a la casa de Jaime:** You will never ever go to Jaime's house.

➤ **¿Cuántas personas serán?:** How many people will you be (in your group/party)?

➤ **Veremos qué pasará:** We'll see what happens.

➤ **Servirán comida durante el vuelo:** They will serve food during the flight.

➤ **Vosotros comprenderéis todo mañana:** You all will understand everything tomorrow.

➤ **¿De veras irás a Nicaragua de vacaciones?:** Are you really going to Nicaragua for vacation?

➤ **Perderás tu mochila si la dejas en el autobús:** You will lose your backpack if you leave it in the bus.

➤ **Qué será, será:** Whatever will be, will be.

The Conditional Tense

In daily speech, the conditional tense is more common than the future tense. I like to think of it as the *Mr. Rogers' Neighborhood* tense: "Would you be mine, could you be mine, won't you be my neighbor?" The conditional tense is used where we use the helping verbs *would* and *could* in English. As with the future tense, conditional tense endings are slapped on to the end of the infinitive. Review them as needed in Appendix A or elsewhere:

➤ **Yo hablaría con el guía, pero ahora no tengo tiempo:** I would talk with the tour guide, but I don't have time now.

➤ **Hoy me gustaría ir a la selva:** I would like to go to the jungle today.

➤ **Les gustaría viajar a las once de la noche:** They would like to go at 11:00 P.M.

Ten Cuidado

You'll notice that the *yo* form and *él/ella/usted* form are the same in the conditional and imperfect tenses. Usually, the context makes it clear who the subject of the sentence is. But you can always add the subject pronoun to your sentence to avoid any ambiguities: *yo hablaría, él hablaría, ella hablaba.*

➤ **Compraríamos dos boletos de tren, pero no tenemos dinero:** We would buy two train tickets, but we don't have any money.

➤ **¿No sería posible llegar a la Ciudad de Panamá a las dos?:** Wouldn't it be possible to arrive in Panama City at 2:00?

Many verbs that have stem changes in the present indicative (such as *pensar*, with *pienso*), are quite regular in the future and conditional (*pensará, jugaría*). However, several common verbs do change their stem when forming the conditional and future tenses: *hacer = har; tener = tendr; saber = sabr;* and so on. The change is exactly the same for both tenses. You'll find a more complete list on the Reference Card in the front of this book.

Acuérdate

The conditional can be used to soften a request. For example, *¿Me puede ayudar con mi equipaje?* = "Can you help me with my luggage?" is a fine sentence. But you can make the request even more courteous by using the conditional: *¿Me podría decir usted si el tren llegará a las seis y media, por favor?* = "Could you please tell me if the train will arrive at 6:30?"

Haz Clic Aquí

Get a good dose of grammar practice online at www.colby. edu/personal/bknelson/grammar. html. If you need extra help with the future and conditional tenses, this is the place to get it.

Risa del Día

Okay, this is the last joke that has anything to do with kids in school, I promise. But this joke is actually funny:

El padre de un niño va a la escuela a investigar por qué a su hijo le pusieron un cero en el examen.

—Lo que pasó -dijo la maestra- es que su hijo copió del examen de otro niño. Es tan claro que los dos exámenes son casi iguales.

El padre, sintiendo su orgullo herido reclamó:

—Pero si los dos exámenes son casi iguales, pudo haber sido el otro niño que copiara de mi hijo.

La maestra siguió explicando:

—Nos dimos cuenta que fue su hijo que copió porque en una de las preguntas, el otro niño escribió: "YO NO SÉ," y su hijo escribió: "YO TAMPOCO."

Vocabulario Útil:

➤ **investigar:** to investigate; to research

➤ **cero:** zero; an F

➤ **examen:** test

➤ **lo que pasó:** what happened; the thing that happened

➤ **igual:** the same

➤ **orgullo:** pride

➤ **herido:** wounded

➤ **darse cuenta:** to realize

➤ **yo tampoco:** neither do I; I don't either

El Cuiz

Give the Spanish translations of the following words. Cheating is not recommended, but do what you feel is best:

1. to deepen; to go into depth _____
2. minister _____
3. defense _____
4. threat _____
5. common _____
6. related to _____
7. to meet; to get together _____
8. army _____
9. commander _____
10. integration _____
11. leader; "boss" _____
12. to review; to look over _____
13. security _____
14. to constitute; to make up _____
15. drug-trafficking _____
16. period; time _____
17. armed forces _____

Tareas

1. Write the future tense endings on a separate sheet of paper.
2. Write the conditional tense endings on a separate sheet of paper.
3. Write the preterite tense endings on a separate sheet of paper.
4. Write the imperfect tense endings on a separate sheet of paper (boy, you sure use a lot of paper).
5. Create sentences in the past tense, and practice forming and using the Spanish preterite. Refer to the previous examples and explanations if you need guidance.
6. Create as many sentences as you can where you need the future and/or conditional tense. Use your dictionary for vocabulary. Think of things that you "will do," "would do," and "could do" (*poder = podr–*). Learn and practice the verbs that change their stem in the future and conditional tenses.

The Least You Need to Know

➤ There are five Spanish-speaking countries in Central America.

➤ The preterite is the simple past and describes things that are over and done with.

➤ The imperfective past describes events that took place over a period of time.

➤ The future and conditional tenses are added to the verb after the ending.

➤ Several common verbs form irregular future/conditional stems.

Chapter 12

Los Estados Unidos de América

As I mentioned way back in Chapter 1, "¡Vamos!", the United States is one of the largest Spanish-speaking countries in the world. This is not simply due to recent developments; Hispanics have had a long history in the United States.

Esteban's History Lesson (Abridged)

In 1848, Mexico lost its war with the United States, and the United States acquired nearly half of Mexico's territory. When the land known as the Mexican Cession became the American Southwest (Texas, Arizona, Nevada, California, New Mexico, Utah, and part of Colorado), the Mexicans who lived there became American citizens. As part of the Treaty of Guadalupe-Hidalgo, the new Mexican-Americans were to be guaranteed the same basic civil rights and freedoms of all citizens, including the possession of their land and the freedom to retain their cultural identity, language, and religion, without interference. However, much of this treaty was ignored, and many of the Mexicans living in these territories lost their land and eventually became second-class citizens.

During World War I, the expanding defense industry and the drafting of American men into the military created a labor shortage in agriculture. At the request of U.S. growers and industrialists, nearly 73,000 Mexicans were legally admitted to the United States to be employed in agriculture and other industries.

The demand for Mexicans ended quickly during the Great Depression. With 25 percent unemployment, the U.S. government decided that it would be less expensive to repatriate Mexicans than to include them in the public welfare programs of the New Deal. Thus, many Mexicans, some of whom had become legal residents or even U.S. citizens, were repatriated (sent back) to Mexico during the 1930s.

With the coming of World War II, American growers again began to lobby the government to bring Mexican workers back to the United States to work on American farms. In 1942, Mexico and the United States signed the Bracero Agreement. Under the terms of this agreement, Mexican workers were recruited in specified centers in Mexico to work in the United States. The Bracero Program was to last for the duration of the war only, but was extended in 1951 and continued until 1964.

Agriculture quickly began to rely on undocumented Mexicans to provide cheap labor. In 1986, the Immigration Reform and Control Act (IRCA) granted amnesty to millions of undocumented aliens, most of whom were Mexican, and allowed them to apply for legal residence. However, even though IRCA made it a crime for businesses to hire undocumented workers, illegal immigration still continues today.

Cultura Latina

The term *chicano* is used by some Mexican-Americans with pride. Other Mexican-Americans feel that they are not *chicanos* and may even take offense at the word. Generally, *chicanos* are Mexican-Americans who have lived in the United States (mostly in California) for several generations. It is always best to ask if a Mexican-American considers himself or herself to be *chicano/a* before using the word. Visit www.chicano.org for more information.

At the end of the Spanish-American War (1898), Spain lost control of Cuba and Puerto Rico. Puerto Ricans eventually became U.S. citizens. During the 1940s and 1950s, many Puerto Ricans left the island for economic reasons. Today there are almost as many Puerto Ricans living in New York City as there are in San Juan. Most are second- and third-generation *neo-yorqeños*.

In 1959, Fidel Castro came to power in Cuba with popular support. The Batista regime that preceded him was indeed very corrupt and did little for the poorer people of the island. However, when Castro turned to the Soviet Union for help in his collectivization of the island's resources, many Cubans felt betrayed and fled the island for Spain and the United States. In 1980, Castro signed an agreement with the United States that allowed Cubans to legally immigrate to the United States. The next day, 120,000 Cubans met at the Port of Mariel and sailed to Florida. This event became known as the Mariel Boat Lift, and Cubans who came at that time are known as *marielitos*. Today, many Cubans still brave the waves in their attempt to flee the island for Florida.

Hispanics from other nations have also come to the United States in recent years. During the decades of civil war in Central America, many Guatemalans, Salvadorans, and Nicaraguans fled their countries as political refugees. Washington, D.C., has one of the largest Salvadoran communities outside of El Salvador.

Lectura: Estudios de Discriminación

The following reading is an opinionated editorial, written from the perspective of a Hispanic living in the United States. Of course, you are free to agree or disagree with the opinions expressed in the passage. But I think the text makes a good *lectura*:

Haz Clic Aquí

A great source of information on Hispanics living in the United States is www.hispanic.com. The site is mostly in English, but it contains many links to Spanish-language sites as well.

> *A pesar de los esfuerzos que los gobiernos federales y estatales de los Estados Unidos han hecho para eliminar el racismo en los campos de la vida social y cultural, la discriminación racial sigue siendo una práctica constante.*

> *Por ejemplo, se puede observar el trato que la principal fuente de noticias, entretenimiento e información de los EE.UU. le da a la minoría más numerosa del país; los latinos permanecen virtualmente invisibles en la televisión.*

> *Algunos estudios recientes han mostrado que cuando la televisión de habla inglesa finalmente informa sobre los latinos, generalmente muestra*

Acuérdate

When Americans say that we're going "south of the border," we mean Mexico. When Canadians say this, they mean the United States. It's obvious, but I bet you've never thought of it, eh?

estereotipos negativos. Evidenciaron también que en la actualidad los programas televisivos comúnmente conocidos como "programas basados en la vida real" han hecho que la situación sea aún peor, dado que solamente muestran a los pocos latinos que tienen problemas con la ley o que han cometido algún delito.

Vocabulario Útil:

➤ **esfuerzo:** effort

➤ **estatal:** state (adj.)

➤ **trato:** treatment

➤ **racismo:** racism

➤ **campo:** field; area

➤ **permanecer:** to remain

➤ **minoría:** minority

➤ **entretenimiento:** entertainment

➤ **estereotipo:** stereotype

➤ **invisible:** invisible

➤ **estudios:** studies; investigations

➤ **evidenciar:** to show evidence that

➤ **informar:** to inform; to give news

➤ **actualidad:** at this time; these days

➤ **comúnmente:** commonly

➤ **cometer:** to commit

➤ **delito:** crime (other than murder)

➤ **ley:** law

Análisis del Texto

Okay, let's take a look at some words and phrases from the *lectura*:

➤ *A pesar de*

This idiomatic phrase means "in spite of." It can also be seen as *a pesar de que*, when it may be followed by a subjunctive form of the verb: *a pesar de que Miguel lo sepa* = "in spite of the fact that Miguel might know it."

➤ *sigue siendo una práctica*

Seguir can take a present perfect *–ing* form of a verb. Here it means "continues to be." Remember that the *u* after the *g* is just an orthographic convenience. It makes no sound and is just there to make sure the *g* doesn't go soft and sound like an English *h*.

➤ *la principal fuente de noticias, entretenimiento e información de los EE.UU.*

Notice that this entire phrase just means "the television." We learn this at the end of the sentence. This is just more elegant variation.

➤ *de habla inglesa*

This is how you say "English-speaking" in Spanish. *Habla* is feminine but will take *el* because of the stressed *a* sound at the beginning.

➤ *Evidenciaron también*

This is a good example of how a Spanish verb can need a long translation in English. *Evidenciar* means "to show evidence of."

➤ *en la actualidad*

This is just a fancy way of saying "now." Remember that *actual* is a false cognate and means "at present," not "actual." The adverb *actualmente* doesn't mean "actually," but rather "at this present time."

➤ *programas basados en la vida real*

Sometimes Spanish can't come up with the short buzz words that we create in English. This means "reality-based."

➤ *han hecho que la situación sea aún peor*

Notice the subjunctive *sea*, which gives us, "have made (that) the situation (may be) worse." There is a force being generated on another subject here (*la cituación*), so a subjunctive verb form is required. More on the subjunctive in *un momento*.

Vista Panorámica de los EE.UU.

➤ **Nombre oficial:** *Estados Unidos de América*

➤ **Gobierno:** *República federal de 50 estados y un distrito federal*

➤ **Capital:** *Washington, Distrito de Columbia*

➤ **Estados con alto porcentaje de hispano-hablantes:** *California, Nueva York, Florida, Texas (Tejas), Illinois, Colorado, Arizona, Nuevo México, Washington, Nuevo Jersey, otros*

➤ **Ciudades con alto porcentaje de hispano-hablantes:** *Nueva York; Los Ángeles; Miami; Houston; San Diego; Washington, D.C.; Phoenix; Chicago; Dallas; San Antonio; El Paso; Boston; otras.*

➤ **Tamaño:** *9.4 millones de kilómetros cuadrados*

Cultura Latina

Spain fought alongside the Yankees during the American Revolution (1775–1783). More than 4,000 Spanish soldiers died while prisoners of war on English prison ships in New York Harbor after being captured while fighting for American independence. Spanish ports in Europe and the Caribbean were safe havens for American ships being harassed by the British.

Ten Cuidado

I've seen far too many mistranslations of the word "crime" as *crimen*. The word *crimen* in Spanish means "murder," and *cometer un crimen* means to "commit murder." If someone commits a crime that is not murder, call it *un delito*. A traffic violation would be *una infracción*. Don't say *violación*, which means "rape."

➤ **Población de hispanos:** *Aproximadamente 40 millones*

➤ **Producto Nacional Bruto:** *5 billones de dólares estadounidenses*

➤ **Exportaciones:** *Maquinaria, computadoras, software, maquinaria industrial, instrumentos científicos, equipo telefónico, equipo de transporte, medicinas, plástico, productos elaborados y productos agrícolos, otras*

➤ **Importaciones:** *petróleo crudo, automóviles, textiles, zapatos, radios, estereos, televisores, electodomésticos, equipo fotográfico, ropa, papel, café, mariscos, otras*

Gramática: The Spanish Subjunctive

Many students of Spanish head for *las montañas* when the topic turns to the subjunctive. But the good news is that with careful explanation, it really isn't that bad. Meet my "kinder, gentler subjunctive."

So, What Is the Subjunctive?

The subjunctive is not a tense. It's more of a "mood." The subjunctive is the "alter ego" of the indicative. It is a second form of the verb that serves an entirely different grammatical function.

The subjunctive removes the subject a few steps away from the certainty of the action or state of the verb: "I did it" (indicative), compared with "It is possible that I might have done it, but nobody is really sure at this moment in time" (subjunctive). While the indicative mood is certain, quantifiable, and solid, the subjunctive is possible, doubtful, indirect, emotional, pliable, opinionated, and contrary to fact.

There are both present and past forms of the subjunctive. There's also a future subjunctive, but it's only used in legal writings. We'll focus on the present subjunctive in this chapter.

Algo Nuevo

Perhaps you didn't know that English also has a subjunctive. We use it most often in "contrary to fact" sentences such as: "I wish I were in the land of cotton" (but I'm not). Nowadays, many people incorrectly say "I wish I was in Dixie," which technically should be "I wish I were in Dixie" (because I'm not). The verbs *may* and *might* also help to form the English subjunctive: "May he rest in peace."

Forming the Present Subjunctive

Making the present subjunctive is sort of like putting the wrong ending on the verb. With his "shoes on backwards," you can imagine how the poor verb feels: unsure, vulnerable, plagued by self-doubt. In the subjunctive, *–ar* verbs take the endings that you worked so hard to learn for the *–er* and *–ir* verbs, and the *–er* and *–ir* verbs take the endings used by *–ar* verbs. The only real deviation from this paradigm is that the first-person singular *yo* form is now the same as the third-person (*él, ella, usted*). If you need to review the subjunctive endings, consult your beginning text or Appendix A, "Basic Grammar Resource."

The key to forming the present subjunctive is to start with the *yo* form of the verb in the indicative and then build your subjunctive from there. I'll show you why in a minute. In most cases, the whole thing is pretty straightforward.

For example, let's say we're dealing with our regular old friend *hablar*. Here are the steps you'll need to follow to form the present subjunctive:

1. Recall the endings for *–er* verbs (remembering the change in the *yo* form).

2. Form the *yo* form of the verb in the indicative (*hablo*).

3. Remove the *–o,* and put the subjunctive ending in its place: *hable.*

The steps you'll need to follow for *–er* and *–ir* verbs are the same. Only the endings have changed:

1. Recall the endings for your *–ar* verbs (remembering the change in the *yo* form).

2. Form the *yo* form of the verb (*comer = como; vivir = vivo*).

3. Remove the *–o,* and put the subjunctive ending in its place: *coma, viva.*

The only hard part to remember is that you must start with the indicative *yo* form (until you have

Haz Clic Aquí

I highly recommend that you visit http://spanish.about.com/education/spanish/mpremail.htm. This about.com site is run by Gerald Erichsen and is your About.com guide to the Spanish language. You can read about the subjunctive in great detail. There's a bulletin board for frequently asked questions, and you can even send e-mail and have some of your questions answered directly.

Acuérdate

Verbs that end in *–cer,* such as *conocer, establecer* (to establish), *parecer* (to seem/to appear), and *crecer* (to grow) change to *conozco, parezco, establezco,* and *crezco* in the first person *yo* form. When forming the subjunctive of such verbs, you must maintain this ending throughout: *conozca, establezcas, parezcan, conozcamos,* and so on.

memorized the subjunctive forms, when they will come naturally to you) and use it as your template for the subjunctive. Any changes in the stem that occur there will be reflected in the present subjunctive form.

The Subjunctive and Those Spelling Rules

Adding this "wrong" ending can necessitate some spelling changes. Take for example the verb *pagar*. If we follow the steps for forming the present subjunctive, we start with *pago*. Now, because this is an *–ar* verb, we remove the *–o* and add *–e,* which gives us *page*. But this would be pronounced as *"pah hay"* because the *g* goes soft before *e* and *i*. Therefore, we must add *u* after the *g* to protect it from the softening effects of the *–e*. So, the present subjunctive of *pagar* is *pague*. The *u* remains a silent partner.

Right and Wrong Spelling with the Subjunctive

Verb	First Person Indicative	Wrong!	Right!
sacar	*saco*	*"sace"*	*saque*
arrancar	*arranco*	*"arrance"*	*arranque*
jugar	*juego*	*"juege"*	*juegue*

When to Use the Subjunctive

Forming the subjunctive is relatively straightforward. The real confusion tends to come when trying to figure out how to use it. I hope the following section clears up any remaining questions that you might have.

Usted *Commands*

Directly telling someone to do or not to do something is known as a command or imperative. When you're addressing someone in the *usted* form (or *ustedes*, for more than one person), you must use the subjunctive form of the verb for all commands:

➤ **Hable con el cocinero, por favor:** Please speak to the cook.

➤ **Paguen la cuenta en la caja, señores:** Pay the bill at the cashier, gentlemen.

➤ **Dígame por favor si Adela está lista o no:** Please tell me if Adela is ready or not.

➤ **No vayan al restaurante que está detrás del hotel:** Don't go to the restaurant behind the hotel.

➤ **Hágame el favor de decirme la hora:** Please give me (do me the favor of telling me) the time.

➤ **Tráigame un nuevo tenedor:** Bring me a new fork.

150

Indirect Commands

When someone's will is directed at or imposed upon something or someone else, the subjunctive form of the verb must be used. If I say: "I want Jorge to eat the bread," I'm expressing my will that Jorge do something. It doesn't matter whether Jorge and I use *tú* with each other. I am placing my will and desire on something other than myself. And if Jorge replies that he's not hungry and wants me to leave him alone about the bread, the subjunctive must also be used when he places his will on me:

➤ **No quiero que Jorge *coma* todo el pan:** I don't want Jorge to eat all the bread.

➤ **El jefe quiere que Julio *venga* temprano al trabajo:** The boss wants Julio to come to work early.

➤ **Deseamos que los ciudadanos *sean* felices:** We wish the citizens to be happy.

➤ **María no permite que su esposo *tome* cerveza:** María doesn't allow her husband to drink beer.

➤ **Juan desea que el mesero *vuelva* en unos minutos:** Juan wishes the waiter to return in a few minutes.

➤ **Nosotros insistimos en que tú nos *pagues* el dinero ahora:** We insist that you pay us the money now.

➤ **Mis padres quieren que yo *haga* los quehaceres:** My parents want me to do my chores.

➤ **Su novia quiere que yo *conozca* a su hermana:** His girlfriend wants me to meet her sister.

Ten Cuidado

Even though the *usted* command forms are more polite than the direct *tú* commands, you should still add courteous phrases such as *por favor* when using them. The *por favor* doesn't have to come next to the command: *Hágame el favor de decirme la hora, por favor* = "Please tell me what time it is." Nobody likes being told what to do, and *por favor* should be used as much as possible.

Acuérdate

When one noun places its will on a different noun, the subjunctive is required: *Quiero que tú vayas* = "I want you to go." But, when the noun places its will on itself, there is no need for the subjunctive, and an infinitive is all you'll need: *Quiero ir* = "I want 'myself' to go."

Impersonal Expressions

It doesn't always have to be a person doing the wanting. The subjunctive must also be used in "impersonal" expressions showing opinion or emotion such as "It's wonderful that …" or "It's too bad that …."

151

Acuérdate

Some people like to use "NEEDS PAWS" as a device to remember under what conditions the subjunctive is used. These letters stand for: **N**ecessity, **E**motion, **E**xaggeration, **D**emanding, **S**eeming, **P**ossibility, **A**sking, **W**ishing, **S**upposing. If this sort of thing helps you, learn **NEEDS PAWS.**

Ten Cuidado

Notice that the *que* that begins impersonal wishes is not the same *qué* that starts phrases such as *¡Qué bueno!* The accented *qué* means "what" and "how," and the unaccented *que* means "that" or "which." There's no difference in pronunciation, but be careful not to confuse them when writing Spanish.

➤ **Es fantástico que Antonio haya conseguido empleo:** It's great that Antonio has found work.

➤ **Es una lástima que María no conozca mejor a su esposo:** It's a shame that María doesn't know her husband better.

➤ **¡Qué lástima que no puedas venir a la fiesta!:** What a shame you can't come to the party!

Negative Tú Commands

When you tell a child, friend, of family member not to do something, the *tú* form of the subjunctive is required:

➤ **No me digas que vas a vender tu casa:** Don't tell me you're going to sell your house.

➤ **Jaimito, no toques el libro de Juan:** Jaimito, don't touch Juan's book.

➤ **Juanito, no juegues con tu comida:** Juanito, don't play with your food.

➤ **No me dejes solo, mi amor:** Don't leave me alone, my love.

Impersonal Wishes, Hopes, and Letting Someone Else Do It

You'll see what I mean by the examples. These are usually preceded by *que*. In sentences expressing hope, the verb *esperar* ("to wait"; "to hope") or *ojalá* ("it is hoped") are optional:

➤ **Que la pague mi cuñado:** Let my brother-in-law pay it. (*la cuenta*)

➤ **Que lo repare el gobierno:** Let the government fix it.

➤ **(Espero) Que sirvan la comida ahora mismo:** I hope they serve the food right now.

➤ **(Ojalá) Que gane mi equipo:** I hope my team wins.

➤ **¡Que coman pastel!:** Let 'em eat cake!

➤ **Que descanse en paz:** May he rest in peace.

➤ **¡Viva el Rey! (*the que is understood*):** Long live the King!

Unspecified Future Time

Use the subjunctive when the exact time a future event will (or may) occur is uncertain or unimportant. These sentences often translate as "whenever" in English:

➤ **Pagaremos la deuda cuando llegue el cheque:** We'll pay the debt whenever the check gets here.

➤ **Te llamo cuando pueda:** I'll call you whenever I can.

➤ **Nadie sabe cuando vaya a acabar el mundo:** Nobody knows when the world will end.

➤ **Felipe dice que lo hará cuando termine la cena:** Felipe says that he'll do it whenever he finishes dinner.

➤ **María, cuando crezcas serás presidente. (crecer):** María, when you grow up you'll be president.

After Certain Stock Phrases

By their very nature, some phrases take the subjunctive. Most end in *que*. Here are few examples:

➤ **aunque:** although

➤ **es posible que:** it's possible that

➤ **hasta que:** until

➤ **después de que:** after

➤ **es importante que:** it's important that

➤ **puede ser que:** it may be that

➤ **tan pronto que:** as soon as

➤ **en cuanto:** as soon as

➤ **a pesar de que:** in spite of the fact that

Ten Cuidado

Avoid stand-alone subjunctives such as: *Yo haga, Él no sepa,* and *Ellos vayan.* You'll need to start these with phrases such as *Es posible que* or *Es importante que* to make them work. You can, however, say *Lo que sea,* which means, "Whatever."

Cultura Latina

Knowing how to use the subjunctive correctly is essential to being able to speak Spanish well. However, in most cases people will still understand you if you accidentally use the indicative when you should have used the subjunctive. Don't let the issue of "subjunctive vs. indicative" prevent you from trying to communicate with people in Spanish.

Here are some additional subjunctive situations. The examples will serve as explanation:

➤ **Something unlikely or uncertain:** *Es posible que mi equipo gane mañana.* It's possible that my team may win tomorrow. (Who knows if they will …)

Acuérdate

Use the subjunctive whenever there is doubt and the subject of the second verb is different from the subject of the first verb: *Yo dudo que Juan pueda hacerlo* ("I doubt that Juan can do it.") You can say *Yo dudo que puedo hacerlo* without a subjunctive because the subject of the two verbs is the same.

Haz Clic Aquí

No matter how you slice it, using the Spanish subjunctive isn't always easy. For more practice, visit the Spanish subjunctive tutorial at www.unc.edu/courses/span003/gram.html.

➤ **After expressions of doubt:** *No creo que mi hermano vaya a poder cruzar la frondera solo.* I don't think that my brother will be able to cross the border alone. (He's not too bright.)

➤ **Statement colored by emotion:** *Estoy tan triste de que tú me hayas abandonado.* I'm so sad that you have abandoned me.

➤ **Statement doubtful or not true:** *Es poco probable que María tenga el dinero para pagarlo.* It's unlikely that María has the money to pay it.

Sometimes both the indicative and the subjunctive are possible in a particular sentence. The decision to use the one or the other depends on how certain, opinionated, or emotional the speaker feels. For example:

➤ **Aunque Julio es inteligente, no puede solucionar el problema:** Although Julio is intelligent, he can't solve the problem. (There is no doubt that Julio is an intelligent man.)

➤ **Aunque Julio sea inteligente, no puede solucionar el problema:** Although Julio may be intelligent, he can't solve the problem. (Here the speaker is casting some doubt as to Julio's intelligence.)

➤ **No es cierto que existe Papá Noel. (existir):** Santa Claus does not exist. (We now have scientific proof.)

➤ **No es cierto que exista Papá Noel:** There is no Santa Claus. (But some people still believe in him, and I can't prove that he doesn't exist.)

Unknown But Potential Existence

➤ **¿Hay alguien aquí que hable el inglés?:** Is there anyone here who speaks English?

The reason that *hablar* is in the subjunctive (*hable*) here is that we're not sure whether such a person exists. Even if there is an English speaker around, we can't know (and don't particularly care) who he or she might be. Another translation of this sentence might be: "Is there anyone here who might be able to speak English?" If we replace *hable* with the indicative *habla,* the sentence might mean: "So, there's someone here who speaks English? Well, good. I look forward to meeting this person."

Risa del Día

I'm not sure why, but there seems to be no shortage of jokes in Spanish about ducks. Most of these ducks talk. Here is an example:

Entra un pato a un bar y dice:

—Un sandwich de pollo y un refresco, por favor.

El barman se queda estupefacto y con la voz temblorosa le dice:

—¿Cómo puede ser que un pato hable?

—¿Y qué? ¿Usted no habla acaso?

—Sí, bueno …. ¿Y cómo descidió honrarme entrando a mi bar?

—Es que trabajo de albañil en la obra de aquí a la vuelta y vine a comprar la comida. ¿Qué tiene de raro?

El Pato paga y se va. El barman se va corriendo al circo y le cuenta lo sucedido al dueño. Juntos se van a la obra a buscar al pato y lo encuentran construyendo una pared. El dueño del circo le dice:

—Por favor señor pato, véngase conmigo a trabajar en el circo.

El pato contesta: ¿Y para qué necesitan a un albañil en el circo?

Vocabulario Útil:

➤ **refresco:** soft drink; soda

➤ **quedarse:** to become; to remain

➤ **estupefacto:** astonished

➤ **voz:** voice

➤ **tembloroso:** shaky

➤ **acaso (no):** by chance; "I suppose you don't"

➤ **honrar:** to honor

➤ **albañil:** mason; bricklayer

➤ **a la vuelta:** around the corner; nearby

➤ **tener de raro:** be strange

➤ **obra:** work; project; construction site

➤ **circo:** circus

➤ **dueño:** owner

➤ **lo sucedido:** what had happened

El Cuiz

Give the Spanish translations of the following words. Cheat only if you really need to:

1. field; area _____
2. efforts _____
3. state (adj.) _____
4. treatment _____
5. racism _____
6. entertainment _____
7. to remain _____
8. minority _____
9. today; the present _____
10. stereotype _____
11. law _____
12. studies; investigations _____
13. to show evidence that _____
14. invisible _____
15. commonly _____
16. "reality-based" _____
17. crime (other than murder) _____
18. to commit _____

Tareas

1. Explain to someone the use of the Spanish subjunctive. If there is no one around, write down your explanation.
2. Write the present subjunctive endings on a piece of paper.
3. Create sentences using the present subjunctive tense. Follow the rules as outlined here, and use the examples as your guide. Consult your dictionary for any additional vocabulary that you might need.

The Least You Need to Know

➤ Spanish-speakers have a long history in the United States.

➤ Forming the subjunctive is a bit like putting the wrong ending on the verb.

➤ Build the subjunctive by using the first-person singular indicative as your template: *salgo, salgas,* and so on.

➤ The subjunctive must be used when someone's will is imposed on someone or something else.

➤ The subjunctive must also be used when there is doubt or emotion and there is a change of subject of the second verb.

Part 3
La Vida Cotidiana

The title of this part means "Everyday Life." The lecturas *in the following chapters are about friends, family, food, religious customs, and* fiestas. *After all, why bother learning Spanish in the first place if you can't have fun, meet new people, and deepen your knowledge of the culture? The grammar sections will be slightly shorter than those in Part 2. This time I'll go into greater detail about* haber, tan, *and* tanto, *the present progressive, prepositions,* por *vs.* para, usted *vs.* tú, *and a few other sundries about grammar and usage.*

Chapter 13

La Familia Latina

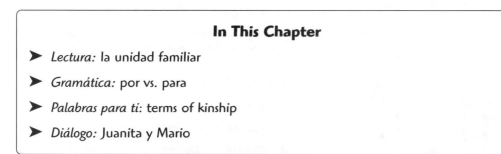

In This Chapter

➤ *Lectura:* la unidad familiar

➤ *Gramática:* por vs. para

➤ *Palabras para ti:* terms of kinship

➤ *Diálogo:* Juanita y Mario

The family unit is one of the most important social institutions in the Spanish-speaking world. The *familia hispánica* often extends beyond the nuclear family, and it is not uncommon for one's grandparents, uncles, aunts, cousins, and other family members to be living under the same roof—or at least nearby. It is also quite acceptable for children to continue to live at home with their parents until they marry.

Many families in Spain and Latin America still follow the traditional family model with respect to gender roles. It is quite common for mothers in middle-class families to remain at home, tending to the needs of the family, while the father works outside the home. However, many women have found it necessary to find work outside the home for economic reasons. In larger cities, Spanish and Latin American women have had successful professional careers.

Lectura: La Unidad Familiar Hispánica

Here is a short reading about the Latin family. It is challenging, so you may want to read it a few times:

Cultura Latina

Godparents are very important to the Latin family structure. The institution of godparenthood is known as *el compadrazgo*. The godparents, or *padrastros*, are usually friends or relatives of the family who do all they can to treat their godchildren as if they were their own. This can include gifts for holidays and special events, and the promise to be helpful throughout the lives of their godchildren.

La familia es una de las instituciones sociales más importantes para el individuo hispano. De ella procede en gran medida su identidad y bienestar personales y su sentido de seguridad y estabilidad. La familia latina representa un apoyo para el individuo a la vez que reafirma su dignidad y posición en la sociedad. Une a todos los miembros, incluso a los parientes, y les hace sentir como parte de una unidad íntima y fuerte, en la que pueden tener confianza. Por eso, en muchos casos, un joven hispano puede permanecer en la casa de sus padres hasta que se case.

La unidad familiar hispana incluye el concepto de la familia extendida. No es raro que, por razones económicas, sociales o personales, los parientes de cierta familia (abuelos, tíos, primos) vivan una temporada o permanentemente con ésta en su casa. Es una costumbre común y aceptada y demuestra la solidaridad e intimidad de la familia hispánica.

Vocabulario Útil:

- **institución**: institution
- **proceder:** proceed; to come from
- **identidad:** identity
- **bienestar:** well-being
- **temporada:** season
- **sentido:** sense; feeling
- **seguridad:** security
- **estabilidad:** stability
- **apoyo:** support
- **reafirmar:** to reaffirm
- **dignidad:** dignity
- **posición:** position
- **sociedad:** society
- **unir:** to unite; to tie

➤ **permanecer:** to remain

➤ **miembro:** member

➤ **costumbre:** custom; way of doing something

➤ **común:** common

➤ **aceptado:** accepted

➤ **demostrar (o → ue):** to demonstrate; to show

➤ **solidaridad:** solidarity

➤ **intimidad:** intimacy

➤ **pariente:** relative (not "parent")

➤ **unidad íntima:** intimate unit

➤ **fuerte:** strong

➤ **confianza:** trust; confidence

Análisis del Texto

Now let's take a closer look:

➤ *La familia es una de*

Did you notice that *una* is feminine? This ties it to *familia:* "The family is one of the ...."

➤ *el individuo hispano*

Here is an example of how you sometimes need to expand your thinking about cognates. The word *individuo* is indeed a cognate with the English word *individual*. But in English, using the word *individual* to mean "a person" sounds a bit formal. In Spanish, *individuo* doesn't sound quite as stilted as *individual* might in English. It just means "person."

➤ *De ella procede en gran medida*

Here, *ella* means "it" and refers to *familia* (linked by gender). The subject pronouns can also stand in for inanimate and abstract nouns. The phrase *en gran medida* literally means "in great measure." A better translation would be: "for the most part."

➤ *identidad y bienestar personales*

The adjective *personales* is pluralized by the *s* to show that it modifies both *identidad* and *bienestar*. If it had been left in the singular, it would have modified only *bienestar,* which would have made sense but wouldn't have been what the author wanted to say.

163

➤ *a la vez que reafirma*

The phrase *a la vez que* literally means "at the time that." A better translation is "while."

➤ *incluso a los parientes*

The word *incluso* means "even," as in "Even I can understand this." It is used adverbially and thus doesn't change to *inclusa*.

➤ *en la que pueden tener confianza*

Note that *en la que pueden* literally means "in that (feminine thing) in which they can ...." The *la* is linked to *unidad* by its gender. A better translation is "in which."

➤ *hasta que se case*

The verb *casar* is subjunctive here. *Hasta que* always takes a subjunctive: "Until whenever they may marry."

➤ *no es raro que ... vivan*

Another subjunctive here is *vivan* (from *vivir*). *No es raro que* takes a subjunctive. *Raro* here means "strange," not "rare." All together the phrase means "It isn't unusual that ...." The idea to follow is doubtful and uncertain, and the statement is in the negative. So, the whole thing just "feels" subjunctive: "It isn't unusual that the relatives might ...."

➤ *con ésta en su casa*

Where on earth did this *ésta* come from? Good question. Well, it must be linked to something feminine, so we'll have to look back in the sentence. This *ésta* is linked to *cierta familia* and is acting as a pronoun (note the *tilde*). Translated, it just means "it."

Gramática: *Para* vs. *Por*

Of the many Spanish prepositions, *para* and *por* seem to cause more grief and confusion than all the others. Why? Both are translated as "for" in English, so it's no surprise that many people have difficulty knowing when to use one and not the other.

Para

Para definitely translates as "for" in most cases. It indicates where things are going and what things are used for. Study the following examples closely to learn how to use *para* correctly:

Acuérdate

Just a reminder that *y* changes to *e* before words that begin with an "ee" sound (*i, hi,* and occasionally *y* when followed by a consonant and sounding as "ee," as in *Ybarra*). We see this in the text in *solidaridad e intimidad*.

➤ **Destination:** *Mañana saldré para Bogotá.* I leave for Bogota tomorrow.

➤ **Use:** *Necesito comprar mucha ropa para niños.* I need to buy a lot of children's clothes ("clothes for children").

➤ **Purpose:** *Habrá una reunión para festejar tu cumpleaños.* There will be a party to celebrate your birthday.

➤ **Comparisons:** *Para un inglés, usted baila muy bien.* You dance pretty well for an Englishman.

➤ **Future time:** *La fiesta está programada para el próximo lunes.* The party is scheduled for next Tuesday.

➤ **Tell it like it is:** *Para mí, esto es un evento maravilloso.* This is marvelous event for (to) me.

Algo Nuevo

One device that you can use to remember how to use *para* is to think of "DUPCFT" = "Don't Use Para Carelessly: Follow these Tips." The letters stand for: Destination, Use, Purpose, Comparison, Future time, and Tell it like it is.

(This one isn't mine. It's an old trick. You're welcome to improve upon it if you can.)

Por

Por is used more in the sense of "by," "by means of," "through," and "on behalf of." Study the following examples to see what I mean:

➤ **Motive:** *Lo hacen por necesidad.* They do it out of need (for necessity's sake).

➤ **Favor:** *Voté por el otro candidato.* I voted for the other candidate (in favor of).

➤ **Reason:** *¿Por qué no vas al baile?* Why aren't you going to the dance?

➤ **Behalf:** *Lo hice por mi esposa.* I did it for my wife.

➤ **Exchange:** *Me dieron diez pesos por un dólar.* They gave me 10 pesos for 1 dollar.

➤ **Time (duration):** *Voy a estar en este pueblo por una semana.* I'll be in this town for a week.

Por is also used to express the passive "by" and "by means of." It is used where we would say "per," as in "per year." Observe:

➤ **La canción fue compuesta por mi cuñado:** The song was composed by my brother-in-law.

➤ **Te enviaré el archivo por correo electrónico:** I'll send you the file by e-mail.

➤ **Me cobran diez pesos por hora:** They charge me 10 pesos per hour.

Acuérdate

The expression *para nada* does indeed mean "for nothing," as in *No sirve para nada* = "It isn't good for anything." It can also mean "not at all" and can serve to intensify a negative: *¿Te gusta la salsa picante?* ("Do you like spicy salsa?") *No, para nada.* ("No, not at all").

Acuérdate

To help you with *por*, think of "MFRBET": Must Fix the Roof for Bernardo, use Esteban's Tools. These stand for: Motive, Favor, Behalf, Reason, Exchange, and Time duration.

Palabras Para Ti

Here's a complete list of the ways that someone can be your *pariente*.

You know they're in your *familia* when they're your …

➤ **abuelo/a:** grandfather/mother

➤ **ahijado/a:** godson/daughter

➤ **bisabuelo/a:** great-grandfather/mother

➤ **bisnieto/a:** great-grandson/daughter

➤ **comadre:** "like a sister"

➤ **compadre:** "like a brother"

➤ **concuño:** spouse's sister's husband

➤ **concuña:** spouse's brother's wife

➤ **cuñado/a:** brother/sister-in-law

➤ **esposo/a:** spouse

➤ **hermano/a:** brother/sister

➤ **hijo/a:** son/daughter

➤ **madrastra:** stepmother

➤ **madre:** mother

➤ **madrina:** godmother

➤ **marido:** husband

➤ **medio/a hermano/a:** half-brother/sister

➤ **nieto/a:** grandson/daughter

➤ **nuera:** daughter-in-law

➤ **padrastro:** stepfather

➤ **padre:** father

➤ **padrino:** godfather

➤ **primo/a:** cousin

➤ **sobrino/a:** nephew/niece

➤ **sobrino/a politico/a:** spouse's nephew/niece

➤ **suegro/a:** father/mother-in-law

➤ **tatarabuelo:** great-great-grandfather/mother

➤ **tatarnieto:** great-great-grandson/daughter

➤ **tío/a:** uncle/aunt

➤ **tío/a político/a:** uncle/aunt-in-law

➤ **yerno:** son-in-law

Acuérdate

You know that *¿por qué?* means "why?" You probably also know that *porque*, written together, means "because." The word *porqué*, with the *tilde*, is a noun and can mean "reason" or "motive," as in: *No me dijo el porqué de su comportamiento* = "He didn't tell me the reason for his behavior." The word can even be pluralized: *porqués*.

Cultura Latina

If you call someone your *co-madre* or *compadre*, this means that you feel that this person is a special friend and you would treat them as if you were siblings.

Diálogo: Mario y Juanita

Here is your first *diálogo*. Mario and Juanita are friends at a high school in Santiago, Chile. They are just getting to know each other. Let's listen in:

Mario: *Hola, Juanita. ¿Cómo estás?*

Juanita: *Muy bien, Mario. Gracias. ¿Y tú?*

Mario: *Bien, pero estoy muy ocupado hoy día. Oye, te quería hacer una preguntita, ¿tienes hermanos?*

Juanita: *Sí, dos. Un hermano y una hermana. Aquí tengo una foto de mi familia (ella saca una foto de su bolsa). Mira, él es mi padre, y ella es mi madre. La que está a la derecha es mi hermana, Adelita, y el que está a la izquierda es mi hermano, Roberto. Atrás están los primos, los tíos, los abuelos y los padrinos. Soy yo ahí, sentada en el piso.*

Mario: *Parece que tu familia es grande. La mía también es grande. Tengo cinco hermanos y muchos parientes. Mañana te enseño una foto.*

Juanita: *Está bien. Nos vemos entonces. Chau.*

Mario: *Chau, Juanita. Hasta mañana.*

Now, here's a translation of the *diálogo*. See how well you did:

Mario: Hi, Juanita. How are you?

Juanita: Very well, Mario. Thanks. And you?

Haz Clic Aquí

Need another opinion? Visit http://powayusd.sdcoe.k12.ca.us/ espanolvirtual/Por%20vs%20Para% 202.html or www.columbia. edu/~fms5/hpor.html for a different look at *por* and *para*. You can also search for *por* and *para* and find other Web sites.

Mario: Fine, but I'm very busy these days. Hey, I wanted to ask you a question. Do you have (any) brothers and sisters? (siblings)

Juanita: Yes, two, a brother and a sister. Here, I have a picture of my family (she takes a photo out of her bag). Look, he is my father, and she is my mother. The (person) on the right is my sister, Adelita, and the one who is on the left is my brother, Roberto. Behind are (my) cousins, aunts and uncles, grandparents, and godparents. That's me there, sitting on the floor.

Mario: It seems that your family is big. Mine is also big. I have five brothers (and sisters?) and a lot of relatives. I'll show you a picture tomorrow.

Juanita: Okay. We'll see each other then. Bye.

Mario: Bye, Juanita. See you tomorrow.

Risa del Día

All its strengths aside, the Latin family also seems to be a great source of humor. There are many jokes about relationships, marriage, in-laws, and related topics. Many of these jokes are definitely not tasteful and thus are unsuitable for publication in this book. Here are two fairly harmless examples:

1. *Se encuentran dos amigas y una llorando le dice a la otra:*

   —*Mi médico me dio una semana de vida.*

   La otra le contesta:

   —*Bueno, te dejo a mi marido por esta semana.*

   —*¿Pero para qué lo quiero a tu marido?*

   —*Porque con él en tu casa la semana te va a parecer una eternidad.*

2. *Conversaban dos hombres en un bar cuando uno pregunta:*

   —*Disculpa la pregunta, ¿pero a ti te cae bien tu suegra?*

   —*No, para nada.*

   —*Entonces ¿por qué llevas una foto de ella en el paquete de cigarros?*

   —*Ah! Es que quiero dejar de fumar.*

Vocabulario Útil:

➤ **se encuentran:** are found

➤ **llorar:** to cry

➤ **médico:** doctor

➤ **una semana de vida:** "a week to live"

➤ **parecer una eternidad:** seem like an eternity

➤ **caerle bien:** to like (a person)

➤ **para nada:** not at all; "no way"

➤ **dejar de fumar:** to quit smoking

El Cuiz

Provide the Spanish equivalents for the following words. Cheat only if it's a *lunes, miercoles,* or *viernes:* i.

1. season _____

2. institution _____

3. proceed; to come from _____

4. identity _____

5. stability _____

6. support _____

7. sense; feeling _____

continues

continued

  8. security _____

  9. to demonstrate; to show _____

10. dignity _____

11. to reaffirm _____

12. well-being _____

13. position _____

14. society _____

15. to unite; to tie _____

16. to remain _____

17. member _____

18. custom _____

19. common _____

20. strong _____

21. solidarity _____

22. intimacy _____

23. relatives _____

24. accepted _____

25. trust; confidence _____

Tareas

1. Think of all the members of your family, including your extended family. Now determine what their relationship to you would be in Spanish.

2. Explain to someone the differences between *para* and *por*. Give examples. If there isn't anyone around, write it down in a notebook.

The Least You Need to Know

➤ Family life is very important in Spanish and Latin American cultures.

➤ *La familia* usually extends beyond the nuclear family.

➤ *Para* and *por* both mean "for" but have different uses.

Chapter 14

Nuevos Amigos

In This Chapter

➤ *Lectura:* Un joven español en busca de amigos

➤ *Usted* vs. *tú*

➤ *Diálogo:* María, Alejandro, y Tom

One of the most exciting things that comes with learning a new language is being able to meet new people and converse with them in their language. Today, even if there's no one around you who speaks Spanish, communicating with others in *el español* is easier than ever. As I mentioned previously, the Internet is full of Spanish chat rooms and bulletin boards.

Close friendships seem to play an even greater role in the lives of Spanish-speakers than they often do in the world of the Anglophones (that's us). Statistics show that in the United States, many adults can name only a handful of close friends whom they have had continuous contact with all their lives. But because it is far more common for Spanish-speakers to grow up and live in the city of their birth, they usually can list far more lifelong friends than we can. This attitude toward friendship usually carries over into their long-distance friends as well. Once you've made a good Latin friend, there's a good chance that you will know this person a long time—if you give as much as you receive, of course (ah, the lessons of life).

Lectura: Un Joven Español Busca Amigos

This is an example of a letter you might see posted on an electronic bulletin board. Here we have a young man from Spain who is looking for new friends to exchange e-mail with. This text is a good example of how someone might write about his or her life in the hopes of making new friends. Of course, this guy is fictitious, so don't try sending him any e-mail. But if you're interested, you can find many "real-live" Spanish speakers on the Web. Just search for "*amigos*" or "*chat español*," and surf around until you find something (or someone) interesting.

> *Me llamo Juan Antonio Garza Muñoz, aunque profesionalmente se me conoce como Juan Garza. Tengo 23 años, y soy escorpión.*

Nací en un pequeño pueblo del suroeste de España, El Rocío, (ubicado a 50 klm. de Sevilla) en una casita en la ladera de una colina. Nací a las 10 de la noche, el 13 de noviembre de 1976. Todo fue a la antigua, podemos decir, ya que a mi madre le asistió al parto solamente una partera. Nací en una pequeña cama y mi madre lo pasó mal (supongo que no tan mal, porque le quedaron ganas de tener tres hijos más).

A los cinco años, vinimos a Madrid a vivir, a intentar salir adelante. Éramos una familia modesta (por no decir pobre). Mi padre, Felipe, era conductor de taxi y de camiones. Mi madre se dedicaba a cuidar de la casa y de la família. Mi infancia fue feliz, supongo. Los niños son felices jugando con sus cosas y con sus amigos.

Mi adolescencia no fue tan feliz, ya que estuvo marcada por dos cosas, muy importantes para mí. La primera es que desde que tenía nueve años mis padres empezaron a trabajar el turno de noche, y dormían de día. Yo los veía solamente una hora al día y, al no tener hermanos de mi edad (son menores todos), la lectura y la música me acompañaban. Menos mal que tenía a mi abuelita, que nos cuidaba durante el día. La otra cosa que marcó mi adolescencia fue la muerte de mi hermanita María cuando yo tenía 15 años. Es algo que me ha costado muchos años superar (si es que lo he superado).

Al los 19 años me fuí de la casa para trabajar de taxista en Valencia. Invertía la mayor parte del dinero que ganaba en la Bolsa de Valores. Fue probablemente la mejor decisión que pude tomar en aquella época. Gané mucho dinero, conocí a gente superdivertida, y ayudé a gente a conseguir trabajo. ¿Qué más podía pedir?

A grandes rasgos así soy yo. Siempre me interesa mantener correspondencia con nuevos amigos. Si os interesa escribirme, tengo correo electrónico: jgarza@lux.intercoms.es (éste es el de mi casa), o sino, jgarza.@datbaspn.dingo.com.es (éste es el del trabajo).

Vocabulario Útil:

➤ **escorpión:** Scorpio (zodiac sign)

➤ **nacer:** to be born

➤ **ubicarse:** to be located

➤ **casita:** little house (*casa + ita*)

➤ **ladera:** side; bank

➤ **colina:** hill

➤ **a la antigua:** old-fashioned way; the old way

➤ **asistir a:** to attend (false cognate)

➤ **parto:** birth

➤ **partera:** midwife

➤ **suponer:** to suppose

➤ **modesto:** modest; not rich

➤ **salir adelante:** to get ahead (economically)

➤ **adolescencia:** adolescence

➤ **turno:** shift (here, "night shift")

➤ **acompañar:** to keep one company; to go with

➤ **menos mal:** it was good that ...; I'm glad that ...

➤ **superar:** to get over; to come through

➤ **Bolsa de Valores:** the stock market

➤ **tomar una decisión:** to make a decision

➤ **aquella época:** that time (of my life)

➤ **conseguir:** to get; to acquire

➤ **pedir:** to ask for

➤ **a grandes rasgos:** "in a nutshell"

➤ **correo electrónico:** e-mail

Cultura Latina

Spaniards and Latin Americans tend to stand quite close to one another when they talk. You might find yourself feeling a bit boxed in by your new Latin friends (not your e-friends, of course). But from their perspective, standing close to you is an indication of their concern and politeness. If you keep backing off, they might get the message that you are cold and aloof.

Algo Nuevo

You already know that *pero* means "but." Now learn *sino*, which means "but rather." *No soy inglés, sino canadiense* means "I'm not English, but (rather) Canadian; *Mis padres no hablaban el italiano, sino el portugués* means "My parents didn't speak Italian, but (rather) Portuguese." Use *sino* when the first part of your sentence is negative and you wish to make a correction to something stated or assumed. *Sino* as a noun means "fate."

Análisis del Texto

Okay, now let's take a closer look:

➤ *se me conoce como Juan Garza*

The *se* makes the statement passive, and the *me* is the direct object pronoun "me." So, this means "I am known as Juan Garza."

➤ *a la antigua*

The *a la* + feminine adjective means "in the style of X." You can say, *a la española* ("in a Spanish style") and *a la mexicana* ("in a Mexican style").

Acuérdate

Notice that in the sentence about the midwife, the subject (*la partera*) comes at the end. As I mentioned previously, the subject of a sentence might not always come at the beginning, as it does in English.

➤ *ya que a mi madre le asistió al parto solamente una partera*

You may need to take this apart to understand what's going on. Literally, we have "to my mother to her attended to the birth only a midwife." This, of course, doesn't make sense. The *le* is the INDOP, the *al parto* is the direct object, and the *a mi madre* just clarifies who the *le* refers to. *Ya que* means "since," so a better translation of this would be: "… since only a midwife attended my mother's delivery."

➤ *lo pasó mal*

The neuter pronoun *lo* here refers to the experience of giving birth in general, which has no gender assigned to it in this sentence, so *lo* is used. Translation: "She had a hard time."

➤ *le quedaron ganas de tener más hijos*

The verb *quedar* means "to remain." A literal translation might be "to her there remained desires to have." A better translation would be: "She still wanted (had desire left) to have more children."

➤ *A los cinco años*

The preposition *a* can be used in numerous time expressions: *a las cinco de la tarde* = "at five o'clock in the afternoon." Here, this phrase translates as: "When I was 5 years old." He could also have written *Cuando yo tenía cinco años.*

➤ *modesta (por no decir pobre)*

The use of *por* here is interesting. Juan calls his family *modesta*, almost as a euphemism for *pobre*. So, this might translate as "My family was modest (rather than calling it poor)." There is a bit of tongue-in-cheek attitude here.

➤ *Menos mal que tenía a mi abuelita*

Menos mal is a rather odd but useful phrase for saying "at least" or "It's a good thing that …" or even "It could have been worse."

➤ *me ha costado muchos años*

When someone says *me cuesta* or *me ha costado,* it may not have anything to do with money. *Costar* can also be used in the sense of "to be difficult" or "to cause difficulty," or even "to take a lot out of someone (physically, emotionally, or in some other way)." Here, this sentence might translate as: "It has taken me many years (of my life)."

Gramática: *Usted* vs. *Tú*

As you already learned in your beginning course, you have a choice between two pronouns and verb forms when addressing people: *tú* and *usted*.

In very general terms, *usted* is used with strangers, superiors, and with people for whom you wish to show respect. You also may use *usted* when you

Haz Clic Aquí

You can hook up with new friends at many Web sites on the Internet. Here are a few addresses to get you started: www.amigos-guadalajara.com, www.exam-ta.ac.uk/spanishchat. htm, and www.spanispride. com/search.html. There are many more out there as well; just search under "Spanish chat rooms."

Ten Cuidado

The *usted* vs. *tú* debate is rarely as clear-cut as some textbooks would have you believe. Entire Ph.D. theses have been written on this topic. As your exposure to the language and culture grows, you'll eventually figure out how *usted* and *tú* are being used by the people around you. Until you do, be careful and stick to the general rules about *usted* and *tú*.

Cultura Latina

There's actually a verb that means "to use *tú* with someone." The verb is *tutear*. If someone says "*Me puede tutear,*" it means that you can call him or her *tú* if you wish. No, there's no verb *ustedear*, except, perhaps, as a joke.

Haz Clic Aquí

Need this explained a different way? Visit www.abcdario.force9. co.uk/abcdario/docs/pronouns. htm.

wish to keep a certain distance and professionalism between yourself and someone. *Tú* is used for friends, family members, young children, and one's peers. While *tú* is not in itself disrespectful, it must be used appropriately.

➤ **¿Cómo está usted?:** How are you? (polite)

➤ **¿Cómo estás tú?:** How are you? (familiar)

While *usted* is almost always appropriate when meeting someone for the first time, it also may be used with people whom you have known for years. For example, my dentist lives in Mexico, and I've been hopping across the border to seek his excellent care for nearly 10 years. He calls me Esteban, and I call him Raúl. Nonetheless, we always use *usted* with each other. Why? Because even though our interaction is relatively friendly and relaxed (he even teases me about my old metal fillings), ours is still a professional relationship. I am his client, and he's my healthcare practitioner. He respects me as his patient by using *usted,* and I respect him as a professional by using *usted* back. If we were to start using *tú*, there would be a palpable change in the nature of our relationship from that of a professional one to one of equal friends. If one day Raúl is no longer my dentist, then we might feel comfortable using *tú*. But perhaps not.

Tú is used in these instances:

➤ When speaking to a child

➤ When you are a child and are talking to friends

➤ When speaking to a family member (most of the time)

➤ When praying (supreme beings are addressed as *tú*)

➤ When speaking to a fellow student

➤ When you and the other person have agreed to use *tú*

➤ When someone insists that you use *tú* with them.

Except when addressing children and fellow students (if you happen to be a student yourself), you should begin your conversations with *usted* and the third person singular verb form that goes with *usted*. Unless you have a clear reason for not addressing someone as *usted* (see the previous list), you risk unintentionally insulting people by using *tú*. If you inadvertently start off with *usted* when the situation would have

176

allowed for *tú*, you'll be kindly instructed to use *tú*. As a non-native speaker, it's unlikely that any offense will be taken. However, it's a lot harder to backpedal once you have started using *tú* with someone to whom you should have said *usted* from the very beginning.

Algo Nuevo

In parts of Latin America, there's another word for *tú*. In Argentina, Uruguay, much of Central America, highland Ecuador, and a few other places, people say *vos*. *Vos* is an old form for "you" that disappeared from most Spanish, just as *thou* faded away in English. The *vos* form of the verb is slightly different from the *tú* form. To form the *vos* form in the present indicative (the only tense that matters), remove the final *r* from the infinitive, replace it with *s*, and accent the final syllable: *vos hablás, venís, tenés,* and so on. If you're in a country where people say *vos*, you'll pick it up quickly. Just use *tú* until you do, and you'll be fine.

What They Didn't Tell You About Tú and Usted

Now that I've covered the "textbook" uses of *usted* and *tú,* I must tell you that the ways in which *usted* and *tú* are used in practice can vary considerably from place to place. In parts of Central America, you may hear people using *tú* (or *vos*) and *usted* in the same sentence with the very same person (*usted* can sometimes be used simply to emphasize a point). You may hear Colombians using *usted* with their close friends and pets, and Chileans using *usted* verb forms with their young children. On the other hand, in the Caribbean, *usted* is rarely used at all. Cubans and Puerto Ricans can be heard using *tú* with just about everybody, all the time, from the very beginning.

Nevertheless, in spite of the subtleties involved, it's still best to follow the general rules I've outlined above until you are comfortable with the way the locals do it; use *usted* until you're 100-percent sure that *tú* is appropriate.

Haz Clic Aquí

You can find out more about *vos* at the Web site http://ourworld. compuserve.com/homepages/hlr/ vos.htm. The site is in Spanish, but you'll get the idea.

Diálogo: Nuevos Amigos

Here is another *diálogo*. This one is much longer than the last one. The scene takes place in Peru, in the colonial city of Cuzco, not far from Machu Picchu. Tom is an American backpacker. He has read *The Complete Idiot's Guide to Intermediate Spanish*, so his Spanish is tip-top. While sitting at a table in a café, he is approached by two Peruvians, Alejandro and María. Here's their conversation:

María: *Hola. ¿Qué tal? ¿De dónde eres?*

Tom: *Hola. Soy de los Estados Unidos.*

Alejandro: *¿Así? ¿De cuál estado?*

Tom: *De Ohio. Soy de Cleveland. Me llamo Tom.*

María: *Me llamo María, y mi amigo se llama Alejandro. ¿Podemos tomar asiento aquí contigo?*

Tom: *Sí, cómo no. Ustedes son de aquí, ¿verdad?*

Alejandro: *Pues, sí, somos de acá. Pero no de aquí de Cuzco. Yo soy de Lima y María es de Arequipa. De hecho, somos turistas aquí también. ¿Qué te parece el Perú?*

Tom: *Me encanta. Llegué apenas anteayer. No me he acostumbrado todavía a la altura. Anoche no pude dormir bien y me dio un dolor de cabeza horrible. Ahora, parece que ya me ha pasado todo. Y ustedes, ¿qué están haciendo en Cuzco?*

María: *Pues, tú sabes, estamos haciendo el camino Inca. No es solamente para los turistas extranjeros, ¿verdad?*

Tom: *Claro que no. Es una maravilla.*

Alejandro: *Dime una cosa. ¿Cuánto gana un trabajador por día en los Estados Unidos? Tú sabes, acá la cosa es muy difícil. Uno trabaja muy duro, pero los sueldos son muy bajos. O sea, creo que ustedes están ganando mucho más que nosotros.*

Tom: *Bueno, eso depende de la clase de trabajo que uno haga. Yo, siendo estudiante, vivo en parte de una beca y de lo poco que me están pagando de mi trabajo temporal en la cafetería universitaria.*

Alejandro: *Pero, por hora, ¿cuanto te pagan?*

Tom: *Pues, se trata del sueldo mínimo permitido por ley. Son unos cinco dólares por hora, más o menos.*

Alejandro: *¡Caray! En comparación con lo que se gana aquí, es mucho dinero.*

Tom: *Tal vez. Pero hay que tener en cuenta que allá todo cuesta mucho más. Aunque parezca mucho dinero, en realidad no lo es.*

María: Oye, Alejandro. Basta con las preguntas acerca del dinero. ¿No ves que le estás molestando a Tom?

Tom: *No te preocupes, María. Todo el mundo me hace las mismas preguntas.*

María: *Mira, vamos a ir a una peña esta noche a las 9:00. ¿Quieres ir con nosotros? Sería más divertido si podríamos ir contigo.*

Tom: *¿Conmigo? Bueno, sí, por supuesto. A mí me gustaría ir con ustedes.*

María: *Muy bien. Entonces, vete a la plaza central a las ocho y media. Podemos encontrarnos frente a la catedral y de ahí, podemos ir juntos a la peña.*

Tom: *Perfecto. Nos vemos entonces a las 8:30.*

Alejandro: *¡Sensacional!*

Tom: *Bueno, hasta entonces. Oye, Alejandro, antes de que te vayas, hazme un favor. ¿Me puedes sacar una foto? Aquí tienes mi máquina de fotos. Es muy fácil de usar. Oprimiendo este botón, se saca la foto.*

Alejandro: *¿Listo? (saca la foto) Bueno, ya la saqué.*

Tom: *Gracias. Ah, una última pregunta. ¿Qué es una peña exactamente?*

María: *Es una fiesta andina con musica tradicional.*

Tom: *¡Qué bueno! Nos vemos entonces.*

Alejandro: *Muy bien. Hasta luego.*

Now here's the text of the *diálogo* translated:

María: Hi. How are you? Where are you from?

Tom: Hi. I'm from the United States.

Alejandro: Really? From which state?

Tom: From Ohio. I'm from Cleveland. My name is Tom.

María: My name is María, and my friend's name is Alejandro. Can we take a seat here with you?

Tom: Yes, of course. You're from here, right?

Alejandro: Well, yes we're from here. But not from here in Cuzco. I'm from Lima, and María is from Arequipa. In fact, we're tourists here, too. What do you think of Peru?

Cultura Latina

In some Spanish-speaking countries, it's expected that a man should kiss a woman on one cheek the first time they are being introduced (if the two are about the same age and social standing). Men may hug if they are good friends. However, it's always best to spend some time observing what the people around you are doing before you start running around hugging and kissing people.

Tom: It's great. I just arrived the day before yesterday. I haven't gotten used to the altitude yet. Last night I couldn't sleep well, and I got a horrible headache. Now it seems that it has all passed. And you? What are you doing in Cuzco?

María: Well, you know, we're doing the Inca trail. It's not just for the foreign tourists, you know ....

Tom: Of course not. It's wonderful (a wonder).

Alejandro: Tell me something. How much does a worker earn each day in the United States? You know, things are pretty tough here (the thing is ...). You work very hard (one works), but the wages are very low. I mean, I think (believe) that you all are making a lot more that we are.

Tom: Well, that depends on the kind of work you do (one does). Being a student, I live partly from a scholarship and partly from the little (I earn) from my part-time job at the school cafeteria.

Alejandro: But, per hour, how much do they pay you?

Tom: Well, it's the minimum wage allowed by law. It's about five dollars per hour, more or less.

Alejandro: Wow! In comparison with what (that which) people earn (is earned) here, that's a lot of money.

Tom: Perhaps. But you have to keep in mind that everything costs a lot more there. Although it might look like a lot of money, in reality it isn't.

María: Hey, Alejandro. Enough with the questions about money. Can't you see that you're bothering Tom?

Tom: Don't worry, María. Everybody asks me the same questions.

Alejandro: Look, we're going to go to a *peña* tonight at 9:00. Do you want to come with us? It would be more fun if we could go with you.

Tom: With me? Well, yes, of course. I'd love to go with you.

María: Great. So, go to the central plaza at 8:30. We can meet in front of the cathedral and then we can go together to the *peña*.

Tom: Perfect. We'll see each other then at 8:30.

Alejandro: Cool!

Tom: Well, see you then. Hey, Alejandro, before you go, do me a favor. Can you take a picture of me? Here's my camera. It's really easy to use. Just push this button to take the picture.

Alejandro: Ready? (takes picture) Okay, I just took it.

Tom: Thanks. Uhhh, one last question. What exactly is a *peña*?

María: It's an Andean party with traditional music.

Tom: That's great! We'll see each other later then.

Alejandro: Okay. See you later (until later).

Algo Nuevo

You've probably heard the word *gringo* before as an insult meaning "Anglo-Saxon." In Mexico, it almost always means someone from the United States (*un yanqui*) regardless of ethnic background. But don't automatically assume that you are being insulted if someone calls you a *gringo*, especially if it is done in a courteous or even humorous tone of voice. I was once called a *gringo* on Mexican television, and no insult was ever intended. In some countries, it simply refers to an English-speaker, although in Argentina, a *gringo* could mean someone from Italy. The term is not used much in Spain.

Risa del Día

This, I suppose, is a dumb joke. Why? Because I made it up myself. You can see why I didn't go into comedy professionally. I've added a little extra verbiage here and there for you to practice your reading skills. The text is presented to you as it might appear in a book. Notice the dashes to indicate dialogue and breaks in the conversation:

Un amigo a otro:

—Juan, ¿sabes qué?—dijo Miguel.

—No—dijo Juan, molesto. Se giró su cabeza hacia su compañero.

—Que ya va para tres años que nos conocimos y hasta la fecha nunca hemos podido pasar una semana entera sin pelearnos.

—Miguel se quita el sombrero y lo pone sobre una mesa—. Estoy pensando que quizá sea mejor que no sigamos siendo amigos. Me cuesta discutir tanto, y a decirte la verdad, ya no me gusta pasar tiempo contigo. ¿Tú qué opinas?

—Bueno,—le dijo Juan a Miguel—. ¿Pero si tú eres mi mejor amigo?

—¿Cómo puedo yo ser tu mejor amigo si cada semana nos peleamos?

—Pues claro, si con mis otros amigos me peleo cada día ....

Vocabulario Útil:

➤ **molesto:** bothered; perturbed

➤ **girarse la cabeza:** to turn one's head

➤ **va para tres años:** it's going on three years

➤ **hasta la fecha:** until today; so far

➤ **entero:** entire; whole

➤ **pelearse:** to get into a fight

➤ **discutir:** to argue

➤ **a decirte la verdad:** to tell you the truth

➤ **opinar:** to think; to have an opinion

➤ **pues claro:** Well, sure ...

➤ **cada día:** every day

El Cuiz

Give the Spanish for the following words. Cheat if you have to, but don't tell your friends:

1. birth _____

2. to be born _____

3. shift _____

4. hill _____

5. adolescence _____

6. to attend _____

7. old-fashioned way; the old way _____

8. midwife _____

9. to suppose _____

10. to get ahead _____

11. to be located _____

12. the stock market _____

13. to keep one company _____

14. to get over; to come through _____

15. e-mail _____

16. to make a decision _____

17. entire; whole _____

18. to ask for _____

19. to get; to acquire _____

20. bothered; perturbed _____

Tareas

1. Go online and surf around for Spanish Web sites with chat rooms or bulletin boards. You don't have to do anything else. Just look at what's there. If you don't have Internet access at home, see if you can log on at your local library.

2. Explain to someone the differences between *tú* and *usted*. If there's no one around, write your thoughts in your notebook.

3. Go to a public place (the mall, shopping area, library, or other location) where you can sit down and watch people for a while. Look at everyone who walks by and ask yourself whether you would address this person as *tú* or *usted*.

The Least You Need to Know

➤ Latin friends often make friends for life.

➤ The Internet is a good place to meet *e-amigos*.

➤ Many subtleties are involved in deciding whether to use *tú* or *usted*.

➤ Follow the general rules about *tú* and *usted* until you learn otherwise.

La Gastronomía y el Buen Comer

You don't need anyone to remind you that both Latin America and Spain boast some of the best foods on the planet! We've all heard of burritos, tacos, and tostadas. But that's just a tiny fraction of the many delectable dishes that await you from *la buena cocina.*

The Complete Idiot's Guide to Intermediate Spanish is not a cookbook. This is unfortunate. But there are so many different dishes prepared in Latin America and Spain that it would be impossible to discuss them all here and still have room for grammar. If you're getting hungry for some authentic Latin American or Spanish food, see if there are any ethnic restaurants in your area. You can usually find something in the big cities, but if you're in a more isolated or rural area, you may have to cook the food yourself. I'll suggest a few Web sites at the end of the chapter where you can find some great recipes if you're interested in more information about Spanish and Latin American cuisine. You also can find great cookbooks at your local library or bookstore.

Lectura: Receta para Tamalitos Mexicanos

Rather than tease you with a *lectura* about how good all the food is and how much Spanish speakers like to eat it with their friends and family, I decided to use a real

Cultura Latina

The main meal in Latin countries usually comes at midday. Eating with family and friends also tends to take longer than you may be used to because lengthy conversations are always expected once the food is consumed. These conversations are called *la sobremesa.*

recipe as the reading for this chapter. I liked this text in particular because of the interesting style in which it is written and because studying it might help you with other recipes written in Spanish:

Tamalitos Mexicanos

Para 6 personas

Ingredientes:

Para la masa:

> *7 elotes desgranados*
>
> *120 gramos (4 onzas) de mantequilla*
>
> *2 cucharadas de azúcar*
>
> *2 cucharaditas de sal*
>
> *hojas de elote*

Para la salsa:

> *4 chiles poblanos asados, pelados, despepitados y rebanados en rajitas finas*
>
> *½ kilo (un poco más de una libra) de tomate asado y pelado*
>
> *½ cebolla mediana*
>
> *1 cucharada de mantequilla*
>
> *sal al gusto*
>
> *350 gramos (12 onzas) de queso cortado en tiras*

Preparación

> *Las hojas de elote se ponen a remojar en agua fría, se escurren y se secan. En el procesador de alimentos se muelen los granos de maíz. La mantequilla se bate con el azúcar y la sal hasta que esté cremosa y se le añaden los elotes molidos. Se hacen los tamalitos untando una cucharada de pasta en una hoja de elote; se doblan como tamales y se van colocando parados en una tamalera o en una olla con tapa a la que se le habrá añadido un poco de agua y se ponen a cocer durante 45 minutos, aproximadamente. Se sirven acompañados por la salsa y, si lo desea, por un poco de crema ácida.*
>
> *Nota: También se pueden hacer en la olla express, en cuyo caso tardarán aproximadamente 15 minutos.*
>
> *Salsa: El tomate se muele con la cebolla, se cuela y se sofríe en la mantequilla; se le añade sal al gusto y se sazona durante aproximadamente 10 minutos; si queda muy*

espesa se le puede añadir un poquito de agua. A los 10 minutos se le agregan las rajas y el queso y se sirve.

Presentación

Se colocan paraditos sin desenvolver en una cazuela; en una salsera aparte se sirve la salsa y, si lo desea, en otra salsera crema ácida. También se pueden servir en un platón ovalado, desenvueltos y bañados con su salsa.

Acuérdate

The word for "bean" varies widely throughout the Spanish-speaking world. In Mexico and most of Central America, it's *frijol*. In Venezuela, it's *caraota*; in Colombia, it's *fríjol* (*tilde* on the *i*); and in Ecuador, it's *fréjol*. *Argentinos* and *Uruguayos* call them *porotos*.

Vocabulario Útil:

➤ **masa:** dough; filling

➤ **elote:** corn cob (Mexico and Central America)

➤ **desgranar:** to remove kernels/grains

➤ **gramo:** gram

➤ **libra:** pound

➤ **onza:** ounce

➤ **mantequilla:** butter

➤ **mediano:** medium-sized

➤ **cucharada:** tablespoonful

➤ **cucharaditas:** teaspoonful

➤ **hoja:** leaf; husk

➤ **asadar:** to roast

➤ **pelar:** to peel

➤ **despepitar:** to remove seeds

➤ **rebanar:** to slice

➤ **raja, rajita, tira:** strip

➤ **sal al gusto:** salt "to taste"

➤ **remojar:** soak

➤ **escurrir:** to drip

➤ **procesador de alimentos:** food processor

➤ **tapa:** lid

➤ **batir:** to beat; to mix

➤ **moler:** to grind

➤ **untar:** to spread

➤ **doblar:** to bend; to turn

➤ **colocar:** to place; to put

➤ **parar:** to stand up

➤ **tamalera:** a tamale holder

➤ **cocer:** to cook; to boil

➤ **si lo desea:** if you wish

➤ **crema ácida:** sour cream

➤ **olla express:** pressure cooker

➤ **tardar:** to take (time)

➤ **colar:** to drain; to strain

➤ **sofreír:** to sauté

➤ **sazonar:** to season

➤ **espeso:** thick

➤ **desenvolver:** to unwrap

➤ **cazuela:** casserole

➤ **salsera:** a salsa dish

➤ **platón:** a big plate

187

Cultura Latina

A tip is *una propina*. In most Spanish and Latin American restaurants, the wait staff does not live off tips as in the U.S., and doesn't expect you to leave a tip. Of course, a small tip will always be appreciated if you wish to reward your waiter for good service. Larger tips may be expected in upscale restaurants that cater to tourists. But as a general rule, you don't need to tip the waiters.

Ten Cuidado

Be careful when asking for butter. *Mantequilla* is the usual word, but in some countries (such as Argentina and Uruguay) the word is *manteca*, which elsewhere means "pork lard." Also, be careful when talking about corn. Most people say *maíz* for corn, but words such as *jojoto*, *elote*, *masorca*, and *cholco* are also possible.

Análisis del Texto

Getting hungry? Me, too. Let's take a quick look at what this recipe has to teach us:

➤ *cucharadas … cucharaditas*

These words mean "tablespoonful" and "teaspoonful." As you know, *cuchara* means "spoon." The suffix *–ada* means "an amount of" or "–ful." We'll talk a bit more about suffixes in a later chapter.

➤ *se ponen a remojar*

There are many *se* passives in this text. *Poner* can be followed by *a* + infinitive to mean "to put to" or "to make X," as in "to put it to soaking:" *El jefe me puso a trabajar* = "The boss put me (made me) to work." A better translation usually leaves the word "put" out of it all together.

➤ *hasta que esté cremosa*

Hasta que is always followed by a subjunctive.

➤ *se hacen los tamalitos untando*

Untar means "to spread." Here, the present participle *untando* means "by spreading."

➤ *se van colocando parados*

This is a compound tense with *ir* + present participle, and translates as "going along doing something." Here we have, "are being placed standing up." You'll learn more about this in Chapter 16, "La Iglesia y la Religión."

➤ *en una olla con tapa a la que se le habrá añadido*

I love this construction! Confused? Let's break it up. The first part is easy enough: "in a pot with lid." Then we have *a*, which means "to." Next is the *la que*. The *la* must stand in for something feminine: *olla*. After that is the *se* (passive), the *le* (to it), the future of *haber*, and the past participle of *añadir* ("to add to"), which is *añadido*. Literally this works out as "in a pot with lid to which (feminine) will have been added." A better translation: "In a lidded pot to which you will have added …."

➤ *la olla express, en cuyo caso*

Now and then you may see the words *cuyo, cuya,* and its plural forms. These mean "of which," "in which," "of whom," and "whose," and mostly are used in the written language: *Un hombre cuyo caballo es veloz* means "A man whose horse is fast." You needn't worry about *cuyo* in the spoken language because there are always ways around it: *un hombre que tiene un caballo veloz* = "a man who has a fast horse." Here we have "a pressure cooker, in which case …."

➤ *se colocan paraditos*

You have seen the *–ito* suffix before: *Casa* changes to *casita*. This ending can also be added to adjectives. Because the *tamalitos* are already smaller than regular old *tamales,* the writer decided to also use the *–ito* suffix on the adjective. This makes 'em sound more dainty.

➤ *platón*

The suffix *–ón* is an enlarger. *Plato* (plate) is made bigger by calling it a *platón*. If you think this book is big, you could call it a *librón*. We'll talk more about suffixes in a later chapter.

Algo Nuevo

You know that *desayuno* is breakfast, *almuerzo* is lunch, and *cena* is dinner. But there's a lot of variation from country to country. In Cuba and Peru, dinner is *la comida*. In Mexico, *la comida* is definitely lunch, and *un almuerzo* is a light snack eaten around 10:00 in the morning. This would be called *las mediasnueves* or *la mediamañana* in Colombia. In Ecuador, dinner is *la merienda*, which in most other countries would mean "a snack." If a person from Ecuador says "*Nátaly merendó medio pollo,*" this would mean "Nataly ate half of a chicken for dinner." In Spain and most of Latin America, this same sentence would mean "Nataly had half of a chicken for a snack." In Spain, a *merienda* is a light afternoon meal, which in Colombia would be called *las onces*.

Gramática: Las Preposiciones

Just a quick bite of grammar this time—about those little morsels we call prepositions.

A preposition is defined as an "invariable particle that unites two words or phrases establishing a dependent relationship between them." In plain English, a preposition is a short word or phrase that tells you where something belongs, where something is positioned, or how something is related to something else.

You already know many Spanish prepositions. Here's a list to help you fill in the gaps. Some can take infinitives, as in *antes de comer,* which means "before eating." You should be able to translate the examples on your own:

Using Prepositions

Preposition	Definition	Example
a	to	*al doctor*
alrededor (de)	around	*alrededor de mí*
ante	before	*ante el juez*
antes (de)	before	*antes de comer*
a través de	across; through	*a través del parque*
bajo	under	*bajo la ley*
cerca (de)	near	*cerca de mi casa*
con	with	*con las manos*
contra	against	*contra la pared*
de	of, from	*de mi familia*
desde	from	*desde la montaña*
debajo (de)	under	*debajo de la cama*
delante (de)	in front of	*delante de mí*
después (de)	after	*después de comer*
detrás (de)	behind	*detrás de él*
en	in	*en mi casa*
encima (de)	on top of	*encima de la mesa*
entre	between	*entre nosotros*
frente a	in front of	*frente a la casa*
hacia	toward	*hacia las montañas*
lejos (de)	far (from)	*lejos de aquí*
según	according to	*según el texto*

Preposition	Definition	Example
sin	without	*sin saber; sin tí*
so	under (legal)	*so pena de muerte*
sobre	over; about	*sobre la tierra*
tras	after	*día tras día*

Diálogo en el Restaurante "La Fonda"

Let's see what happens to José and María when they stop for lunch at a small restaurant:

El mesero: *Bienvenidos a La Fonda.*

María: *Gracias, joven. Una mesa para dos personas, por favor.*

El mesero: *Cómo no, señora. Síganme por favor. Su mesa está cerca de la ventana.*

José: *¿Así? Excelente. Tenemos mucha hambre. (Toman asiento.)*

El mesero: *Muy bien. Díganme, ¿qué desean tomar?*

María: *Para mí, una limonada. Ya sé que mi esposo va a querer un jugo de naranja.*

José: *No, querida, no quiero nada de eso. Joven, tráigame una cerveza bien fría.*

María: *Pero, mi amor, no te olvides de tu salud, y del problema que tienes con el hígado y todo, tú sabes ....*

José: *Pues, tienes razón. Entonces, déme un vaso de leche, por favor. (Sale el mesero ... vuelve con las bebidas.)*

El mesero: *Aquí tienen las bebidas. Ahora, ¿qué van a querer? (also: pedir, ordenar, comer)*

José: *Es que no estamos listos todavía, joven. Dénos la oportunidad para estudiar (leer) el menú, y vuela en dos minutos, si no sería gran molestia.*

El mesero: *Está bien. (Sale el mesero. Regresa 15 minutos después). Bueno, ¿ya están listos?*

María: *Sí, joven, ya. Yo voy a probar el filete de pescado.*

Cultura Latina

The word for "waiter" changes from place to place: *mesero* (most of Latin America), *mesonero* (Venezuela), *garzón* or *mozo* (Argentina), *camarero* (Spain, the Caribbean). You may need to ask the locals *"¿Cómo se dice 'mesero/camarero' aquí?"* to find out what word people use where you are.

José: *Y yo el caldo de res, y el pollo rostizado. Pero dígame una cosa, joven. ¿Es picante el caldo?*

El mesero: *No, señor. No tiene nada de picante.*

José: *Está bien, entonces. Usted sabe … por lo del estómago … hay que tener cuidado.*

El mesero: *Sí. El pollo va acompañado de frijoles y arroz.*

José: *Eso está muy bien. Ahora, lleve los vasos vacios a la cocina y dígale al cocinero que prepare la comida de una vez. Es que tenemos mucha prisa.*

El mesero: *Sí, señor. Como usted quiera.*

José: *Espere, tengo una pregunta más. ¿Qué pasa con los cubiertos?*

El mesero: *Enseguida se los traigo. (va a la cocina; le grita al concinero) ¡Oye, Juan! Hay un tipo en la cinco que quiere que hagas la comida de una vez.*

El cocinero: *¿Así? ¡Qué lástima! Es que estoy muy cansado. Ya no quiero cocinar. Que espere hasta que me dé la gana.*

Acuérdate

When referring to something abstract, we need *lo*, the neuter pronoun.. In the dialogue, José says, *"lo del estomago"*. This translates literally as "the thing about the stomach." As other examples, *lo de Juan* means "the issue (problem, idea) with Juan"; *lo único que no sé hacer* means "the only thing I don't know how to do"; and *lo que me dices* means "the thing (subject, issue) you are telling me."

Translation

El mesero: Welcome to La Fonda.

María: Thanks. You're very kind. A table for two, please.

El mesero: Very good. Please follow me. Your table is near the window.

José: Is that right? Excellent. We're very hungry.

El mesero: Great. What would you like to drink?

María: For me, a lemonade. I already know that my husband is going to want orange juice.

José: No, dear, I don't want anything like that. Young man, bring me a very cold beer, please.

María: But honey, don't forget about your health, and the problem with your liver, you know ….

José: Well, you're right. In that case, I'm going to order a glass of milk. (waiter leaves; returns)

El mesero: Here are your drinks. Now, what are you going to order?

José: Well, we're not ready yet. Give us a chance to study the menu, and come back in two minutes, if it wouldn't be too much trouble.

El mesero: All right. (exit waiter; returns 15 minutes later). So, are you ready now?

María: Yes, young man, we are. I'm going to try the fish fillet.

José: And I'm going to try the beef stew and the rotisserie chicken. But tell me something, young man. Is the stew spicy?

El mesero: No, sir. There's nothing spicy in it.

José: Well, that's fine then. You know … my stomach problems … you have to be careful.

El mesero: Right. The chicken comes with beans and rice.

José: That's fine. Now, take these empty glasses to the kitchen and tell the cook to prepare the food at once. We're in a hurry. ("We have a lot of hurry")

El mesero: Yes, sir. As you wish.

José: Wait, one more thing. What about the silverware?

El mesero: I'll bring it to you right away. (goes to kitchen; yells to the cook) Hey, Juan! There's a guy (*tipo* = "type") at table five (*la* refers to *mesa*) who wants you to make his food right away.

El cocinero: Oh yeah? What a shame! You see, I'm very tired. I don't want to cook anymore. Let him wait until I feel up to it.

Acuérdate

Intentar, tratar de, and *probar* all mean "to try," but *intentar* and *tratar de* + infinitive are more common for actually trying to do something: *Voy a tratar de cocinarlo bien* means "I'm going to try to cook it well." Although *probar* sometimes can be used this way, it works best in the context of "to taste something" *¿Quiere probar la comida?* means "Do you want to try the food?"

Acuérdate

The word for a drinking straw also changes from place to place. In Mexico it's a *popote.* Most other places call it a *pitillo* or *pajilla,* but *pajita, sorbete,* and *carrizo* are also possible. In Argentina, Uruguay, and Paraguay, a *bombilla* is a metal straw for drinking *mate,* a green tea that is popular there. Elsewhere, a *bombilla* is usually a light bulb. Go figure.

Algo Nuevo

Literally, *Es que* means "It's that ...." But a better translation might be "You see ...,"
"What's happening is that ...," "The thing is that ...," and so on. By starting with *Es que*,
the cook is explaining his actions or situation. In the right context, the statement *Es que
Elias no tiene dinero* could mean "You see, the problem is that Elias doesn't have any
money, so that's why he can't buy/do the thing we're talking about."

Risa del Día

I suppose that these are old jokes. Food is held in such
high regard that there aren't too many jokes about
food. So, here are a couple of short ones:

➤ *Jaimito a su maestra* (with *vos* verb form, indicat-
ing that this joke is probably from Argentina)

> —*Jaimito, ¿vos rezás antes de comer?*

> —*No, maestra. Mi mamá no cocina muy
> bien, pero no es para tanto!*

➤ *En el restaurante*

> —*Camarero, ¡el pollo está crudo!*

> —*¿Como lo sabe, si no lo ha probado?*

> —*Es que se está comiendo mi ensalada.*

➤ **rezar:** to pray

➤ **cocinar:** to cook

➤ **para tanto:** that bad; "that extreme"

➤ **crudo:** raw; uncooked

Ten Cuidado

Use *hay* (not *tener*) when asking
about eggs and milk. Eggs are
huevos. But that word can also
mean "the male generative or-
gans." If you ask someone
"*¿tiene huevos?*" you aren't asking if there are eggs available,
but if he (or she!) has testicles.
Also avoid "*¿Tiene leche?*",
which translates as "Are you lactating?" Say "*¿Hay huevos?*" and
"*¿Hay leche?*" instead.

El Cuiz

Provide the Spanish for the following words. Rather than cheat, study the
Vocabulario Útil again before taking the quiz if necessary:

1. lid _____

2. butter _____

3. dough; filling _____

4. corn cob _____

5. gram _____

6. to roast _____

7. strip _____

8. salt "to taste" _____

9. food processor _____

10. tablespoonful _____

11. teaspoonful _____

12. leaf; husk _____

13. to peel _____

14. to slice _____

15. soak _____

16. to drip _____

17. a tamale holder _____

18. to beat; to mix _____

19. to grind _____

20. to spread _____

21. to bend; to turn _____

22. sour cream _____

23. pressure cooker _____

24. to stand up _____

25. to place; to put _____

26. to cook; to boil _____

27. to sauté _____

28. to take (time) _____

29. to drain; to strain _____

30. thick _____

31. to season _____

32. a salsa dish _____

33. to unwrap _____

Haz Clic Aquí

Visit these Web sites for more recipes and information about Spanish and Latin American food:

www.afuegolento.com/portada. ats mexicodesconocido.com.mx/ comida/2070.htm

www.ourense.com/gastronomia. html

www.koldoroyo.es/portada.ats

margaritaonline.com/pages/ Gastronomia.htm

dyred.sureste.com/piramide/ piramid2.htm

www.geocities.com/Paris/Bistro/ 7445/comida.html

www.laguia.com.ve/informatvas/ gastronomia/HomeGastronomia. html

Tareas

1. Host an authentic Latin American or Spanish dinner. Surf online or visit your library for recipes and any cookbooks that feature recipes from the Spanish-speaking world. Invite friends and family. Enjoy *sobremesa* after eating.

2. During your dinner, discuss what you have learned about meals and food. If you need more information, do more research on the Internet or at the library.

3. Create sentences for practicing your prepositions. Use the list here as your guide, and utilize new vocabulary or words from your dictionary as you build your sentences.

The Least You Need to Know

➤ The main meals in Spanish-speaking countries tend to come at midday.

➤ The words for some foods change from country to country.

➤ The words for the main meal of the day change from country to country.

➤ Prepositions show relationship and position; some can take an infinitive.

Chapter 16

La Iglesia y la Religión

In This Chapter

➤ *Lectura:* La Virgen de Guadalupe

➤ *Gramática:* the present progressive tense

➤ *Palabras para ti*

Historians of both Spain and Latin America have long identified the Roman Catholic Church as one of the most important forces in culture, society, and politics. In 1492, the Spanish *reconquista* finally came to an end when the last of the Moors were ousted from Granada and the entire Iberian Peninsula came under the religious control of the church. That same year, Catholicism was introduced to the New World (or maybe it was the other way around).

Catholicism and Latin American Culture

The Catholic Church brought profound changes to *las Américas*. It introduced a new moral code, baptism, the holy sacraments, the notion of heaven and hell, the Virgin, the saints, monogamy, and, of course, the crucified Christ. The human sacrifices and cannibalism practiced by some native peoples were replaced by the consumption of the host (body and blood of Christ). Cathedrals were built on the sites of the old native worshipping grounds, and native deities were replaced by Christian saints.

Today, the Roman Catholic Church is still an integral part of the cultural and religious life of most Spaniards and Latin Americans. Naturally, not all Spanish-speakers are Roman Catholics. Protestant denominations, Judaism, Mormonism, Native American religions, and atheism (just to mention a few) are also represented throughout the region. Nonetheless, statistics show that 99 percent of Spaniards and 87 percent of all Latin Americans are at least nominally Roman Catholic, and that nearly 40 percent of the world's Catholics speak Spanish as their first language. Thus, even if you aren't religious, you should have at least a passing understanding of the role the church plays in Ibero-American history and society.

If you plan to travel to Spain or Latin America, there's a good chance that at some point you'll find yourself in a church or cathedral during a religious service, as Masses are held every day of the week. I have included the Spanish versions of the *Ave María* and the *Padre Nuestro* as sidebars in this chapter just so that you might have a clue as to what's going on during the service.

Algo Nuevo

To give you an idea of the kind of language you'll find in a religious text, here's "In the beginning ..." from the *Book of Genesis:*

En el principio creó Dios los cielos y la tierra. Y la tierra estaba desordenada y vacía, y las tinieblas (darkness) estaban sobre la faz del abismo, y el Espíritu de Dios se movía sobre la faz de las aguas. Y dijo Dios: Sea la luz; fue la luz. Y vio Dios que la luz era buena; y separó Dios la luz de las tinieblas. Y llamó Dios a la luz Día, y a las tinieblas llamó Noche.

Lectura: La Virgen de Guadalupe

Our Lady of Guadalupe, also known as *la guadalupana*, is Mexico's patron saint. Her image can be seen in cathedrals, churches, chapels, and just about anywhere else you could possibly imagine: kitchen walls, key chains, napkins, candle holders, posters, hats, T-shirts, automobiles, you name it. Faith in the apparition of *la guadalupana* runs deep in the Mexican religious psyche, and her image is a constant reminder of the miracles she still performs (testimonials appear daily in newspapers) and of Mexican national pride.

According to legend, *la Virgen* appeared to Juan Diego, a Mexican Indian, in 1531 on a hill outside Mexico City called *Tepeyac*. The *Virgen* appeared several times to Juan

Diego over the course of several days. She told him that she had a special love for the native Mexican people, and that a shrine should be built on the hill in her honor.

Whether you believe the story or not, this event gave the Catholic Church a much stronger message to deliver to the indigenous population—that *la Virgen* appeared directly to one of their own people and that she cared about the welfare of the native Mexicans.

Today, the Basilica of the Virgin of Guadalupe is still on *Tepeyac* hill and is visited by 10 million pilgrims each year. The original cloth on which her image miraculously appeared is on display, and pilgrims shuttled past on a series of people-movers can see it high on the wall. Here's the story:

> *La Virgen de Guadalupe se apareció al indio Juan Diego el sábado 9 de diciembre de 1531 en las faldas del cerro del Tepeyac, situado a las afueras de la ciudad de México, para anunciarle que deseaba que en ese lugar se construyera un templo en su honor, para en él mostrar su amor, su compasión, su auxilio y su defensa a los hombres, y le pidió que hiciera llegar su mensaje al obispo de México, Juan de Zumárraga. Juan Diego cumplió con el encargo de la Virgen, pero el obispo no le creyó.*

> *Aquella misma tarde Juan Diego volvió a pasar por el Tepeyac, le contó a la Virgen lo sucedido y le pidió que enviara a otro mensajero, pero ella insistió en que Juan Diego lo intentara de nuevo al día siguiente.*

> *Siguiendo las instrucciones de la Virgen, Juan Diego volvió a presentarse ante el obispo, quien entonces le pidió alguna señal que demostrara que lo que decía era verdad.*

> *Ese mismo día por la tarde, Juan Diego tuvo su tercer encuentro con la Virgen. Al hacerle saber la petición del obispo, la Virgen le pidió que volviera a encontrarla al día siguiente, y que entonces le daría la señal que pedía el obispo.*

> *Pero al día siguiente—lunes 11—el tío de Juan Diego, Juan Bernardino, se enfermó gravemente a causa de la peste, y esto impidió a Juan Diego presentarse ante la Virgen. Esa misma noche empeoró el estado de Juan Bernardino, por lo que Juan Diego tuvo que ir a la ciudad de México en busca de un sacerdote.*

> *Transcurrían las primeras horas del 12 de diciembre cuando, en su camino a la ciudad, Juan Diego pasó a la altura del Tepeyac. Avergonzado*

Cultura Latina

Most Latin American countries have a patron saint, and many cities and towns also have their own patron or patroness. Nearly every day of the year is associated with a particular saint (in the United States, we only seem to know St. Patrick's Day and St. Valentine's Day). When your town's saint's day comes up, it's time for a *fiesta*, known as a *fiesta patronal*.

por no haber cumplido la promesa que le había hecho a la Virgen, decidió rodear el cerro para evitar un nuevo encuentro. Sin embargo, la Virgen se apareció a Juan Diego en el llano que se extiende junto al cerro. Le dijo a Juan Diego que no debía temer más por la salud de su tío y le pidió que subiera a la cumbre del Tepeyac, en donde encontraría unas rosas de Castilla—que no florecían en el cerro—las que serían la señal que debía entregar al obispo.

Mientras Juan Diego se dirigía a casa del obispo, la Virgen se apareció ante el moribundo Juan Bernardino y lo sanó. Le explicó el encargo que había dado a Juan Diego, y le pidió que hablara al obispo de su enfermedad y la forma como había sido curado por ella.

Hacia el mediodía de aquel 12 de diciembre Juan Diego le dijo al obispo que le había traído la señal que le había pedido. Entonces desenvolvió su ayate y las rosas de Castilla cayeron al suelo, y en la manta apareció la imagen de la Virgen de Guadalupe.

Vocabulario Útil:

- **aparecer**: to appear
- **falda**: bank; skirt
- **cerro**: hill
- **auxilio**: help
- **mensaje**: message
- **obispo**: bishop
- **cumplir**: to keep; uphold; make good on
- **encargo**: mission; assignment; task
- **lo sucedido**: what had happened
- **mensajero**: messenger
- **siguiente**: following
- **volver a + infinitive**: to repeat X; to do it again
- **de nuevo**: again; another time
- **presentarse**: to come before; to present oneself
- **señal**: sign
- **encuentro**: meeting; encounter
- **petición**: request
- **enfermarse**: to get sick

- **gravemente**: gravely; seriously
- **a causa de**: because of; due to
- **peste**: plague; epidemic
- **impedir**: to stop; to impede
- **estado**: condition; state
- **empeorar**: to worsen; to get worse
- **por lo que**: and so; for this reason
- **sacerdote**: cleric; priest
- **transcurrir**: to transpire; to happen
- **avergonzado**: ashamed
- **rodear**: to go around
- **llano**: low, flat land
- **temer**: to fear
- **cumbre**: top; summit
- **florecer**: to grow; to flower; to bloom
- **dirigirse**: to head toward; to go toward
- **moribundo**: deathly ill
- **sanar**: to heal; to cure
- **enfermedad**: sickness
- **manta**: rug; carpet; cloth on the floor

Análisis del Texto

Now let's look at our text more closely:

➤ *deseaba que en ese lugar se construyera un templo*

This is a simple past tense with a past subjunctive—just thought I'd point it out. *Construir* needs that *y* to form the past subjunctive because its stem ends in a vowel. The literal translation is, "She wanted that in that place be built a temple." A better translation would move the "in that place" to the end: "She wanted them to build a temple in that place."

➤ *para en él mostrar su amor*

The *él* stands in for *templo*.

➤ *y le pidió que hiciera llegar su mensaje*

Hiciera is past subjunctive of *hacer*. *Hacer* can be used with another infinitive as a helping verb: "She asked him to get the message to him" (to make it arrive).

➤ *pero el obispo no le creyó*

Believing is done with the indirect object pronouns (INDOPs) in Spanish: *No te creo* means "I don't believe (to) you." In this example, we know that the Bishop didn't believe Juan Diego personally. If the text had read *"pero el obispo no lo creyó,"* this would have meant that he didn't believe what Juan Diego said ("didn't believe it") rather than not believing that Juan was an honest person. The INDOP, as you know, is invariable for gender: *No le creo a María* means "I don't believe María." You may sometimes see *No se lo creo,* which means "I don't believe him/her/*usted,* and I don't believe what he/she/*usted* said, either."

➤ *Aquella misma tarde*

This phrase means, "that very same afternoon." The use of *aquella* helps to distance the reader from the event. This did happen in 1531, after all ....

Cultura Latina

An *ayate* is a traditional bag made from a cloth woven from the fibers of the agave plant. Unless you've got a super dictionary, you probably won't find it. The word comes from the *Náhuatl* language spoken by the Aztecs. Many such Native American words (*petate*, *elote*, and so on) originally ended in a –*tl* but were changed to –*te* by the Spanish.

➤ *al día siguiente*

This should be understood as "on the following day," not "to the following day."

➤ *le pidió alguna señal que demostrara*

Here we have the past subjunctive in *demonstara*. The *obisbo* is unsure of what sign might be given: "asked him for a sign that might show ...." Because it is unknown what kind of sign *la Virgen* might give, the subjunctive is required.

➤ *por lo que Juan Diego tuvo que ir*

The *lo* refers to the whole situation of the illness of Juan Diego's uncle, and offers a cause-and-effect link between the two statements: "Juan Bernardino's condition worsened, and so (for this reason) Juan Diego had to go ...."

➤ *Transcurrían ... cuando ... Juan Diego pasó*

This is a fine example of how a preterit tense (*pasó*) can interrupt the events being described in the imperfect (*transcurrían*).

Gramática: The Present Progressive Tense

When something or someone is involved in an activity in a particular moment (often, but not always, the present moment), Spanish uses what is known as the present progressive tense. This tense corresponds to the –*ing* tenses we use all the time in English.

You have seen several verbs in the present progressive in previous *lecturas* and examples. Now let's look at the tense in greater detail:

Forming the Present Progressive Tense

Verb	Ending	Present Participle	Definition
hablar	–*ando*	*hablando*	"talking"
cantar	–*ando*	*cantando*	"singing"
comer	–*iendo*	*comiendo*	"eating"
vivir	–*iendo*	*viviendo*	"living"
oír	–*yendo*	*oyendo*	"hearing"

The present progressive in Spanish is basically the same as the English construction "someone or something *is* doing:" *estar* (to be) + present participle. Most verbs form regular present participles. But, of course, a few common *–er* and *–ir* verbs have slightly irregular forms. Stem-changing *–ir* verbs such as *pedir* (pido) and *dormir* (duermo) change the *e* to *i* and the *o* to *u* in the present participle:

➤ *venir* changes to *viniendo*

➤ *decir* changes to *diciendo*

➤ *sentir* changes to *sintiendo*

➤ *pedir* changes to *pidiendo*

➤ *dormir* changes to *durmiendo*

➤ *morir* changes to *muriendo*

➤ *poder* changes to *pudiendo*

If the verb stem ends in a vowel (*creer, caer, oír, leer*), then the *i* in *–iendo* becomes *y: creyendo, cayendo, oyendo, leyendo*. Verbs ending in *–eír*, such as *reír* ("to laugh") and *sonreír* ("to smile"), lose both the *e* and the *tilde: riendo, sonriendo*.

Here are some basic sentences using the present progressive tense:

➤ **Estoy escribiendo una carta a mi viejo amigo:** I'm writing a letter to my old friend.

➤ **Antonio está viajando por España:** Antonio is travelling through Spain.

➤ **Están recibiendo comunión:** They are receiving communion.

➤ **Estamos construyendo una nueva iglesia:** We are building a new church.

The present participle can also be used after verbs such as *seguir* and *continuar* (both mean "to continue") and the verb *ir* ("to go"):

➤ **Siguen charlando:** They're still talking.

Ten Cuidado

Although *ser* also means "to be," it isn't used with the present progressive. You can't say *Juan es hablando.* You must use *estar*.

Ten Cuidado

The participle is always invariable. No matter who you are or what you're doing, the *o* at the end never becomes *a*. It also is never pluralized with an *s*.

Acuérdate

The present participle of *ser* is *siendo*. It isn't used often, but it's handy for saying "Being X ...," as in: *Siendo hombre, no pudo entender los dolores de parto de su esposa* ("Being a man, he couldn't understand his wife's labor pains.")

Cultura Latina

Here is the Spanish text for the "Lord's Prayer":

Padre Nuestro que estás en el Cielo, santificado sea Tú nombre; venga a nosotros tu reino y hágase Tu voluntad en la tierra como en el cielo; danos hoy nuestro pan de cada día y perdona nuestras ofensas, como también perdonamos a los que nos ofenden, no nos dejes caer en tentación, y líbranos del mal. Amén.

➤ **Voy entendiendo un poco mejor el español:** I'm getting to understand Spanish a bit better.

➤ **Continuarán reparando la capilla durante toda la semana:** They will be continuing to repair the chapel during the entire week.

The present participle also has some uses by itself. Use it to say "By doing X …," as in the following examples:

➤ **Trabajando se gana la vida:** You live by working (one lives …).

➤ **Leyendo un poco cada día, tu español mejorará:** By reading a little every day, your Spanish will improve.

Algo Nuevo

The verb *ir* works well with the present participle: *Voy caminando por la calle* means "I am walking along the street (and making progress)." Its use implies motion. I could also say *Estoy caminando por la calle,* but with *estar* the focus is more on *what* I am doing rather than on the fact that I am getting somewhere. I could be walking in place. Sometimes the sense of motion is figurative: *Voy entendiendo* means "I'm moving toward understanding" (I understand more and more each time).

Note that the tense of *estar* can vary. You can use it in the imperfect, conditional, future, or even the subjunctive:

➤ **Juan estaba hablando con el cura cuando sonó el teléfono:** Juan was talking to the priest when the phone rang.

➤ **Había estado mirando la televisión durante una hora cuando se me cortó la luz**: I had been watching television for an hour when the power went out on me.

➤ **Es posible que esté leyendo**: It's possible that he is reading.

➤ **Estaré viajando durante el próximo mes**: I will be travelling during the coming month.

Palabras Para Ti

Here are some more words related to religion and religious life:

➤ **orar; rezar:** to pray

➤ **misa:** Mass

➤ **misal:** missal; book used for Mass

➤ **crusifijo:** crucifix

➤ **ídolo:** idol

➤ **biblia:** Bible

➤ **pecado:** sin

➤ **cura (masculine):** priest

➤ **culto:** religion other than Catholicism (not a "cult" in the English sense)

➤ **protestante:** Protestant

➤ **judío:** Jewish

➤ **musulmán:** Muslim

➤ **hindú:** Hindu

➤ **templo:** temple

➤ **mezquita:** mosque

➤ **comunión:** communion

➤ **inclinarse la cabeza:** to bow your head

➤ **confesar:** to give confession

➤ **bendecir:** to bless

➤ **ángel:** angel

➤ **espíritu santo:** Holy Spirit

Cultura Latina

Here is the Spanish version of the *Ave María*:

Dios te salve María, llena eres de Gracia, el Señor esté contigo; bendita eres entre todas las mujeres y bendito el fruto de tu vientre Jesús. Santa María, Madre de Dios, ruega por nosotros los pecadores ahora y en la hora de nuestra muerte. Amén.

Haz Clic Aquí

You can get a little more information and practice with the present progressive tense at www.learningspanish.com/progressive.html or www.mssc.edu/comm/faculty/talavera/rev61.htm.

Cultura Latina

Santería, a religion of Afro-Caribbean origin, is practiced in the Caribbean by some segments of the population. It incorporates the worship of the traditional Orisha beliefs of West Africans into Roman Catholicism. *Santería's* origins date back to the slave trade, when African slaves brought to the region kept their old beliefs alive by equating each Orisha with a corresponding Christian saint.

Haz Clic Aquí

If you need more information or vocabulary for Roman Catholicism, go right to the top and visit the Vatican's official Web site at www.vatican.va/phome_sp.htm. It's in Spanish.

Risa del Día

Jokes of a religious nature abound in Spanish. Many are *chistes verdes*. The following joke was among the tamest I could find. I think it's pretty funny:

> *Un misionero va caminando por la jungla cuando de repente se topa con un tigre de aspecto feroz y muerto de hambre. Ante la desesperación se arrodilla y reza:*
>
> *— ¡Oh, Padre, infunde sentimientos cristianos a esta fiera!*
>
> *El tigre, sorprendido, mira a su alrededor y a continuación se arrodilla y dice:*
>
> *—¡Oh, Padre, bendice este alimento que voy a recibir!*

Vocabulario Útil:

- ➤ **misionero:** missionary
- ➤ **de repente:** all of a sudden
- ➤ **toparse:** to run into; to come upon
- ➤ **muerto de hambre:** dying of hunger; famished
- ➤ **ante:** "faced with"
- ➤ **desesperación:** despair
- ➤ **arrodillarse:** to kneel down
- ➤ **infundir:** to fill with
- ➤ **fiera:** wild beast
- ➤ **a continuación:** next; and then
- ➤ **bendecir:** bless
- ➤ **alimento:** food
- ➤ **recibir:** to receive

El Cuiz

You know what to do. If you cheat this time, you risk punishment by a higher being:

1. to keep; uphold; make good on

   _____

2. to appear

   _____

3. sign

   _____

4. bishop

   _____

5. message

   _____

6. following

   _____

7. to come before; to present oneself

   _____

Cultura Latina

The Festival of Our Lady of Guadalupe falls on December 12th and is celebrated throughout Mexico. The main event is held at *Tepeyac*, in the great atrium of the *Basilica de Guadalupe*. Many groups specializing in different native dances arrive from all over the country to perform during the festival. The most famous native dance is called *los matachines*.

8. again; another time _____
9. meeting; encounter _____
10. request _____
11. to get sick _____
12. top; summit _____
13. ashamed _____
14. because of; due to _____
15. to transpire; to happen _____
16. and so; for this reason _____
17. to go around _____
18. to pray _____
19. chapel _____
20. cleric; priest _____
21. mosque _____
22. communion _____
23. to grow; to flower; to bloom _____

24. to bless _____

25. condition; state _____

26. to give confession _____

27. to fear _____

28. to heal; to cure _____

29. to head toward; to go toward _____

30. Jewish _____

31. Muslim _____

32. to worsen; to get worse _____

Haz Clic Aquí

Obviously, this chapter only touches the surface of this topic. If you're interested in more information about religious practices in Spain or Latin America, perform an Internet search using your favorite search engine under "religion + Latin America" or "religion + Spain."

Tareas

1. Create sentences using the present progressive tense. If you want, start with a few "somebody-is-doing-something" sentences in English, then try to translate them into Spanish. Use the examples and the explanations as your guide. Vary the tense of the helping verb to express more complex ideas of time.

2. Write a brief essay about yourself and your religious background. You don't need to share it with anyone. If you have no religious preference or affiliation, write about that.

The Least You Need to Know

➤ Roman Catholicism is the predominant religion in Spain and Latin America.

➤ The Virgin of Guadalupe is Mexico's patroness.

➤ The present progressive is the *–ing* form of the verb.

➤ You can change the tense of the helping verb (*estar, contiunar, ir,* and so on) to create more complex tenses.

Chapter 17

Las Fiestas

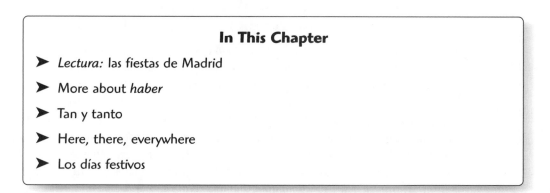

> **In This Chapter**
>
> ➤ *Lectura:* las fiestas de Madrid
>
> ➤ More about *haber*
>
> ➤ Tan y tanto
>
> ➤ Here, there, everywhere
>
> ➤ Los días festivos

How would you like to tie a red bandana around your neck and run for dear life within a few feet of several angry bulls with hundreds of people yelling at you and no way to escape? Sounds crazy, right? And yet each July people from all over the world travel to Pamplona to participate in the Running of the Bulls and the Festival of San Fermín, one of the most internationally celebrated festivities in Spain.

What If I Don't Like Bulls?

If running from vicious *toros* is not your style, then maybe you should consider the Tomatina, a much more "civilized" festival where everyone gets together and throws tomatoes at each other. Can't believe it? Well, as columnist Dave Barry would say, "I swear I'm not making this up." Since 1944, each year on the last Wednesday of August in the little town of Buñol (30 miles west of Valencia), people flock to fight a war with over-ripe tomatoes. *¿Por qué?* Well, *¿por qué no?*

Both Spaniards and Latin Americans find reasons to celebrate many events throughout the year. Many of the celebrations are religious holidays, even though the tone of the fiestas themselves may not seem overly religious. Other fiestas date back to pre-Christian pagan festivals, or, in the case of Latin America, to pre-Columbian times (that's before Chris Columbus got there).

Lectura: Las Fiestas de Madrid

The following *lectura* discusses Madrid and the various fiestas held in the city throughout the year. It's a challenging text because its tone is a bit more literary than most of your previous readings. Feel free to read it several times if you need to. Have your dictionary on hand for any new words, and take your time:

Madrid es una ciudad muy alegre. Ofrece todo tipo de espectáculos propios de una gran capital. También tiene el encanto de conservar aún el sabor tradicional de "la villa." Y es cierto que en algún sentido y en lo profundo de su alma Madrid sigue siendo esa villa, esa ciudad de barrio que aún ofrece toda la autenticidad de un pequeño pueblo. Encantadora y versátil se presentará al visitante, si tiene la oportunidad de saborear algunas de estas fiestas que acontecen desde los primeros segundos en que comienza el año: El Año Nuevo comienza con el gran espectáculo. Casi 40 millones de españoles estarán pendientes cada año a la media noche del gran reloj de la Puerta del Sol, que emitirá las tradicionales 12 campanadas para las que una gran muchedumbre, allí congregada (y el resto de los españoles que lo siguen por televisión), tomen las 12 uvas a su son, durante los 12 últimos segundos del año. Este momento marcará el inicio de la fiesta que se despliega por toda la ciudad.

El 5 de Enero tiene lugar la tradicional y vistosa Cabalgata de los Reyes Magos, que desfila por la zona de Hortaleza. Parece carnaval y representa la entrada de los Magos en la ciudad. Es también una tradición que se repetirá por numerosas ciudades españolas.

El 15 de Mayo, se celebran las Fiestas de San Isidro, patrón de la ciudad, con numerosos festejos típicos como verbenas, romerías y las mejores corridas de toros del año. También se celebran conciertos de rock y jazz, teatro y ferias de artesanía.

Durante los meses de Julio y Agosto se celebran los Veranos de la Villa, campaña de teatro, cine, y espectáculos musicales organizados por el ayuntamiento. Del 6 al 15 de Agosto se celebra la Verbena de la Paloma, una de las fiestas más castizas de la ciudad, caracterizada por su colorido y el gran optimismo que se respira por la calle.

En ella se resucitarán los típicos trajes del chulo madrileño, bailes, y los bellos mantones de manila, y lo mejor del folklore madrileño.

Septiembre, es la gran temporada de estreno en teatros, cines y espectáculos en general. Durante este més se celebran los Festivales de Otoño y la Fiesta de la Melonera en Arganzuela, cuyos orígenes se remontan al siglo XVIII. Del 8 al 12 de Octubre, se celebra la Fiesta del Pilar. En Noviembre tienen lugar las tan diversas celebraciones de la tradicional Almudena, en contraposición con la Fiesta Internacional de Jazz.

Diciembre cierra el año con la exposición y venta de nacimientos y árboles de Navidad en puestos tradicionales situados en la Plaza Mayor, todo un espectáculo de luz y colorido con todo el encanto y romanticismo que acompaña a tan tradicionales fiestas.

Cultura Latina

In Madrid, a *verbena* is an open-air celebration on the eve of a saint's day. In the south of Spain and elsewhere, this would be called a *feria*. A *romería* is a "pilgrimage," especially popular in the South of Spain. Both *verbenas* and *romerías* are extremely festive occasions with all sorts of activities going on throughout the day and night.

Vocabulario Útil:

- **encanto:** enchantment; charm
- **aún:** still; yet
- **espectáculo:** event; show
- **villa:** village; town
- **sentido:** sense; feeling
- **alma:** soul
- **barrio:** neighborhood
- **encantador:** enchanting; charming
- **visitante:** visitor
- **saborear:** to experience; "to taste"
- **acontecer:** to occur
- **estar pendiente:** to be watchful; be waiting for
- **campanada:** sounding of a bell; chiming
- **muchedumbre (feminine):** crowd

- **son:** sound
- **inicio:** beginning
- **desplegarse:** to unfold; to spread out
- **tener lugar:** to take place
- **vistoso:** bright and colorful
- **cabalgata:** ride (on horses)
- **desfilar:** to parade
- **ayuntamiento:** city government
- **castizo:** traditional; pure
- **colorido:** colorful atmosphere
- **estreno:** debut
- **cuyos:** whose
- **remontarse:** to date back to
- **nacimientos:** nativity scenes
- **puestos:** stand; stall; kiosk

Cultura Latina

The *chulo madrileño* is a typical working-class figure from certain areas of Madrid. The word *melonera* comes from *melón*. So, *La Fiesta de la Melonera* celebrates the late summer melon harvest. *La Virgin de la Almudena* is the patroness of Madrid, and the *almudenas* are *verbenas* held in her honor.

Análisis del Texto

You survived. Wonderful. Let's look at a few phrases from the text—nothing too difficult:

➤ *todo tipo de espectáculos*

Note that the plural of *espectáculos* doesn't require that *tipo* (type; kind) be pluralized. In fact, Spanish often presents us with a singular collective when a plural is understood: *El Cubano habla muy rápidamente* means "Cubans speak very fast." Here, *todo tipo* would be translated in English as "all kinds," even though it's singular in Spanish.

➤ *en lo profundo de su alma*

Lo profundo means "the deep part." So, this means "in the bottom of its soul …."

➤ *Encantadora y versátil se presentará al visitante*

Here is a great example of how you can't always find the subject of the sentence in the sentence itself. In fact, we have to go way back to the beginning of the previous sentence to see that *encantadora y versátil* and the verb *se presentará* are all referring back to *la villa de Madrid*. To translate this effectively into English, we almost need to bring the subject back into the sentence. And the charming and versatile part actually would come later in an English sentence: "The village of Madrid will appear charming and versatile to the visitor who …."

➤ *estarán pendientes … del gran reloj*

Estar pendiente is a great way to say that someone is waiting for something, or is expecting something, or is being watchful with great expectation.

➤ *12 campanadas para las que … tomen las 12 uvas a su son*

This construction can be a little tricky if you aren't careful. The *las* refers back to *campanadas* (chimes of the bell). So, at each chime of the big bell, Spaniards eat a grape until the New Year arrives.

➤ *el gran optimismo que se respira por la calle*

You have to use your imagination here—there is no shortage of flowery language in Spanish: "The great optimism that is breathed on the street." A better translation might substitute something like "can be felt" for "breathed."

➤ *cuyos origenes se remontan al siglo XVIII*

Here is *cuyo* again. It means "whose" and is generally used only in writing. The gender is not affected by the subject, but rather by the thing possessed—in this case, *origenes*. Centuries ago, *cuyo* was actually a possessive: *Cuyo es aquél caballo* meant "Whose is that horse." But people haven't used it that way since the days of Don Quixote.

Gramática: More About *Haber*

We have already discussed the helping verb *haber* as part of the *Yo he hablado* ("I have spoken") construction. *Hay* and *hubo* also come from *haber*. But *haber* can do a lot more for you because it can legitimately take any tense. It also takes a subjunctive mood in *haya* (present) and *hubiera/hubiese* (past). You can use *haber* + past participles to form the more complex "compound tenses."

Usually your instincts will guide you as to what these mean because we use similar constructions in English. Take a quick look at the following examples:

➤ **La fiesta habrá terminado a esa hora:** The fiesta will have finished at that time.

➤ **Si yo hubiera ido a la reunión, te habría podido dar este regalo:** If I had gone to the party (but I didn't), I would have been able to give you this present.

➤ **Habiendo terminado su bebida, lanzó la copa al piso:** Having finished his drink, he threw the glass to the floor.

➤ **María lo habría hecho, pero no hubo tiempo:** María would have done it, but there wasn't time.

➤ **Es posible que no haya fiesta manãna:** It is possible that there isn't a fiesta tomorrow.

Haz Clic Aquí

El Día de los Muertos, or the "Day of the Dead," is not a low-budget horror movie. Rather, it's a holiday on November 2nd to celebrate the memory of one's ancestors. It is especially popular in Mexico but is also celebrated elsewhere. For more information on this holiday, visit www.tlane. edu/~latinlib/deaddays.html, or research the topic at your local library.

Acuérdate

Use *hacer* with a time expression + *que* to say that something has been going on for a specific time period and is still continuing: *Hace tres días que leo esta novela* means "I've been reading this novel for three days (and I still am)." *Hace tres años que no fumo* means "I haven't smoked in three years (and still haven't)." With a preterite verb, *hacer* means "ago": *Ocurrió hace dos semanas:* "It occurred two weeks ago."

Here, There, Everywhere

Most of these you have already seen. This is just a quick review with added explanation. You'll need these to express where and directions:

➤ **aquí:** here

➤ **acá:** here, over here (see sidebar)

➤ **ahí:** there (in general)

➤ **allá:** there (in general)

➤ **allí:** there (more specific)

➤ **más allá:** beyond

➤ **allende:** beyond (literal)

➤ **atrás:** behind

➤ **a la derecha:** on the right

➤ **a la izquierda:** on the left

➤ **a un lado:** to one side

➤ **derecho, recto:** straight ahead

➤ **en frente:** in front

Both *aquí* and *acá* mean "here." In parts of South America (Argentina, Uruguay, and Chile), *acá* is more common than *aquí*. Purists will tell you that *aquí*, however, is the preferred word. *Acá* can be correctly used when the "here" you're talking about is rather general: *Acá en los Estados Unidos se fuma mucho, pero no aquí en me casa* means "Here in the United States, people smoke a lot, but not in my house." Use *acá* with verbs of motion: *Vente para acá* (often sinalefized as *vente paracá* or even *vente pacá*)—"Come over here."

Acuérdate

In Mexico, *tanto* can mean "an amount," and *tantito* is "a little bit." So, you'll hear people say *¿Me das tantito?* for "Can you give me a little bit (of something)?" This usage is most popular in Mexico and may not be understood elsewhere.

Tan y Tanto: *So, So Much*

The adverbs *tan* and *tanto* are used to say "so much" and "how much." *Tanto* also can be used as an adjective, placed before a noun or nouns, and must match gender and number. When used adverbially (*Te quiero tanto* means "I love you so much"), it remains in the masculine singular.

➤ **La fiesta fue tan divertida:** The fiesta was so fun.

➤ **Tantos libros, tan poco tiempo para leerlos:** So many books, so little time to read them.

➤ **Tanta fue su emoción que comenzó a llorar. Y lloró tanto:** He felt so much emotion that he started to cry. And he cried so (too) much.

Algo Nuevo

After nearly a year of preparations, the Spanish city of Valencia overflows with excitement from the 13th to the 19th of March during the celebration of its major festival: *las Fallas*. *Fallas* are creations of paper maché, wood, and wax that the Valencians build in the streets and burn on the night of the feast of St. Joseph. These figures, called *ninots* by the locals, represent critical and often humorous expressions of important events of the year. The figures are burnt on the night of March 19th in a tower of flames, and each bonfire is a temple devoted to this colossal festival of fire.

The Holidays

Here's a list of the major holidays celebrated throughout Latin America and Spain. Of course, there are hundreds more regional holidays, but these are the big ones. Most are religious:

➤ **Miércoles de Ceniza:** Ash Wednesday

➤ **Domingo de Ramos:** Palm Sunday

➤ **Viernes Santo:** Good Friday

➤ **Día de Pascua:** Easter

➤ **Día de Todos los Santos:** All Saints Day

➤ **Nochebuena:** Christmas Eve

➤ **La Navidad:** Christmas Day

➤ **Noche Vieja:** New Year's Eve

➤ **El Año Nuevo:** New Year's Day

Acuérdate

You already know that *feliz* means happy. Thus, *Feliz Navidad* means "Merry Christmas"; *Felices Pascuas* means "Happy Easter"; and *Feliz cumpleaños* means "Happy birthday." For a more general "Happy holidays," you can say *Felices fiestas*.

Cultura Latina

El Día de los Reyes Magos ("Day of the Wise Men") falls on January 6th (the Epiphany). It is on this day, rather than on Christmas, that most gift-giving takes place. On a different note, the equivalent of Friday the 13th in Latin countries is Tuesday the 13th. Don't ask me why.

Cultura Latina

Los puertorriqueños celebrate two special days: November 19th, the day Christopher Columbus discovered the island or *Borinquen*; and July 25th, the day the Puerto Rican constitution was signed. Some Puerto Ricans also celebrate the 4th of July.

Fiestas Patrias: Independence Days

Of course, every Spanish-speaking country other than Spain was once ruled by the Spanish crown. Over the course of the nineteenth century, each gained its independence. Sounds like a good reason to throw a party to me. Here's a list of the independence day holidays for Spain's former colonies:

➤ **Argentina:** *el 9 de julio*
➤ **Bolivia:** *el 6 de augosto*
➤ **Chile:** *el 18 de septiembre*
➤ **Colombia:** *el 20 de julio*
➤ **Costa Rica:** *el 15 de septiembre*
➤ **Cuba:** *el 20 de mayo*
➤ **La República Dominicana:** *el 22 de febrero*
➤ **El Ecuador:** *el 3 de octubre*
➤ **Las Filipinas (Philippines):** *el 12 de junio*
➤ **El Salvador:** *el 15 de septiembre*
➤ **Guinea Ecuatorial:** *el 12 de octubre (1968)*
➤ **Guatemala:** *el 15 de septiembre*
➤ **Honduras:** *el 15 de septiembre*
➤ **México:** *el 16 de septiembre*
➤ **Nicaragua:** *el 15 de septiembre*
➤ **El Panamá:** *el 28 de noviembre* (from Spain), *el 3 de noviembre* (from Colombia)
➤ **El Paraguay:** *el 14 de mayo*
➤ **El Perú:** *el 28 de julio*
➤ **Uruguay:** *el 25 de augosto*
➤ **Venezuela:** *el 5 de julio*

Risa del Día

Here are two short jokes to brighten your *día*:

Mamá, mamá ….

—¿Puedo ir a una fiesta de 15 años?

—No, nena, es demasiado larga.

Un ladrón a otro:

—Rápido, que viene la policía. ¡Salta por la ventana!

—Pero si estamos en el piso 13 ....

—¡Éste no es el momento para ser supersticioso!

Vocabulario Útil:

➤ **nene/nena:** child

➤ **demasiado:** too

➤ **saltar:** to jump

➤ **piso:** floor

➤ **supersticioso:** superstitious

Cultura Latina

The most memorable day in the life of a Mexican girl is her 15th birthday party, known as *la quinceañera*. Traditionally, a girl can marry at the age of 15 (although this is highly unusual outside of the most rural areas). The family prepares a large celebration and, if it can afford to, rents a hall for dancing and other festivities.

El Cuiz

Please provide the Spanish. If you cheat, you won't be invited to the party ....

1. still; yet _____

2. village; town _____

3. soul _____

4. to experience; "to taste" _____

5. sense; feeling _____

6. enchantment; charm _____

7. neighborhood _____

8. sounding of a bell; ringing _____

9. visitor _____

10. enchanting; charming _____

11. to occur _____

12. to be watchful; be waiting for _____

13. crowd _____

14. to take place _____

15. to unfold; to spread out _____

16. to parade _____

17. traditional; pure _____

18. city government _____

19. stand; stall; kiosk _____

20. beginning _____

21. debut _____

22. colorful atmosphere _____

23. to date back to _____

Tareas

1. Create sentences using various tenses of *haber*. Use the examples in the chapter as your guide. Try incorporating some of the new vocabulary you have learned here.

2. Make more sentences (they can be really short) using *tan* or *tanto*.

3. Make even more sentences using words from the "Here, There, Everywhere" section.

4. Invite some friends over for a little *fiesta* of your own. Talk about how exciting this book is and suggest that all your guests run out and buy a copy ASAP.

The Least You Need to Know

➤ In both Spain and Latin America, *fiestas* are common and lots of fun.

➤ The helping verb *haber* takes many tenses and can be used with the past participle to express complex ideas.

➤ *Tan* is an adverb that means "so" and sometimes "such."

➤ *Tanto* means "so much" and is both an adjective and an adverb. When used as an adjective, it must agree in gender and number.

➤ There are several words for "here" and "there," such as *aquí, acá, allí,* and *allá.*

Part 4

Arts and Leisure

¡Olé! *It's time to enjoy some of the finer things in life.*

In this part, your lecturas *will discuss literature, sports, art, music, and handicrafts. There's also a chapter devoted to travel-related dialogues. Our grammar sections will cover the past subjunctive, numbers, fractions, percentages, and interrogatives. You'll also learn the magic of Spanish prefixes and suffixes. Amaze your* amigos *by being able to accurately guess what a word means—even if you've never seen it before!*

You're doing great. ¡Manos a la obra! *(Let's get to it!)*

Don Quixote de la Mancha

In This Chapter

➤ *Lectura:* El Ingenioso Hidalgo Don Quixote de la Mancha

➤ *Gramática:* the past subjunctive

➤ *Diálogo:* Quixote, Sancho Panza, y los molinos de viento

Miguel de Cervantes Saavedra (1547–1616) is considered by many to be the greatest Spanish author who ever lived. Some call him the "Spanish Shakespeare"; others call Shakespeare the "English Cervantes." *El Ingenioso Hidalgo Don Quixote de la Mancha*, first published in 1605 (a second part was published in 1615) is most certainly one of the masterpieces of world literature. The book has had a tremendous influence on the development of prose fiction and the modern novel, and has been translated into all modern languages.

The Man from La Mancha

The tale of Don Quixote describes the adventures of an idealistic Spanish *hidalgo* (nobleman) named Alonso Quijano who, after reading far too many books about knights, dragons, and chivalry, goes a bit *loco* and comes to believe that he himself is a knight who must battle against the injustices of the world. Together with his loyal *escudero* (squire), Sancho Panza, Quixote travels through the arid landscape of La Mancha in search of adventure, dedicating his noble deeds to a Dulcinea (known in every sense by the locals as Aldonza), whom he sees as his lady and eternal love. Quixote's imagination often runs away with him. He sees windmills as giants, flocks of sheep as enemy armies, and country inns as castles. His romantic view of the world, however, is balanced by Sancho Panza's down-to-earth perspectives on life.

The tale of Don Quixote paints a rich picture of Spanish life as it presents the reader with countless philosophical insights. Quixote's idealism seems like madness in a world that often views heroism and love as forms of insanity. This has led many readers to consider *Don Quixote* a tragedy despite its humorous style and many satirical episodes. But others have found the story to be uplifting, as evidenced by the 1965 Broadway hit musical *Man of La Mancha* (music by Mitch Leigh), renewed by the message that "life should not be lived as it is, but rather as it should be."

Lectura: Don Quixote: Capítulo Uno

This *lectura* is a condensed and simplified version of the opening chapter of *Don Quixote*. Reading it in the original sixteenth-century Spanish is extremely tedious. (Imagine reading Shakespeare if you're not a native English-speaker.) Pay close attention to the first sentence: *En un lugar de la Mancha* …. This line is as famous in Spanish as "To be or not to be" is in English. Don't worry if you don't understand some of the words in the text; even this version is difficult and old-fashioned:

En un lugar de la Mancha, de cuyo nombre no quiero acordarme, vivía no hace mucho tiempo un hidalgo de los del antiguo estilo. Con él vivían un ama que no pasaba de los cuarenta y una sobrina que no llegaba a los viente, además de un hábil mozo de campo y plaza.

La edad de nuestro hidalgo rondaba los cincuenta años; era de complexión recia, seco de carnes, enjuto de rostros, gran madrugador y amigo de la caza. Alonso Quijano era su nombre. Este hidalgo, los ratos que estaba ocioso (que eran los más del año), se daba a leer libros de caballería. Tanta era su afición a dichos libros que llegó a olvidarse de la caza y a descuidar la adminstración de su hacienda. Incluso vendió una parte de sus tierras para adquirir todos los libros de caballerías que pudo.

Leía en aquellos libros cosas como ésta: "La razón de la sinrazón que a mi razón se hace, de tal manera mi razón se enflaquece, que con razón me quejo de vuestra hermosura".

Con estas razones perdía el pobre el juicio. Enfrascado en sus lecturas, se le pasaban las noches y los días, viendo cada vez más turbio lo claro y menos claro lo turbio. Y así, del poco dormir y del mucho leer se le secó el cerebro.

Su fantasía se llenó de todo lo que leía en los libros: de encantamientos y pendencias, de batallas y desafíos, de heridas y amores, de tormentos y disparates imposibles. Y todos estos disparates se convirtieron para él en la histora más cercana del mundo.

Rematado ya su juicio, en la cabeza se le metió el loco pensamiento de hacerse caballero andante. Le pareció que debía irse con sus armas y caballo a buscar aventuras que le dieran eterno nombre y fama.

Y lo primero que hizo fue limpiar unas armas que habían sido de sus bisabuelos, que desde hacia siglos estaban olvidadas en un rincón. Fue luego a ver a su rocín, y aunque era éste flaco y desgarbado, le pareció que le pareció que ningún otro caballo le igualaba. En su imaginación buscó un nombre que le fuese bien y, tras larga reflexión, vino a llamarlo Rocinante.

Después, y durante ocho días, buscó otro nombre para sí. Al cabo de su deliberación se dio el de Don Quijote. Pero, acordándose que el valeroso Amadís no se había contentado con llamarse Adamís a secas, sino que añadió el nombre de su reino y patria, para hacerla famosa, y se llamó Amadís de Gaula, así quiso, como buen caballero, añadir al suyo el nombre de la suya y llamarse Don Quijote de la Mancha.

Algo Nuevo

The name of Don Quixote's horse is actually a play on words. *Rocín* means "an old nag." The *ante* part comes from *antes*, which means "before." So, *Rocinante* means "used to be a nag." This makes sense, because the horse now belongs to a famous knight errant. Sancho Panza is also a humorous name. The word *panza* means "belly" or "stomach." If you remove the *s* from Sancho, you get *ancho*, which means "wide" or "stretched out." Need I say more?

Vocabulario Útil:

- ➤ **un ama (feminine):** mistress
- ➤ **hábil:** capable; skillful
- ➤ **rondar:** to round out to; to be about
- ➤ **recio:** robust; sturdy
- ➤ **enjuto:** lean; gaunt

- ➤ **rostro:** face; countenance
- ➤ **madrugador:** gets up early
- ➤ **caza:** hunting
- ➤ **ocioso:** idle; leisurely
- ➤ **darse a:** to be given to

223

➤ **caballería:** chivalry

➤ **aficción:** love of

➤ **dichos:** said; aforementioned

➤ **descuidar:** to neglect; opposite of *cuidar*

➤ **hacienda:** estate

➤ **adquirir:** to acquire

➤ **razón:** reason

➤ **sinrazón:** injustice; wrong

➤ **enflaquecer:** to become thin

➤ **enfrascado:** immersed; bottled up

➤ **turbio:** unclear; murky

➤ **cerebro:** brain; mind

➤ **encantamiento:** spell; enchantment

➤ **pendencia:** fight; scuffle

➤ **batalla:** battle

➤ **desafío:** challenge

➤ **herida:** wound

➤ **tormento:** torment

➤ **disparate:** nonsense; a foolish thing

➤ **cercano:** close; nearby

➤ **rematado:** finished off; "gone"

➤ **pensamiento:** thought

➤ **caballero:** knight

➤ **andante:** errant; going from place to place

➤ **aventura:** adventure

➤ **limpiar:** to clean

➤ **armas:** arms

➤ **rincón:** corner

➤ **flaco:** skinny; weak

➤ **desgarbado:** ungainly; unsteady on foot

➤ **igualar:** to equal; to be as good as

➤ **sí:** here, "himself"

➤ **al cabo de:** after; at the end of

➤ **deliberación:** deliberation; thinking

➤ **contentarse:** to be happy with; to content

➤ **a secas:** alone; by itself

➤ **patria:** homeland

Análisis del Texto

Let's take a look at what we got out of this *lectura*:

➤ *de cuyo nombre*

This means "of whose name ...."

➤ *un hidalgo de los del antiguo estilo*

A *hidalgo* was the lowest rank of nobility in seventeenth-century Spain. It comes from *hijo de algo* which means "son of something." *Del antiguo estilo* means "of the old style." Today, Hidalgo is a popular *apellido* (surname).

➤ *que no pasaba de los cuarenta y una sobrina que no llegaba a los viente*

Understanding this sentence requires a little extra thinking. You know that the articles can stand in for nouns, using gender and number as a link between them. But until now, the noun being referenced has always been around somewhere. Here, *los* refers to a masculine plural noun. But where is the noun? You won't find it anywhere in the passage.

The noun, in this case, is implied by the context: *no pasaba de los cuarenta* means that the subject "wasn't over forty." So, *los* refers to *años*.

➤ *un hábil mozo de campo y plaza*

This is an old-fashioned expression meaning that the young man (*mozo*) is as capable at physical labor (*el campo*) as he is at taking care of the duties of the house.

➤ *que llegó a olvidarse*

Here *llegar a* is acting as a helping verb. It translates as "to come to" or "to happen to," as in "I came to realize that my wallet had been stolen." So here, our *hidalgo* "came to forget" or even "came to the point of forgetting."

➤ *"La razón de la sinrazón que a mi razón se hace, de tal manera mi razón se enflaquece, que con razón me quejo de vuestra hermosura"*.

Forget this! It doesn't make sense. And it isn't really supposed to: "The reason of the unreason with which my reason is afflicted so weakens my reason that with reason I complain of your beauty."

The idea is so confusing that it pushes Quijano over the edge. Don't try to understand it, or you'll soon find yourself doing battle with windmills.

Cultura Latina

Don Quixote and Sancho Panza have been the subjects of many works of art. Quixote has also been the inspiration for two operas, a symphonic poem by German composer Richard Strauss, several motion pictures, a ballet by American choreographer George Balanchine, and, of course, the 1965 musical *Man of La Mancha*.

Acuérdate

The *se le* (*se me, se te,* and so on) configuration is used frequently in Spanish to express what I call the "don't look at me, it wasn't my fault" concept: *Se me olvidó tu nombre* literally means "Your name forgot itself on me." This is how many Spanish-speakers would say "I forgot your name"; *Se te cayeron las llaves* means "The keys dropped themselves on you," which really means "You dropped your keys."

➤ *cada vez más turbio lo claro y menos claro lo turbio*

I like this. *Cada vez más* means "more and more." *Cada vez menos* means "less and less," even though the *cada vez* is only stated once. So, this means that he saw "more and more clearly what was unclear, and more and more unclearly what was clear."

➤ *en la cabeza se le metío el loco pensamiento*

This means, "The crazy idea got into his head."

➤ *aunque era éste flaco*

Note that *éste* stands in for his *rocín* (old nag). When *éste* or *ésta* is used as a pronoun, it is often translated as "the latter." To say "the former," one would use *aquél* or *aquélla*.

Cultura Latina

The word *flaco* is also a popular nickname for anyone who is skinny: *Oye Flaco, ¿cómo te va?* means "Hey, Skinny, how's it going?"

Acuérdate

La Mancha is a region of Spain southeast of Madrid on the *meseta* between Albacete, Ciudad Real, Toledo, Valdepeñas, and Cuenca. Interestingly, the word also means "stain," as in *Mi camisa tiene una mancha* ("My shirt has a stain on it.").

➤ *durante ocho días*

Why eight days? Good question. The answer is that in Spanish, *ocho días* is synonymous with "one week."

➤ *buscó otro nombre para sí*

You know that *sí* means "yes." *Sí* also has an interesting secondary usage as a third-person pronoun meaning "self." It can be singular or plural: *entre sí* (among themselves).

It can be modified by *mismo/a/os/as* for clarity: *Compró un juguete para sí misma* means "She bought a toy for herself." Check your dictionary under *sí* for additional examples.

➤ *se dio el de Don Quijote*

Dar has many secondary uses in addition to "to give." Here, *se dio* means "it gave itself," meaning "it presented itself," or, actively, Don Quijote "came up with it." The *el* refers back to *nombre*.

➤ *Amadís de Gaula*

Amadis of Gaul is the title of a series of medieval romances of chivalry, written in prose and relating the adventures of a legendary hero of the same name. The story was first published in 1508. In many ways, *Don Quixote* is a satire of the tales of Amadis de Gaula and other such works.

➤ *añadir al suyo el nombre de la suya*

You have learned *suyo* as the third person possessive adjective "his," "hers," and so on. With the article, *suyo* and its permutations can serve as a noun: "to add to his (name) the name of his (homeland)."

Gramática: The Past Subjunctive

Many basic texts don't cover the past subjunctive tense, but I personally think it's fun. So, let's take a look:

Forming the Past Subjunctive

For regular verbs, the past subjunctives are made by adding the following endings to the verb stem:

Forming the Past Subjunctive *–ar* Verbs

Ending	Verb	Example
–ara	*hablar*	*hablara*
–aras	*pagar*	*pagaras*
–ara	*contar*	*contara*
–áramos	*cantamos*	*cantáramos*
–arais	*mandar*	*mandarais* (Spain)
–aran	*pensar*	*pensaran*

And for *–er* and *–ir* verbs, we have these:

Forming the Past Subjunctive with *–er* and *–ir* Verbs

Ending	Verb	Example
–iera	*comer*	*comiera*
–ieras	*vivir*	*vivieras*
–iera	*salir*	*saliera*
–iéramos	*entender*	*entendiéramos*
–ierais	*meter*	*metierais* (Spain)
–ieran	*ocurrir*	*ocurrieran*

Verbs that form irregular preterites will form irregular past subjunctives. Start with the *yo* form of the preterite verb, remove the ending, and add the past subjunctive *–er* and *–ir* endings, even for *–ar* verbs:

Forming the Irregular Past Subjunctives

Verb	Stem	Subjunctive
hacer	*hice*	*hiciera*
saber	*supe*	*supiera*
poder	*pude*	*pudiera*
andar	*anduve*	*anduviera*
estar	*estuve*	*estuviera*

Acuérdate

You'll notice that the first-person and third-person singular forms for the past subjunctive are the same. Usually the context makes it clear who the subject of the sentence is. But whenever there is a risk of confusion, simply add the subject pronoun *yo, él, ella,* or *usted.*

There is an alternate form for the past subjunctive that uses the following endings:

➤ For *–ar:* –ase, –ases, –ase, –ásemos, –aseis, –asen

➤ For *–er* and *–ir:* –iese, –ieses, –iese, –iésemos, –iesen

This form is slightly less popular than the *–ara/–iera* forms that we are discussing in this chapter. You may hear it in the *Cono Sur* or read it from time to time in a text. This secondary form (which is actually older than the *ara/iese* form) is becoming less common, and many people never use it at all. You should know about it, but you don't have to learn it if you don't want to. The other form will be understood everywhere.

The verbs *ir* and *ser* have the same form in the past subjunctive: *fuera, fueras, fuera, fuéramos, fueran.* The context of the sentence will always indicate which verb it is.

Using the Past Subjunctive

The past subjunctive works like the present subjunctive, only in the past. What I mean is, if you want someone to do something in the present, you use the present subjunctive: *Quiero que Juan lo haga* = "I want Juan to do it." But if you wanted someone to do something in the past, you need to use the past subjunctive form: *Quería* (imperfect past) *que Juan lo hiciera* = "I wanted Juan to do it." All the rules that you learned previously about how and when to use the subjunctive apply to the past subjunctive—only now, the time or action of the sentence must have occurred in the past.

One of the most common uses you'll have for the past subjunctive is in "contrary to fact" sentences. When you say "if something were possible (but it's not)" or "if this were true (but it isn't)," you will use the past subjunctive, even if the situation is going on currently. Often, it is used with the conditional tense. Observe:

➤ **Si yo pudiera hablar el francés, ganaría mucho dinero:** If I could speak French (but I can't), I could make a lot of money.

➤ **Si estuvieramos en la Argentia, podríamos ir a la Tierra del Fuego:** If we were in Argentina (but we're not), we could go to Tierra del Fuego.

➤ **Si yo fuera Don Quixote, compraría un nuevo caballo:** If I were Don Quixote (but I'm not), I would buy a new horse.

Acuérdate

The *–ir* verbs with stem changes in the present indicative change to *i* in the past subjunctive tense: *pedir = pidiera, sentir = sintiera.*

Acuérdate

Ojalá can be used with a past subjunctive: *Ojalá que fuera así* means "I wish it were so (but it isn't)"; *Ojalá que José lo hubiera sabido* means "I wish that Jose had known (but he didn't)."

Diálogo: Los Molinos

I suppose that this isn't a true-to-life dialogue. But here we have Don Quixote and Sancho Panza in their conversation during Quixote's famous "battle" with the windmills/giants. Note the use of the dashes to open and close the dialogue:

—*La ventura va guiando nuestras cosas; porque ves allí, amigo Sancho Panza, donde se descubren treinta o pocos más, desaforados gigantes, con quienes pienso hacer batalla y quitarles a todos las vidas.*

—*¿Qué gigantes? —dijo Sancho Panza.*

—*Aquellos que allí ves —respondió su amo— de los brazos largos.*

—*Mire vuestra merced —respondió Sancho— que aquellos que allí se parecen no son gigantes, sino molinos de viento, y lo que en ellos parecen brazos son las aspas.*

—*Ellos son gigantes; —respondió Don Quijote— y si tienes miedo, quítate de ahí, y ponte a rezar que yo voy a entrar con ellos en fiera y desigual batalla.*

229

Y con esto, dio de espuelas a su caballo Rocinante, sin atender a las voces que escudero Sancho. Iba diciendo a grandes voces— ¡No huyáis, cobardes y viles criaturas; que un solo caballero es el que os acomete!

Se levantó en esto un poco de viento, y las grandes aspas comenzaron a moverse; lo cual visto por Don Quijote dijo— ¡Pues aunque mováis más brazos que los del gigante Briareo, me lo habéis de pagar!

Y encomendándose de todo corazón a su señora Dulcinea, con la lanza en ristre, arremetió a todo el galope de Rocinante, y embistió con el primer molino, dándole una lanzada en el aspa. El viento volvió el aspa con tanta furia que hizo la lanza pedazos, llevándose tras sí al caballo y al caballero, que fue rodeando muy maltrecho por el campo. Acudió Sancho Panza a socorrerle, a todo el correr de su asno, y cuando llegó le halló que no se podía menear.

—¡Válame Dios! —dijo Sancho—. ¿No le dije yo a vuestra merced que mirase bien lo que hacía, que no eran sino molinos de viento?

—Calla, amigo Sancho —respondió don Quijote—; que las cosas de la guerra; que aquel sabio Frestón ha vuelto estos gigantes en molinos por quitarme la gloria de su vencimiento: tal es la enemistad que me tiene.

Vocabulario Útil:

- ➤ **ventura:** fortune
- ➤ **se descubren:** "are revealed"
- ➤ **desaforado:** terrible; monstrous
- ➤ **vuestra merced:** your mercy
- ➤ **amo:** master
- ➤ **molinos de viento:** windmill
- ➤ **aspa:** blade/wing of a windmill
- ➤ **fiera (adjective):** fearsome
- ➤ **desigual:** unequaled
- ➤ **espuelas:** spurs
- ➤ **a grandes voces:** shouting
- ➤ **huir:** to flee; to run away
- ➤ **cobarde:** coward
- ➤ **acometer:** to attack
- ➤ **encomendarse:** to entrust oneself

- ➤ **lanza:** lance
- ➤ **pedazos:** pieces
- ➤ **en ristre:** at the ready
- ➤ **arremeter:** to charge (in battle)
- ➤ **embestir:** to charge (same as *arremeter*)
- ➤ **furia:** rage
- ➤ **tras sí:** behind itself; after itself
- ➤ **maltrecho:** in bad shape; exhausted
- ➤ **socorrerle:** to help him
- ➤ **menear:** to move one's body
- ➤ **¡Válgame Dios!:** "Lord, give me strength!"
- ➤ **enemistad:** enmity (opposite of *amistad*)

Análisis del Texto

Normally, I'd probably just provide you with a translation of a dialogue, but since we're dealing with literature, I think some analysis is required:

➤ *con quienes pienso hacer batalla*

This would mean "with whom I plan ("am thinking") to do battle."

➤ *quítate de ahí y ponte a rezar*

Literally, this means "remove yourself from there." It's still a common way in Spanish to say "get out of the way."

Algo Nuevo

Vuestra merced ("Your mercy" or "Your grace") was a common form of address from inferior to superior in the sixteenth and seventeenth centuries. The modern formal *Usted* is a contraction: *vuestra merced,* which is why it can be abbreviated either *Vd.* or *Ud.*

➤ *Briareo*

This is a mythological giant with 100 arms and 50 heads.

➤ *haber de pagar*

The verb *haber* + *de* means about the same thing as *tener que*. It is an older form to express obligation, but is still used today by many speakers (*Has de hacerlo = Tienes que hacerlo*). It could also be translated as a future expression: "You'll pay for this!"

Haz Clic Aquí

If you travel to Spain, you can follow the steps of Don Quixote himself along the *Ruta de El Quijote*. Check out the map at www.citelan.es/quixote/2ruta22.html.

Risa del Día

The word for tongue-twister in Spanish is *trabalenguas*. Here's one that would have made Quixote proud. The word *dicho* as a noun means "an old saying." It is also the past participle of "to say." So, this starts out with "They tell me that I have said a saying …."

> *"Me han dicho que he dicho un dicho,*
> *pero ese dicho no lo he dicho yo,*
> *porque si ese dicho*
> *que han dicho que he dicho yo*
> *lo hubiera dicho yo,*
> *estaría bien dicho*
> *por haberlo dicho yo".*

El Cuiz

I pray thee, that thou shalt provide the Castillian for the following locutions, if it pleaseth thou muchly …. Cheateth not, lest thee be eaten by dragons:

1. face; countenance _____
2. idle; leisurely _____
3. chivalry _____
4. said; aforementioned _____
5. to acquire _____
6. reason _____
7. injustice; wrong _____
8. estate _____
9. brain; mind _____
10. battle _____
11. knight _____
12. himself; oneself _____
13. after; at then end of _____
14. wounds _____
15. to be happy with; to content _____
16. homeland _____
17. errant; going from place to place _____
18. corner _____
19. to equal; to be as good as _____
20. your mercy _____
21. master _____

22. windmill _____

23. fearsome _____

24. a knight's helper _____

25. coward _____

26. to attack _____

Tareas

1. Surf the Internet or visit your local library and search for more information about *Don Quixote*. Even if you read the book in English, it will still help you to understand a very important part of Spanish culture.

2. Create sentences using the past subjunctive tense. Use the examples as your guide. Make sentences using a "contrary to fact" construction: "If I were a knight from La Mancha (but I'm not), ..."

The Least You Need to Know

➤ *Don Quixote (Quijote)* is one of the masterpieces of world literature.

➤ The past subjunctive follows the same rules for usage as the present subjunctive, only for past actions or events.

➤ The past subjunctive is used for "contrary to fact" statements such as "If I were king (but I'm not) ...."

Chapter 19

El Museo del Prado

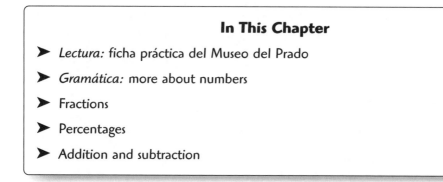

In This Chapter

➤ *Lectura:* ficha práctica del Museo del Prado

➤ *Gramática:* more about numbers

➤ Fractions

➤ Percentages

➤ Addition and subtraction

Many exceptional art museums are located throughout the Spanish-speaking world. And yet Madrid's *Museo del Prado* continues to welcome more visitors than any other art museum in Spain or Latin America. The Prado houses more than 3,000 works of the finest paintings, sculptures, drawings, furniture, and decorative art, and is one of Spain's most popular attractions.

El Prado

Construction of the Prado began in 1810 during the reign of King Fernando VII and his wife, Doña Isabel de Braganza. The original building has had numerous extensions added to it since then. Today the collection is divided between the original Villanueva building, which houses paintings from the Middle Ages to the nineteenth century, and the *Casón del Buen Retiro*, which houses nineteenth-century works formerly displayed in the Modern Art Museum.

Haz Clic Aquí

If you can't travel to Madrid any time soon, you can visit the Prado online at the museum's official Web site: museoprado. mcu.es.

The museum's collection consists principally of works donated to the Spanish royal collection between the sixteenth and nineteenth centuries. Of particular interest are the paintings by Titian, commissioned by Charles V and Philip II in the sixteenth century, and a series painted by Rubens for Philip IV in the early seventeenth century. The Prado also houses an exceptional collection of paintings from the Spanish school, including works by El Greco, Velázquez, and Goya.

Lectura: Ficha Práctica del Museo del Prado

If you've started to feel that your previous *lecturas* have been a bit too theoretical, here's a reading I'm sure you'll find quite practical. This time we have the visitor information guide from the Prado Museum itself. It contains all the facts about touring the museum that you'd ever need to know. Even if you won't be traveling to Spain anytime soon, the vocabulary in the text will be helpful at any museum you might visit during your travels:

Direcciones:

> *Edificio Villanueva*
> *Paseo del Prado, s/n. 28014 Madrid.*
> *Tel. (91) 330 28 00. Fax: (91) 330 28 56*

> *Casón del Buen Retiro*
> *c/ Alfonso XII, 28. 28014 Madrid.*
> *Tel. (91) 420 05 68 - (91) 429 29 30*

Sede Administrativa:

> *c/ Ruiz de Alarcón, 23. 28014 Madrid*
> *Tfnos. (91) 330 28 00. 330 29 00. fax (91) 330 28 56.*
> *Correo electrónico: museo.nacional@prado.mcu.es*

> *Con motivo de las obras de remodelación y ampliación del edificio del Casón del Buen Retiro (c/ Alfonso XII, 28), las Salas de Exposiciones de dicho edificio permanecerán cerradas al público a partir del 2 de Agosto de 1997.*

Teléfono de Información:

> *(91) 330 29 00.*

> *Teléfono de Información del Ministerio de Educación y Cultura (24h): 906 32 22 22.*

Horario:

Martes a Sábado: 9,00–19,00

Domingos, festivos, 24 y 31 de diciembre: 9,00–14,00

Lunes: Cerrado

Primer día de enero, Viernes Santo, 1 mayo y 25 diciembre: Cerrado

Transportes:

Metro: Estaciones de Banco de España y Atocha

Autobuses: 9, 10, 14, 19, 27, 34, 37, y 45

Ferrocarril: Estación de Atocha

Precio de entrada:

500 ptas: Tarifa general

250 ptas: Titulares Carnet Joven, estudiantes o sus equivalentes internacionales; grupos culturales y educativos (previa solicitud).

Gratis: Mayores de 65 años o jubilados; menores de 18 años.

Miembros de la Fundación Amigos del Museo; voluntarios culturales y educativos; desempleados.

Gratis a todos: Sábados de 14,30 a 19,00 y Domingos de 9,00 a 14,00

Planos del Museo:

Disponibles en las taquillas del Museo.

Gratis los siguientes Días:

18 de Mayo. Día Internacional de los Museos 12 de Octubre. Fiesta Nacional de España 6 de Diciembre. Día de la Constitución.

Abonos: Paseo del Arte:

1.275 ptas.

Incluye una visita al Museo del Prado, Fundación Thyssen Bornemisza y Museo Nacional Centro de Arte Reina Sofía.

Cultura Latina

Spain has produced some of the world's most famous painters: Salvador Dalí, Pablo Picasso, El Greco, Goya, Velázquez, and others. You can find lots of information on each of these artists and see examples of their *obras* (works) at any library and on the World Wide Web. Just seek, and you shall find.

Tarjeta 4.000: 4.000 ptas.

Con este abono se puede acceder al Museo de Prado durante un año.

Tarjeta 6.000: 6.000 ptas.

Con este abono se puede acceder, durante un año, a todos los Museos de Titularidad Estatal. Todas estas tarjetas se pueden adquirir en las taquillas de Museo.

Condiciones de entrada para grupos escolares:

Los grupos escolares (máximo de 25 alumnos por profesor) deberán de ir provistos de su correspondiente (y obligatoria) autorización del Museo. Los profesores deben solicitarla con anticipación—al menos dos semanas—a la Oficina de Visitas de Grupos del Museo de Prado.

Cafetería:

El horario de la cafetería es de 9,30 a 18,00

Autoservicio:

Martes a Sábados 11,30–16,00

Librería y Tienda:

Martes a Sábado 9,00–18,30

Domingo y festivos 9,00–13,30

Otros servicios:

Accesos especiales para minusválidos

Salón de actos

Vocabulario Útil:

- ➤ **ficha:** file; card
- ➤ **práctico:** practical; useful
- ➤ **dirección:** address
- ➤ **s/n:** sin número (no number)
- ➤ **c/:** calle (street)
- ➤ **sede:** seat; office; headquarters
- ➤ **administrativo:** administrative
- ➤ **con motivo de:** due to; "with the reason of"
- ➤ **a partir de:** as of
- ➤ **horario:** schedule; timetable
- ➤ **festivo:** holiday (*día festivo*)
- ➤ **ferrocarril:** rail; train
- ➤ **tarifa:** fee; price

➤ **titular:** holder of; named owner of

➤ **carnet:** ID card

➤ **educativo:** educational

➤ **previa:** having obtained previously

➤ **solicitud:** request; application

➤ **gratis:** free; no cost

➤ **mayores de:** older than

➤ **jubilado:** retired person

➤ **menores de:** younger than

➤ **voluntario:** volunteer

➤ **desempleado:** unemployed; out of a job

➤ **plano:** map; plan

➤ **disponible:** available

➤ **taquilla:** ticket window

➤ **siguiente:** following

➤ **abono:** season ticket; payment

➤ **escolar:** school (adjective)

➤ **provisto:** to carry; to be equipped with

➤ **correspondiente:** corresponding

➤ **obligatorio:** obligatory; mandatory

➤ **autorización:** permission

➤ **deber:** to be obligated to

➤ **solicitar:** to apply

➤ **con anticipación:** in advance

➤ **al menos:** at least

➤ **autoservicio:** self-service

➤ **librería:** bookstore

➤ **minusválido:** disabled; handicapped

➤ **salón de actos:** event hall; conference hall

Análisis del Texto

This text isn't too difficult; just a few minor points here and there:

➤ *28014 Madrid*

Notice that the *código postal* (ZIP code or postal code) comes before the name of the city, not after it. Most Spanish-speaking countries follow this order, although Puerto Rico and Mexico do not. Some smaller countries do not have postal codes.

➤ *Con motivo de las obras de remodelación y ampliación*

Motivo is indeed related to the English word "motive," but while "motive" seems a bit formal, the Spanish word *motivo* can be used in everyday conversation. It simply means "reason," as in *¿Cuál es el motivo de su llamada?* ("What is the reason for your call?").

➤ *9,00–19,00*

The use of the 24-hour clock in Spanish-speaking countries is more common than in the United States. Note also that the comma is used here instead of the colon. Both the colon and the comma can be used for times 9,00 or 9:00 in Spanish.

Ten Cuidado

You must write a *tilde* over the letter *o* when it comes between numbers: *345 ó 592* = "345 or 592." This is to distinguish the letter *o* from the number zero.

Acuérdate

Durante does mean "during," but with a specified time it also can mean "for X amount of time." So, *durante un año* would translate as "for a year," not "during a year."

Acuérdate

Remember that *primero* and *tercero* become *primer* and *tercer* before singular masculine nouns.

➤ *previa solicitud*

The word *previo* does mean "previous." However, when placed before the noun, it can also convey the idea of "having fulfilled the requirement of ...." For example, *consulta previa petición de hora* means "consultation by appointment only"; and *Sus pertenencias se entregarán previo pago de la suma mencionada* means "Your belongings will be handed over upon receipt of the aforementioned amount." So here, *previa solicitud* would mean "upon having filed an application." This construction is usually found in formal writing only.

Gramática: More About Numbers

I know that you've learned the numbers already. But there may be a few things about them that you didn't get to when you were a beginning student. So, let's take a closer look.

The Ordinals: First, Second, Third, and So On

The ordinal numbers are all adjectives, and thus must match the gender and number of the noun or nouns they modify. They are usually (but not always) placed before the noun:

➤ **primero (primer):** first

➤ **segundo:** second

➤ **tercero (tercer):** third

➤ **cuarto:** fourth

➤ **quinto:** fifth

➤ **sexto:** sixth

➤ **séptimo:** seventh

➤ **octavo:** eighth

➤ **noveno:** ninth

➤ **décimo:** tenth

➤ **undécimo/decimoprimero:** eleventh

➤ **duodécimo/decimosegundo:** twelfth

➤ **decimotercero:** thirteenth

➤ **decimocuarto:** fourteenth

➤ **decimoquinto:** fifteenth

➤ **decimosexto:** sixteenth

➤ **decimoséptimo:** seventeenth

➤ **decimoctavo:** eighteenth

➤ **decimonoveno:** nineteenth

➤ **vigésimo:** twentieth

➤ **vigesimoprimero:** twenty-first

➤ **vigesimosegundo:** twenty-second

➤ **vigesimotercero:** twenty-third

➤ **tregésimo:** thirtieth

➤ **cuadragésimo:** fortieth

➤ **quincuagésimo:** fiftieth

➤ **sexagésimo:** sixtieth

➤ **septuagésimo:** seventieth

➤ **octogésimo:** eightieth

➤ **nonagésimo:** ninetieth

➤ **centésimo:** hundredth

Algo Nuevo

The ordinal numbers beyond *décimo* (tenth) are rarely used in conversation and may be replaced by the cardinal number: *el cuarenta aniversaro* or *el cuadragésimo aniversario* both mean "the fortieth anniversary." Cardinal numbers are also used in titles when the number is above 10: Luis XII = *Luis doce;* Juan Carlos XX = *Juan Carlos viente.*

Here are a few examples:

➤ **El primer pintor español de la etapa:** The first Spanish painter of the period.

➤ **La tercera exhibición del año:** The third exhibition of the year.

➤ **Juan Pablo Segundo:** Pope John Paul the Second.

➤ **Es el segundo Juan Pablo que he visto hoy:** He's the second guy named John Paul I've seen today.

Ten Cuidado

Ordinal numbers are usually placed before the noun they modify, but they must be placed after the noun if it is part of a title: *Juan Carlos Segundo* means "Juan Carlos the Second." Make sure that you don't translate these as "the second Juan Carlos."

Acuérdate

You know that the words *mayor* and *menor* mean "older" and "younger," respectively. But with numbers, *mayor* means "greater than," and *menor* means "less than."

Fractions

You may not have learned these as a beginner, so here are the fractions that you are most likely to use in daily conversation:

➤ ½: *un medio*

➤ ⅓: *un tercio*

➤ ¼: *un cuarto*

➤ ⅕: *un quinto*

➤ ⅔: *dos tercios*

➤ ¾: *dos cuatros*

When a fraction is not used in a strictly scientific or mathematical sense, it may be expressed in the following ways. Notice that gender may come into play:

➤ **un kilo y medio:** one and a half kilos

➤ **media naranja** or **la mitad de una naranja:** half an orange

➤ **dos de cada tres médicos:** two out of three doctors

➤ **la quinta parte del dinero:** one fifth of the money

Addition and Subtraction

A few good examples should suffice here:

➤ 2 + 3 = 5: *dos más tres son cinco*

➤ 7 – 3 = 4: *siete menos tres son cuatro*

➤ 2 × 9 = 18: *dos por nueve son diesiocho*

➤ 20 ÷ 5 = 4: *veinte dividido por cinco son cuatro*

Percentages

When giving the percent (%) of a number, you must use an article. The indefinite article translates as "by." Here's what I mean:

➤ **el quince por ciento de la población:** 15 percent of the population

➤ **Mis ingresos han subido un 10 por ciento:** My income has increased by 10 percent.

Algo Nuevo

Longer numbers such as telephone numbers or ID numbers are usually read in groupings of two, unlike in the United States, where we tend to read each number individually. Odd numbers that can't be paired up may be read alone. So, if my phone number is 921-547-3601, I would read it as *nueve veintiuno, cinco cuarenta y siete, treinta y seis cero uno.* Of course, people will understand you if you read the numbers one by one, but it sounds more natural in Spanish the other way.

Risa del Día

Here we have a joke about modern art:

Un tipo en un museo de arte moderno está explicando un cuadro a un amigo:

—Pues esto es un amanecer, como indican sus colores cálidos que rompen la imagen clásica del cubismo y arte abstracto para plasmarse más allá de la realidad que involucra el sueño que uno tiene por la mañana ....

En esto que se acerca otro tipo y dice:

—¡Huy! ¡Pero si eso es un atardecer!

—¿Cómo que un atardecer? ¡Esto es un amanecer!

—¡Pero cómo puede usted asegurar que es un amanecer!

—Mire, yo he estudiado en Cambridge y Harvard, he hecho tres masters en arte moderno, así que estoy seguro que es un amanecer.

—Pues mire, yo conozco al pintor y ése jamás se levanta temprano, así que estoy seguro que es un atardecer.

Vocabulario Útil:

➤ **tipo:** guy; person

➤ **cuadro:** painting

➤ **amanecer:** sunrise

➤ **plasmarse:** to be expressed

➤ **involucrar:** to involve

➤ **uno:** one; a person; "you"

➤ **atardecer:** sunset

➤ **asegurar:** to assure

➤ **jamás:** never ever

➤ **levantarse:** get up

➤ **temprano:** early

El Cuiz

You know what to do. Spanish words, por favor.

1. address _____
2. due to; "with the reason of" _____
3. seat; office; headquarters _____
4. younger than _____
5. holiday _____
6. as of _____
7. having obtained previously _____
8. older than _____
9. fee; price _____
10. holder of; named owner of _____
11. ID card _____
12. educational _____
13. schedule; timetable _____
14. retired person _____
15. unemployed; out of a job _____
16. available _____
17. following _____
18. ticket window _____
19. season ticket; payment _____
20. to carry; to be equipped with _____
21. school (adjective) _____
22. at least _____
23. disabled; handicapped _____

24. in advance _____

25. to apply _____

26. to be obligated to _____

27. painting _____

28. sunrise _____

29. beyond _____

30. to involve _____

31. sunset _____

32. to assure _____

33. get up _____

Tareas

1. Create sentences that use ordinal numbers. If needed, try using the word *vez* (time, occurrence) if you get stuck: *la primera vez, la quinta vez* ("the first time," "the fifth time") and so on.

2. Create sentences that help you practice your fractions, percentages, and the reading of longer numbers such as phone numbers. Use your telephone directory, if needed.

3. Visit the Prado's Web site and learn more about the museum's collection. Or, check out what's available at your local library about Spanish and Latin American artists.

The Least You Need to Know

➤ The Prado is Spain's no. 1 art museum.

➤ Ordinal numbers are adjectives and usually are placed before the noun.

➤ Percentages require an article.

➤ Fractions can be expressed in several ways.

➤ *Más, menos, por,* and *dividido por* mean "plus," "minus," "times," and "divided by," respectively.

Chapter 20

La Música Latina

> **In This Chapter**
>
> ➤ *Lectura:* salsa y cumbia
>
> ➤ *Gramática:* prefixes
>
> ➤ *Cielito Lindo*

Both Spain and Latin America present a rich variety of musical heritages—from Andalucian flamenco music, to the classical guitar concertos of Joaquín Rodrigo; from the haunting sounds of the Andean pan flute, to the many rhythms of Latin jazz and popular song: *rumba, mambo, cumbia, cha-cha-chá, canto, bolero, guaguancó, plena, timba, toque, bamba, merengue, bachata, son, guajira* … just to name a few.

The Sound of Many Cultures

The popular music of the Spanish-speaking world has always been an expression of the meeting of diverse peoples. The Moors and Gypsies shaped the tonality and harmonic structure of the flamenco. New World musicians incorporated European instruments into their music-making, including the accordion, harp, guitar, trumpet, and woodwinds. West Africans and Native Americans contributed new instruments such as the marimba and the conical drum, as well as their native dances and rhythms, to create what we know collectively as Latin American music. The influence of Latin music has reached far beyond its borders. American jazz has been greatly influenced by Latin styles.

Cultura Latina

The *bolero* originated in Cuba in the late 1800s, but it had also become extremely popular in Mexico by the 1940s and 1950s. Boleros are essentially ballads of love or love lost. Interestingly, a *bolero* in Mexico is also "a shoeshiner." So, if you call out for someone to play you a *bolero*, you may find someone coming to shine your shoes as well.

Today, numerous crossover stars have made significant in-roads into American pop culture with hits such as the *Macarena, La Vida Loca,* and *Mambo No. 5.* And, of course, who could ever forget the very first crossover rocker, Richie Valens, and his hit *La Bamba.*

Lectura: Salsa y Cumbia

It wasn't easy to pick a *lectura* for this chapter; the various styles of Latin music are practically endless, and it seemed a shame to skip over so many different genres of Latin music. However, both salsa and cumbia have become quite popular outside of their countries of origin, so I thought that the following text might be appropriate.

Salsa is associated primarily with Puerto Rico, and the size and vibrancy of the *boricua* communities in the United States has done much to popularize this art form. Cumbia, although originally an Afro-Colombian beat, has become so popular in Mexico that it can be heard on Spanish-language radio stations along the border as well as in any large U.S. city with a sizeable Mexican population.

Salsa es un estilo de música latinoamericana que surgió en Nueva York como resultado del choque de la música afrocaribeña traída por puertorriqueños, cubanos, colombianos, venezolanos, panameños y dominicanos, con el Jazz y el Rock de los norteamericanos. Desde ese entonces, vive deambulando de isla en isla, de país a país, incrementando de tal manera, su riqueza de elementos.

La salsa no es una moda pasajera, sinó una corriente musical establecida, de alto valor artístico y gran significado sociocultural: en ella no existen barreras de clase ni de edad.

La cumbia, en cambio, es el aire musical más representativo de Colombia. Es producto del aporte de tres culturas: negra africana, indígena y blanca. La cultura negra aportó la estructura rítmica y la percusión (tambores); la indígena aportó las flautas (caña de millo y las gaitas) y parte de la línea melódica; la blanca, por su parte, las variaciones melódicas y coreográficas, y la vestimenta de los danzantes. La cumbia expresa claramente el mestizaje de la cultura colombiana. El ritmo se ha popularizado también en México.

Definitivamente, pues, la música es parte de nuestra raíz, nos identifica con un determinado momento y lugar. Y, en gran medida, nos identifica como raza. La musica es, para nosotros los latinos, un vehículo de cultura, la esencia misma de lo que nos hace ser quienes somos.

Vocabulario Útil:

➤ **surgir:** to arise

➤ **resultado:** result

➤ **choque:** collision

➤ **afrocaribeño:** Afro-Caribbean

➤ **entonces:** time; period

➤ **deambular:** to roam

➤ **incrementar:** to increase

➤ **tal manera:** such a way

➤ **riqueza:** richness

➤ **moda:** fashion; style

➤ **pasajero:** fleeting (adjective)

➤ **sino:** but rather

➤ **corriente:** current; style

➤ **significado:** meaning

➤ **barrera:** barrier

➤ **clase:** here, social class

➤ **en cambio:** "in comparison"

➤ **aire:** aspect; "air"

➤ **representativo:** representative

➤ **aporte:** contribution

➤ **indígena:** indigenous; native

➤ **rítmica:** rhythmic

➤ **vestimenta:** clothing; costumes

➤ **definitivamente:** undoubtedly

➤ **pues:** then

➤ **raíz:** root

➤ **determinado:** certain; determined

➤ **raza:** race (ethnicity)

➤ **vehículo:** vehicle

Análisis del Texto

¡Fantástico! Now, let's look a little closer:

➤ *desde ese entonces*

You probably know the word *entonces* as "then" or "so," as in *Entonces, ¿quién me va a llevar al concierto?* ("So, who's going to take me to the concert?") But *entonces* has a secondary meaning as "time" or "period" in phrases such as this one: *En aquel entonces todavía era soltero* = "At that (distant) time I was still a bachelor."

➤ *vive deambulando*

I'll bet you weren't expecting to see the present participle being used with *vivir* as a helping verb.

Haz Clic Aquí

More Latin music Web sites include todomusica.hypermart.net/ links/Latina/Salsa_y_Merengue, www.hispanico.com/en/musica/ latina/index.html, www.artelatino. com/nuestramusica/muestras.html, and www. picadillo.com

Cultura Latina

The *corrido* is a story/song form similar to the American country music ballads. *Corridos* became popular in Mexico during the revolution as a means of retelling historic events or passing along folklore, or as a narrative of battles and revolutionary heroes. Today, any person or event can be the subject of a *corrido;* the lyrics may be satirical, political, or tragic.

It isn't common, but because the verb *vivir* here implies action or motion, it's a natural fit with the present participle: *Vivo durmiendo* = "I'm walking through my life asleep."

➤ *en ella no existen barreras de clase ni de edad*

Just a quick reminder that you'll need to look all the way back to the beginning of the previous sentence to find the noun that is linked to *ella.* Notice here also the use of *ni* for "nor," and that the *de* is repeated.

➤ *la negra africana, la indígena y la blanca*

Notice how much work the writer is getting out of *la.* It is standing in for *cultura,* linked by gender, three times. We could add the word *cultura* in if we wanted to (*la cultura negra africana, la cultura indígena,* and so on), but *la* (or *el,* if it had been a masculine noun) can do the job all by itself once the subject has been stated.

➤ *por su parte*

This is just a way of setting the third element (*la cultura blanca*) a little farther from the first two elements. *Por su parte* means "for its part" but can often be left out of a translation because it usually doesn't add to the meaning of the text. It's a literary device that makes the writer sound smarter.

➤ *definitivamente, pues, la música es parte*

The little word *pues* usually means "well." *Pues, lamento haberme olvidado de los boletos del concierto* means "Well, I'm sorry I forgot the concert tickets." However, at other times *pues* means "then," as it does here: "Without a doubt, then, music is part ...."

➤ *la esencia misma*

You know that *mismo* means "same," but it also can be translated under certain circumstances as "very": *Aquí mismo* means "this very place"; *Eso mismo me dijo* means "He said that very thing to me." In *la esencia misma,* the best translation would be "the very essence," not "the same essence."

Gramática: Prefixes

Let's face it. There are tens of thousands of Spanish words out there, and it would be all but impossible to learn them all. In fact, nobody knows them all. I certainly don't.

But I'm going to share a few tricks with you that can help you expand your vocabulary without having to memorize long lists of words.

Spanish, like English, utilizes many prefixes and suffixes to create new words or to alter the meaning of existing ones. With this in mind, one of the most efficient ways to expand your Spanish vocabulary is to learn the meanings of the various prefixes and suffixes. In this chapter, we'll examine the prefixes; in the next two chapters, we'll tackle the suffixes.

Using Prefixes

You probably already know that a prefix is a letter, particle, or mini-word that can be affixed to the beginning of another word. We use many of them in English: *pre–, sub–, anti–, ex–, ob–, in–,* and so on. Many of these English prefixes are the same (or darn close) in Spanish. This is because most English and Spanish prefixes come from Latin or Greek (we talked about the similarities between the two languages back in Chapter 2, "A Closer Look"). So, in most cases, you'll already know what a prefix means in Spanish because it will sound and look a lot like the corresponding English prefix.

Here's a list of some of the more common prefixes. The meaning of the Spanish examples should be obvious to you:

Common Prefixes

Prefix	Meaning	Example
ante–	before	*antemano*
anti–	against	*antibiótico*
auto–	self	*autoservicio*
bi–, bis–, biz–	two	*bilateral*
cent–	hundred/hundredth	*centavo*
contra–	against	*contrario*
com–, con–	with	*communidad*
de–, des–	take apart; "un"	*desempleado*
entre–	among, between	*entrevista*
ex–	out	*extraer; éxodo*
homo–	same	*homogenizado*
i–, im–, in–	opposite of	*increíble*
inter–	between, among	*intercambio*
mal–, mala–	bad	*malévolo*

continues

Common Prefixes (continued)

Prefix	Meaning	Example
meta–	beyond	*metafísico*
mono–	one	*monolingüe*
para–	together, with	*paramédico*
poli–	many	*polifónico*
pre–	before	*precertificado*
pro–	in favor of (to propose)	*proponer*
re–	with intensity	*revisión; refreír*
re–	again	*repasar* (review)
semi–	medium; half	*semiautomático*
seudo–	false	*seudónimo*
sobre–, super–	above; superior	*superficial*
sub–	under	*subterráneo*
tele–	at a distance	*telescopio*
uni–	one; singular	*unidimencional*

Haz Clic Aquí

For a more complete list of prefixes, visit www.arcom.net/belca/como_esc/c_prefijos.html. The site also tells you if the prefix is from Latin or Greek. (I'm sure you're dying to know!)

Cielito Lindo

I'm not sure why, but of all the lovely songs sung in Spanish, *Cielito Lindo* ("Beautiful Heaven") seems to be the most recognizable to Americans. The song was popularized in the 1940s by Hollywood star Deanna Durbin. But maybe that antacid commercial from the 1980s is to blame? Who knows ....

Either way, it's not that great of a song, folks. In fact, if it weren't for the "Ay Ay Ay Ay" part, this tune would have died a quiet death at the end of the Mexican Revolution. But just get a few *gringos* together in a cantina, add a couple rounds of tequila, and sooner or later someone starts bellowing "Ay Ay Ay Ay." And that's the only part that anyone knows!

Well, here are the real lyrics (some of them, anyway). If you plan on singing this little ditty anytime soon, why not impress your friends by performing the whole thing? You'll be forever remembered as the only one in the room who could get past the "Ay Ay Ay Ay" part.

De la Sierra Morena,
cielito lindo, vienen bajando
un par de ojitos negros,
cielito lindo, de contrabando.

Ay, ay, ay, ay,
canta y no llores,
porque cantando se alegran,
cielito lindo, los corazones.

Pájaro que abandona,
cielito lindo, su primer nido,
si lo encuentra ocupado,
cielito lindo, bien merecido.

Ese lunar que tienes,
cielito lindo, junto a la boca,
no se lo des a nadie,
cielito lindo que a mi me toca.

Ay, ay, ay, ay,
canta y no llores,
porque cantando se alegran,
cielito lindo, los corazones.

Vocabulario Útil:

➤ **ay:** oh

➤ **venir bajando:** coming down

➤ **par:** pair

➤ **contrabando:** contraband

➤ **alegrarse:** to cheer up

➤ **nido:** nest

➤ **merecido:** deserved

➤ **lunar:** mole (on the skin)

➤ **a mi me toca:** it's my turn (for a kiss?)

Haz Clic Aquí

If your computer has audio capability and you need to hear the melody of *Cielito Lindo* again, visit www.n2.net/clairemont/Student/cielito.html.

Cultura Latina

Considered the most romantic music in the Latin world, the style known as *el trio* plays simple but beautiful music that usually combines vocal harmonies with romantic guitars. Most of the songs performed are *boleros*.

Risa del Día

This first joke almost appeared back in the chapter about religion. There are hundreds of *San Pedro* (Saint Peter) jokes in Spanish, usually of the "Three guys die and go to heaven and meet Saint Peter at the pearly gates" variety. The last of the three usually receives some undeserved injustice. As always, *chistes verdes* abound. But this one had a musical punch line, so I've included it here. No offense meant to any fellow musicians out there ....

Cultura Latina

Considered the national music of Mexico, *mariachi* originated in the late nineteenth century as a traditional folk music form. The music evolved into a symphonic ensemble that included harp, trumpet, violin, *guitarrón*, and *vihuela* (small guitar). The outfits—typically tight pants, short jackets, and big sombreros— were derived from the first Mexican *charros*, or cowboys.

Haz Clic Aquí

Interested in more information about mariachi music? Visit www.elmariachi.com, the Internet's most comprehensive mariachi Web site.

San Pedro está recibiendo a los recién llegados a las puertas del cielo, y el primero viene de Texas. "¿Dime, que hacías en vida?" pregunta San Pedro.

El tejano responde, "Bueno, yo extraía petróleo, me hice rico, pero no me senté en los laureles—Repartí todo mi dinero entre toda mi familia, de forma tal que están aseguradas las próximas tres generaciones".

San Pedro responde, "Eso está muy bién. ¡Que pase el siguiente!"

El segundo de la fila había escuchado la conversación y dijo, "Yo gané mucho dinero en la bolsa, pero no quise beneficiarme de ello yo sólo, como hizo el tejano. Así que doné cinco millones a la caridad".

"Maravilloso" dice San Pedro. "Adelante. ¿Quién sigue?"

El tercero también había oído todo, así que dijo tímidamente, "Bueno, yo sólo gané quinientos dólares en toda mi vida".

"¡Cielos!" dice San Pedro. "¿Y qué instrumento tocabas?"

Vocabulario Útil:

➤ **recién llegados:** new arrivals

➤ **tejano:** Texan

➤ **extraer:** to extract

➤ **sentarse en los laureles:** to rest on one's laurels

➤ **repartir:** to distribute

- ➤ **el siguiente:** the next guy
- ➤ **fila:** line
- ➤ **beneficiarme:** to benefit
- ➤ **caridad:** charity
- ➤ **maravilloso:** marvelous
- ➤ **quién sigue:** who's next?
- ➤ **tímidamente:** timidly; with shyness
- ➤ **¡Cielos!:** Heavens!
- ➤ **instrumento:** instrument
- ➤ **tocar:** to play an instrument

Cultura Latina

Perhaps the most well-known form of Spanish music is *el flamenco*. Once considered a low art form, *flamenco* was all but banned during Franco's 40-year reign. But today *flamenco* music and dance have become world-famous, due in part to *flamenco* supergroups such as the Gypsy Kings.

Algo Nuevo

Also called Latino rock, *rock en español* covers several musical styles, from the milder rock-reggae to Spanish hip-hop. In the 1980s and 1990s, new musical fusions emerged that mixed Latin beats with urban elements of hip-hop, rap, house, techno, funk, and more. The lyrics are in Spanish, English, and Spanglish.

El Cuiz

No quiz today .... Go listen to some music instead!

Tareas

1. Go to your local music store and see what's available in the Latin section. Ask about flamenco music as well. But before you spend a lot of *dinero,* see if your local library has any tapes or CDs that you can check out for free.

2. Go online and search for more Web sites about Spanish or Latin American music. It won't take you long to find many good sites in both English and Spanish.

3. Memorize (or at least become familiar with) as many prefixes as you can. Create sentences using words from this chapter (or your dictionary) that begin with a prefix that you learned here.

The Least You Need to Know

➤ There are many different styles of music in Spain and Latin America: *cumbia, bolero, salsa,* and *merengue,* just to name a few.

➤ Prefixes build Spanish words and can help you increase your vocabulary more easily than memorizing long lists of words.

➤ *Cielito Lindo* has more words than just the *"Ay ay ay ay"* part.

Chapter 21

El Fútbol

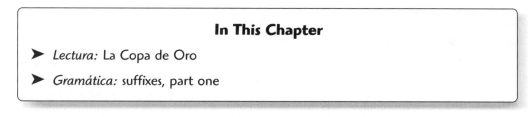

In This Chapter

➤ *Lectura:* La Copa de Oro

➤ *Gramática:* suffixes, part one

In terms of mass appeal and overall participation, sports in Spain and Latin America basically comes down to one thing: *fútbol* (a.k.a. soccer). Sure, *beisbol* is also a serious sport in the Caribbean and parts of Central America. And, yes, here and there, other sports such as rugby, jaialai, horse racing, and basketball are also quite popular. But no other sport—not even bull fighting—can evoke such passion as soccer, in spite of the fact that the game was originally introduced to the Spanish-speaking world by the English.

El Juego Nacional

Children seem to start kicking the soccer ball around practically from the day they learn to walk. Everyone is proud of their national teams and the skill of their players. Universities and cities compete in national championships, and national teams are formed to compete internationally. An important victory can provoke mass hysteria and spontaneous celebrations across the country.

Unfortunately, sometimes *el fútbol* can be taken a bit too seriously, as was evidenced during the 1994 World Cup when a Colombian player was assassinated after accidentally kicking the ball into his own goal during a game against the United States. The loss of an important tournament can have serious repercussions and can even impact a country's economy, suicide rate, and national elections. The bottom line seems to be that it's not how you play the game that counts, but whether you win.

Lectura: La Copa de Oro

Several international tournaments are played in professional soccer. The following text discusses Mexico's disappointing performance against Canada during the Gold Cup playoffs:

Haz Clic Aquí

The International Soccer Federation, known as FIFA (for its French title *Fédération Internationale de Football Association*), maintains its own Web page. You can review the rules of the game and hundreds of important statistics in both English and Spanish at www.fifa2.com.

Cultura Latina

The first World Cup competition was held in 1930 and was won by Uruguay. "*El equipo charrúa*" (a.k.a. the Uruguayans) won again in 1950. Most of the other World Cup games have been won by Argentina, Brazil, and Italy. The World Cup is held every four years.

La Selección de México tuvo un sorpresivo y triste adiós de la Copa de Oro, al caer 2–1 ante Canadá, un rival chico que hizo ver muy mal a los verdes.

México, tres veces campeón de este certamen, tuvo que hacer las maletas en forma prematura, pues casi nadie esperaba que no llegara ni siquiera a la Semifinal del torneo en la que estuvo rodeado de rivales con una calidad supuestamente inferior a la suya.

Antes de los dos minutos del primer tiempo extra el canadiense Richard Hastings anotó el gol de oro con un tiro de zurda por arriba de Óscar "Conejo" Pérez, con lo que culminó un fugaz contragolpe luego de que el equipo de la hoja de maple comenzó mal contra el equipo méxicano, que había cobrado un tiro de esquina.

Los más de 18 mil espectadores que estaban reunidos en el estadio, casi todos ellos mexicanos, reaccionaron con estupefacción ante la anotación.

Mientras que "El Conejo" permanecía congelado en su área y sus demás compañeros salían cabizbajos, en cuestión de segundos, los elementos canadienses se trepaban unos a otros en el suelo en señal de festejo, y Hasting permanecía con los brazos en alto.

México llevó en su pecado una gran penitencia, ya que tuvo el balón durante casi todo el partido, pero casi nunca se atrevió a tirar al arco, si acaso se acercó con un envío en la primera parte que el arquero Forrest le sacó con apuros a Francisco Palencia.

Hasta este lamentable partido el futuro pareció prometedor para un Tricolor que no veía en Canadá a un rival suficientemente peligroso. Pero en lo que ha sido un torneo de sorpresas, el fantasma de lo insospechado parecía rondar en el ambiente y eso se hizo realidad cuando al minuto 83 Martin Nash dio un centro desde la derecha que ni Claudio Suárez ni Rafael Márquez pudieron evitar que fuera rematado por Carlo Corazzin, cuyo cabezazo produjo el 2–1.

Vocabulario Útil:

- **selección:** select team
- **sorpresivo:** surprising
- **Copa de Oro:** Gold Cup
- **campeón:** champion
- **certamen:** competition; contest
- **hacer las maletas:** to pack (their) bags
- **prematuro:** premature
- **torneo:** tournament
- **rodear:** to surround
- **supuestamente:** supposedly
- **tiempo extra:** overtime
- **anotar:** to note; to rack up a goal
- **zurda:** left; from the left foot
- **"Conejo":** a nickname, "the Rabbit"
- **culminar:** to culminate; to end
- **fugaz:** very fast
- **contragolpe:** counterattack
- **cobrado:** here, "made a goal successfully"
- **tiro:** shot
- **esquina:** corner
- **espectador:** spectator

- **reunir:** to come together; to meet
- **estadio:** stadium
- **reaccionar:** to react
- **estupefacción:** astonishment; stupefaction
- **anotación:** racking up of goals
- **permancer:** to remain
- **congelado:** frozen
- **cabizbajo:** heads bowed
- **en cuestión de:** in a matter of
- **elementos:** here, team members
- **treparse:** to climb up
- **suelo:** ground
- **señal:** signal
- **festejo:** celebration
- **en alto:** up in the air
- **pecado:** sin
- **penitencia:** penitence
- **balón:** ball
- **atreverse:** to dare
- **tirar:** here, "to kick; to shoot"
- **arco:** net; goal
- **acaso:** here, "just barely"
- **acercarse:** to get close to
- **envío:** here, "a pass"
- **arquero:** goalie
- **le sacó:** took it out

➤ **con apuros:** hurriedly

➤ **lamentable:** unfortunately

➤ **partido:** game; match

➤ **suficientemente:** sufficiently

➤ **peligroso:** dangerous

➤ **de sorpresas:** "of surprises"

➤ **fantasma:** ghost

➤ **insospechar:** to not expect

➤ **rondar:** here, "to permeate"

➤ **ambiente:** environment; atmosphere

➤ **un centro:** pass to the center

➤ **rematado:** finished off; completed

➤ **cabezazo:** hit with the head

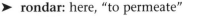

Acuérdate

In soccer, each team has 11 players on the field. Usually there are four forwards (*delanteros*), two players in midfield (*medio campistas*), and four defensive players in the back (*defensas*). Of course, the goalie guards the net (*portería, arco*), and is the only person who can touch the ball with his or her hands. The soccer field itself is delineated by sidelines, which are called *líneas de banda* in Spanish.

Análisis del Texto

It is time now for some analysis:

➤ *al caer 2–1 ante Canadá*

Here the contraction *al* before an infinitive means "upon doing X," as in *Al concluir el partido, nos fuimos del estadio* ("When the game ended [upon ending], we left the stadium").

➤ *hizo ver muy mal a los verdes*

Los verdes is just an elegant variation for the Mexican soccer team (they wear green uniforms). Notice the use of *hacer ver:* "… made the 'Greens' look very bad."

➤ *que había cobrado un tiro de esquina*

You'll find the verb *cobrar* used most often with money to mean "to take money" or "to charge": *Me cobraron tres pesos por los boletos* means "They charged me three pesos for the tickets." Here, *cobrar* has the meaning of "to register against the other team," or "to rack up a point." *Un tiro de esquina* is "a corner shot."

➤ *reaccionaron con estupefacción ante la anotación*

Note the use of the "Night-Before-Xmas" construction: "They reacted with disbelief."

➤ *los elementos canadienses se trepaban unos a otros en el suelo en señal de festejo*

This literally means, "The Canadians climbed on top of each other on the ground in celebration."

Algo Nuevo

Notice the construction *en form prematura* from the *lectura*. This is an adverbial phrase and means "prematurely." Such constructions (*en forma X, de manera X*) are common in Spanish and usually are translated with a regular adverb in English. So, *Maradona envió el balón de manera muy rápida* should not be translated as "Maradona passed the ball in a very quick manner," but simply as "Maradona passed the ball very quickly." In the previous example, *en forma prematura* could have been written as *prematuramente*, but often the *–mente* adverbs are avoided because they can get a bit too long.

➤ *si acaso se acercó*

Acaso is one of those words with several lives. Sometimes the word *acaso* simply adds doubt or reinforces the uncertainty of a question: *¿No sabes acaso si el equipo brasileño ya llegó?* would be translated as "Do you happen to know if the Brazilian team already arrived?" The phrase *por si acaso* means "just in case." In this example, *acaso*, together with *si*, would be translated as "if they ever got near the goal at all." Look up *acaso* in your dictionary for additional examples.

Ten Cuidado

Elegant variation is very common in sports writing. Don't get thrown off by phrases such as *el equipo de la hoja de maple*. You could translate this as "the Maple Leaf team" if you wanted to, but in most situations, simply saying "the Canadians" would sound more natural in English.

➤ *un Tricolor que no veía en Canadá a un rival suficientemente peligroso*

Un Tricolor (there are three colors in the Mexican flag) refers to the Mexican team. It's just more elegant variation. Translated, this means: "A Mexican team who didn't think (see) that Canada was a sufficiently dangerous rival."

➤ *el fantasma de lo insospechado parecía rondar en el ambiente*

Here we have a Spanish metaphor—literally, "the ghost of the unsuspected seemed to permeate the atmosphere." Remember that you may have to look beyond the usual

Haz Clic Aquí

Visit www.maradona.com, a Web site "dedicated to the greatest soccer player of all time and to all those who grew with the magic of Maradona in their eyes." Although he isn't as popular as he once was, Maradona, who grew up in a poor district of Buenos Aires, is still considered by many to be one of the best soccer players who ever lived.

Ten Cuidado

Remember that although a suffix may look exactly the same in English and Spanish, the two are not pronounced the same: For example, *–ble* is "bull" in English and "blay" in Spanish.

meanings of words to understand what is being talked about, and that metaphors and flowery language are common in Spanish.

➤ *no pudieron evitar que fuera rematado por Carlo Corazzin, cuyo cabezazo produjo el 2–1*

Take a quick look at that past subjunctive (*fuera*): "They couldn't avoid that it (the center kick from the left) was finished off by Carlo Carazzin, whose (hit with the) head produced the 2–1." *Evitar* has the effect of placing an impersonal desire (that an event should not happen) on something else, so we need the subjunctive after it: *El medio campista no pudo evitar que se le quitara el balón* = "The mid-field player couldn't avoid having the ball taken from him."

Gramática: Suffixes, Part One

Suffixes are exactly like prefixes, with one major difference: They always show up late at parties. You already know many suffixes, though you may not have realized it. Each suffix has a particular role to play and can alter or expand the meaning of a word.

Unfortunately, the use of suffixes is not an exact science, and it isn't always possible to know what a word means simply by knowing the root word and the suffix. Still, a suffix usually can point you in the right direction and can be a wonderful tool in understanding and creating new words.

We'll be looking at suffixes in both this chapter and the next. Let's begin with a list of suffixes that are cognates of English. The examples should be self-explanatory:

Some Suffix Examples

Suffix	English	Examples
–aje	*–age*	*garaje*
–algia	*–algia*	*nostalgia*
–ancia	*–ance/ancy*	*discrepancia*

Suffix	English	Examples
–arquía	–archy	*anarquía*
–ario	–ary	*sumario*
–ático	–atic	*fanático*
–bio	–b/–ian	*microbio; amfibio*
–ble	–ble	*razonable*
–cida	–cide	*insecticida*
–cidio	–cide	*suicidio*
–ción	–tion	*infección*
–culo	–cle	*obstáculo*
–cultura	–culture	*agricultura*
–cracia	–cracy	*democracia*
–crecía	–cracy	*hipocrecía*
–crata	–crat	*demócrata*
–dad	–ity	*libertad*
–dor	–tor	*pintor*
–endo	–endous	*estupendo*
–esa	–ess	*princesa*
–ectomía	–ectomy	*apendectomía*
–endo	–end	*dividendo*
–fico/a	–fic	*magnífico*
–filo/ia	–phile	*bibliofilo*
–fobia	–phobia	*agorafobia*
–fóbico/a	–phobic	*claustrofóbico*
–fono	–phone	*gramófono*
–génico	–genic	*fotogénico*
–iatra	–ician	*pediatra*
–icio/a	–ice	*justicia; servicio*
–ico	–ic/ical	*rústico; práctico*
–íficar	–ify	*identificar*
–ismo	–ism	*comunismo*
–ista	–ist	*artista*
–ita	–ite	*israelita*
–itis	–itis	*artritis*
–itud	–tude	*actitud*
–iz	–ess	*actriz*
–izo	–ish	*rojizo*

continues

Some Suffix Examples (continued)

Suffix	English	Examples
–logo	–logist	*antropólogo*
–ograma	–ogram	*cardiograma*
–ónimo	–onym/–mous	*sinónimo*
–nomo	–omer	*astrónomo*
–or/a	–er/or	*doctor*
–oso/a	–ous	*escandaloso*
–tivo	–tive	*representativo*
–tomía	–tomy	*anatomía*
–torio	–tory	*laboratorio*
–voro	–vorous	*omnívoro*

Risa del Día

Soccer is especially popular in Argentina. The following joke seems slightly more humorous because it's told in the *vos* form of address, which is common in Argentina. Notice that *escuchame* ("es cu CHA me") and *querés* are the imperative forms when using *vos*. Normally, these would be *escúchame* and *quieres*. *Jugás* is the *vos* present indicative, which in most places would be *juegas*:

➤ *Dos amigos:*

—*Ché Ernesto, escuchame … ¿en el cielo habrá cancha de fútbol?*

—*Yo creo que sí, Jorge, porque si allá todo es perfecto, tiene que haber cancha de fútbol.*

—*Bueno, hagamos una cosa. El primero que muera que se lo diga al otro, ¿eh?*

—*Listo, quedamos así.*

Al cabo de unos años, Jorge muere. Al día siguiente, Ernesto escucha una voz de ultratumba:

—*¡Joooorge, Joooorge, Joooorge! ¡soy Ernesto!*

—*¿Qué querés?*

—*Te tengo dos noticias, una buena y otra mala …. ¿La buena?*

—*Que yo tenía razón, en el cielo hay una cancha espectacular, con plateas, un pasto perfecto y unas instalaciones alucinantes.*

—*¿Y la noticia mala?*

—*Que vos jugás mañana a las 11:00.*

Acuérdate

The word for referee in Spanish is *árbitro*. In soccer, *el árbitro* keeps time on his own watch, not on an official time clock as in most other games.

Vocabulario Útil:

➤ **ché:** "hey" (in Argentina)

➤ **cancha:** field (for sport)

➤ **listo:** here, "all right"

➤ **al cabo:** at the end

➤ **ultratumba:** beyond the grave

➤ **plateas:** benches; bleachers

➤ **pasto:** grass; turf

➤ **instalaciones:** buildings; equipment

➤ **alucinante:** amazing; incredible

El Cuiz

Give the Spanish equivalents of the following words. Any cheating will result in a penalty kick against your team:

1. to surround _____

2. supposedly _____

3. overtime _____

4. to culminate; to end _____

5. surprising _____

6. champion _____

7. competition; contest _____

8. to pack one's bags _____

9. stadium _____

10. to react _____

11. astonishment; stupefaction _____

12. ground _____

13. signal _____

14. celebration _____

15. premature _____

16. tournament _____

17. net; goal _____

18. to get close to _____

19. shot _____

20. corner _____

21. to come together; to meet _____

22. in a matter of _____

23. to climb up _____

24. ghost _____

25. environment; atmosphere _____

26. finished off; completed _____

27. ball _____

28. to dare _____

29. field (for sport) _____

30. at the end _____

31. goalie _____

32. hurriedly _____

33. game; match _____

34. sufficiently _____

35. dangerous _____

36. hit with the head _____

37. to produce; to make _____

38. grass; turf _____

Tareas

1. Visit www.fifa2.com and learn more about the rules of soccer. Read as much as you can in Spanish, and use the English part of the site if you get stuck. If you can't get online, look up soccer ("football" for those of you not in the United States) in an encyclopedia.

2. Write the Spanish suffixes in this chapter on note cards. On the other side, write the English equivalent. Go through the cards and learn the suffixes well enough to recognize them when you see them.

The Least You Need to Know

➤ *Fútbol* is generally the most popular team sport in the Spanish-speaking world.

➤ As with prefixes, many suffixes that come from Greek or Latin are English cognates.

➤ Suffixes build Spanish words and can help you increase your vocabulary more easily than memorizing long vocabulary lists.

Chapter 22

Artesanías Mexicanas

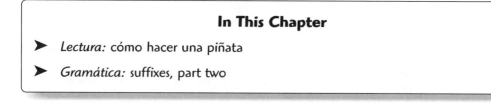

In This Chapter

➤ *Lectura:* cómo hacer una piñata

➤ *Gramática:* suffixes, part two

Mexico produces a broad and most beautiful collection of handcrafted objects. Handicrafts are known collectively as *artesanías,* and someone who makes them is an *artesano* or *artesana.*

Las Artesanías Mexicanas

Each region of Mexico specializes in a particular craft. For example, many ceramic items are made in the state of Jalisco, most notably in the town of Tonalá, which has been long considered as an important center for handicrafts. In the state of Chihuahua, near Casas Grandes, local potters have revived the ancient art of pottery making, known as *alfarería,* in the style of the ancient Paquimé and Mimbreño peoples. In the 1960s, the Seri Indians of Isla Tiburón (located between coastal Sonora and Baja California) began carving figurines in ironwood, depicting natural motifs such as fish, dolphins, whales, turtles, and bears. These figurines have become very popular in recent years, and although their supply of ironwood has dwindled, a few hundred Seri Indians still carve the wooden figurines.

The state of Oaxaca is famous for its brightly colored animal figurines, known as *alebrijes,* and for its *tapetes,* or "woven rugs." The Zapotec Indians are one of the few remaining Native American cultures in Mexico who are still dedicated to the fine art of

Haz Clic Aquí

If you are interested in *artesanías* but are unable to travel to Mexico any time soon, you can see (and even purchase) handicrafts online at www.tezontle.com.mx/Default.htm, www.mexcrafts.com.mx, www.artmexhandicrafts.com, http://xaac.com/mayablue/textiles.htm, www.tucson.com/joba www.mexonline.com/crafts.htm, or www.bazardemexico.com.

Cultura Latina

The village of Tlaquepaque, located just outside Guadalajara, is one of Mexico's largest markets for *artesanías*. Over the years, Tlaquepaque has attracted many of Mexico's most talented *artesanos* and has developed a reputation for the quality and diversity of its wares. You'll find everything from ceramics, to paper maché, to handblown glassware. If you're ever in Guadalajara, a trip to Tlaquepaque is a must.

weaving. Their *tapetes* are considered to be among the finest hand-woven carpets in the world and are highly sought after—not only in the United States, but also around the world. In other states, such as Puebla, Guerrero, and Chiapas, *artesanos* produce a large variety of items made of ceramic, clay, paper maché, glass, tin, wood, wool, straw, stone, metal, and many other materials.

Lectura: Cómo Hacer una Piñata

You probably already know what a *piñata* is. The *piñata* is hung high from a pole or tree by a rope. As it swings from side to side, children put on blindfolds and swing sticks at it until the poor *piñata* is ruptured and its concealed treats fall to the ground. When that happens, children scramble in delightful pandemonium to pick up all the goodies.

While some *piñatas* are relatively simple, others may take weeks to complete and are truly works of art. The following text gives instructions on how to make one:

> *Hay piñatas de todos tamaños y figuras. Las más clásicas son flores, barcos, estrellas, loros, pavos reales, tecolotes, gallos, gallinas, patos, guajalotes, borregos, burros, toros, elefantes, pescados, frutas y vegetales, aeroplanos, payasos, y personajes de moda o políticos.*

> *La piñata tradicional se hace con una olla. Existen pueblos de alfareros que se dedican a hacer "ollas piñateras", como ellos las llaman. Estas ollas llegan a los mercados a donde la gente puede adquirirlas. Posteriormente les aplican engrudo con el que pegan el papel periódico que servirá de base para darle la forma que se desea, usando papeles de colores más apropiados. Hoy día, también se fabrican muchas piñatas de papel y cartón solamente, pero son de una calidad inferior a la tradicional.*

> *Para hacer una piñata tradicional, siga los siguientes pasos:*

1. *Compre una olla piñatera.*

2. *Elija un diseño para su piñata y dibújelo en una hoja de papel en blanco.*

3. *Pegue papel periódico alrededor de la olla para así construir el modelo deseado, ya sea con cartoncillo o papel grueso, usando engrudo.*

4. *Cubra el armazón con papel de china enroscado, papel lustre o crepé.*

5. *De los extremos de la figura, cuelgue tiras largas multicolores de listón para darle mayor lucimiento.*

6. *Llene la piñata de galletas, dulces, cacahuates o frutas de la estación: naranjas, limones, mandarinas, jícamas, y otras.*

Cuando se va a romper la piñata, ésta se cuelga con un lazo sostenido desde sus dos extremos por personas que la mueven tratando de que no la rompan pronto. Por su parte, quienes intentan romperla, deben tener cubiertos los ojos, y les darán vueltas hasta hacerles perder la noción del espacio de manera que no sea fácil romperla.

Vocabulario Útil:

➤ **figura:** figure

➤ **clásico:** classic

➤ **pavo real:** peacock

➤ **tecolote:** owl

➤ **borrego:** lamb

➤ **guajalote:** turkey

➤ **alfarero:** potter

➤ **olla piñatera:** a pot used to form a *piñata*

➤ **posteriormente:** afterward

➤ **engrudo:** paste (flour and water)

➤ **papel periódico:** newspaper

➤ **apropiado:** fitting; appropriate

➤ **calidad:** quality

➤ **siguiente:** following

➤ **paso:** step

➤ **elegir:** to choose

➤ **diseño:** design

➤ **hoja:** page

➤ **en blanco:** blank

➤ **pegar:** to affix; to glue on

➤ **alrededor:** around

➤ **ya sea:** whether it be

➤ **cartoncillo:** construction paper

➤ **grueso:** thick

➤ **cubrir:** to cover

➤ **armazón:** frame

➤ **papel de china enroscado:** coiled Chinese (rice) paper

➤ **papel lustre:** silver paper

➤ **extremo:** end

➤ **listón:** ribbon

➤ **lucimiento:** sparkle; brilliance

➤ **galleta:** cookie; biscuit

➤ **lazo:** a rope in a loop

➤ **sostener:** to hang; to hold

➤ **romper:** to break

➤ **dar vueltas:** to spin around

➤ **noción del espacio:** depth perception

Cultura Latina

Words like *tecolote* (owl) and *guajalote* (turkey) are ancient Nahuatl words passed down from the Aztecs. They are used primarily in Mexico. In most other countries, an owl is *un buho* (sometimes *una lechuza*), and a turkey is *un pavo*.

Ten Cuidado

The word *extremo* is an unreliable *amigo* in many situations. Yes, it is a cognate of the word "extreme" in English, and when used as an adjective, it does mean that: *un caso de extrema gravedad* means "an extremely serious case." But as a noun, it usually means "end," as we see in our *lectura*: *los extremos de la figura* means "the ends of the figure."

Análisis del Texto

Now let's take a closer look:

➤ *La piñata tradicional se hace con una olla*

The *se hace* is translated as "is made." It's a "*se* passive" construction: "The traditional *piñata* is made with a pot."

➤ *posteriormente les aplican engrudo*

Posteriormente looks like a fancy word, but all it means is "then or afterward." Don't try to translate this as "posteriorly."

➤ *servirá de base*

The preposition *de*, which normally might mean "of" or "from," should be translated here as "as." Thus, *servirá de base* would mean "will serve as a base." *Servir* can also take *para*, as in *Esta cosa no sirve para nada*, which means "This thing is useless (doesn't serve for anything)."

➤ *Cuando se va a romper la piñata, ésta se cuelga*

Here we have another example of a gender link: *ésta* refers back to *piñata*, and serves as a pronoun. So, this would translate as "When the *piñata* is going to be broken, it is hung ...." The sentence probably could be understood just fine without the *ésta*, but having the pronoun there makes the sentence sound a bit more formal.

➤ *Por su parte, quienes intentan romperla, deben tener cubiertos los ojos, y les darán vueltas hasta hacerles perder la noción del espacio de manera que no sea fácil romperla.*

This is quite a sentence, isn't it? Let's break it up. First, the *por su parte* is just there to set this sentence apart from the previous one. Before we were talking about the *piñata,* and now we're talking about the people who are going to swing at it. You could translate it as "for their part," or you could just leave it out.

Quienes means "those who." *Deben tener* means "should have." Notice that *cubiertos*, which means "covered," comes before the noun modified (*ojos*). The verb of the sentence, *ser*, is in the subjunctive (*sea*) because we do not know how many times they will have to turn the children around until they lose their depth perception. Translated, this sentence would mean

> "For their part, the people who are going to try to break the *piñata* should have their eyes covered and be spun around until they lose their depth perception so that it won't be easy to break it (the *piñata*)."

Acuérdate

The verb *tener* is actually a cognate for the verbal suffix "–tain" in English. So, "to detain" is *detener*; "to sustain" is *sostener*; "to maintain" is *mantener*; and "to retain" is *retener*.

Gramática: Suffixes, Part Two

Now let's get back to those darn suffixes. In addition to the many suffixes of Latin and Greek origin that Spanish shares with English, there are a number of suffixes that are used in Spanish alone.

For example, let's take the basic word *palo*, which means "stick" or "shovel." Add the suffix *–illo*, and we get *palillo*, which means "a toothpick." *Palito* could be a small shovel or a twig. If we add the ending *–eta* to *palo*, we get *paleta*, which in Mexico is a "Popsicle," and to an artist is a "palette" for mixing paint. If we add *–azo*, a suffix meaning "a hit or blow with," we get *palazo*, which could imply hitting something or someone with a shovel. If you hit somebody with your Popsicle, you'd be giving them a *paletazo*.

Or, how about the popular musical instrument *la guitarra*? If we add the augmentative suffix *–ón*, we get *guitarrón*, a very large guitar used in mariachi bands. We could add another suffix right on to this new word, such as *–ista*, and get *guitarronista*, a person who plays the *guitarrón*. Now, if our *guitarronista* has warm sentiments for his beloved *guitarrón*, he might refer to it lovingly as his *guitarroncito*. And if, after a long night playing in dusty cantinas he decides to hit one of the *trompetistas* over the head with his dear *guitarróncito*, we could say that he gave the trumpet player a *guitarroncitazo*.

The following sections cover a lot of suffixes, and you don't need to memorize all of them. Except for the more common ones, it is quite possible to live without them entirely. But your knowledge of Spanish will always remain incomplete if you don't at least have a passing knowledge of suffixes.

Ten Cuidado

The use and meaning of Spanish suffixes can be filled with subtleties. To use them effectively, you may need considerable practice talking with native speakers. Even if you follow the rules, you may find yourself conveying an unintended idea with the addition of a suffix. But words such as *poquito* and *muchísimo* are pretty standard and can be used at any time.

Acuérdate

Sometimes a diminutive can be added to a word that might seem to result in an oxymoron: *La casa está enormecita* means "The house is a little too enormous"; while *Los zapatos me quedan grandecitos* means "the shoes are just a little too big on me." Don't let this boggle your mind.

Diminutive Suffixes

Diminutive suffixes are common and are used to make a word refer to something smaller. The most common diminutive suffix is *–ito* (and its feminine equivalent, *–ita*). Thus, *un pájaro* is a "bird," and un *pajarito* is a "little bird." In English, we can also make a similar diminutive by adding *–y* or *–ie,* as in "birdie."

Sometimes several suffixes can be added for an increased effect: *poco → poquito → poquitito → poquititito.*

Diminutive suffixes also can be used to create terms of endearment. They can be added to a person's name (*Esteban → Estebanito; Lupe → Lupita*) or to any noun or adjective (*el niñito está pequeñito* = "The dear little boy is teeny weenie.").

Here are some of the more common diminutive suffixes with examples:

➤ **–ito, –cito, –ecito:** I'm sure that you've seen these already: Monosyllabic words that end in a consonant, and words containing diphthongs or that end in *–e* usually take *–cito* or *–ecito.* Thus, *flor* becomes *florecita,* which means "little flower"; *bebé* becomes *bebecito,* which means "a little baby"; and *puerta* becomes *puertecita,* which means "a little door." Notice that the ending must agree in gender with that of the original noun, except in words that end in "the wrong letter," such as *un problema → un problemita.*

➤ **–illo, –cillo:** These are similar to *–ito,* but not quite as common: *un poquillo* means "a little bit." The second version, *–cillo,* is used with multisyllabic words that are accented on the last syllable: *cartón* (cardboard) → becomes *cartoncillo* (construction paper).

➤ **–tico:** Much the same as *–ito,* this is used mostly in the Caribbean and especially in Costa Rica: *Espere un momentico por favor* means "Please wait one little moment."

➤ **–zuelo, –achuelo:** Not particularly common, these suffixes can be added to nouns and sometimes adjectives to create slightly smaller versions of larger things: *río* → *riachuelo* (brook or stream); *cazo* (saucepan) → *cazuela* (casserole dish).

Augmentative Suffixes

The augmentative suffixes are the opposite of diminutives. They have the effect of making something larger or more intense.

➤ **–ísimo:** You probably already know this superlative suffix, which is added to adjectives and some adverbs as an intensifier: *Te quiero muchísimo* means "I love you very much." Similarly, *Fue una tarea dificilísima* means "It was an extremely difficult task." You may even hear it used more than once in the same word, as in *muchisísimo*. The King of Spain isn't just *rico*, he's *riquisísimo*.

➤ **–ote, –ota:** These suffixes are added to nouns and adjectives: *grande* → *grandote* (huge); *perro* → *perrote* (big dog); *abrazo* (hug) → *abrazote* (a huge "bear" hug); *bandera* (flag) → *banderota* (a big flag or banner).

➤ **–ón, –ona:** These are similar to the previous suffixes: *libro* → *librón* (a large book). The *–ón* ending does not need to change to match the gender of the original word (*guitarra* → *guitarrón*), unless it is added to an animate noun (*mujer* → *mujerona*, which means "a big woman"). However, this suffix can also be used adjectivally, when the gender must match the noun described: *oreja* → *orejona* (describes a female with big ears), and *simpática* (friendly) → *simpaticona* (a very friendly girl/woman).

➤ **–azo:** This suffix generally means "a hit or blow with ...," as in *ladrillo* (brick) → *ladrillazo* (a hit with a brick.) The suffix can also be used simply as an augmentative: *hombre* → *hombrazo* (a big and, presumably, good man). *Ella le dio un telefonazo* would mean "She hit him with a telephone."

Cultura Latina

In Mexico and some other Latin countries, the word *ahorita* (*ahora + ita*) is common and can be used in a variety of ways. Depending on the context, *ahorita* can mean anything from "right away" to "in a while (could be hours later)." If you ask "When will (something) be ready?" and the response is *ahorita*, you may want to clarify exactly what the speaker means.

Cultura Latina

The *–tico* suffix is so popular in Costa Rica that *los costaricenses* are nicknamed *ticos*.

Pejorative Suffixes

The pejorative suffixes can be attached to words to indicate contempt or undesirability. They are not terribly common but are nonetheless good to know:

➤ **–uco, –uca, –ucho, –ucha:** *casa* → *casucha* (a house in disrepair); and *hermana* → *hermanuca* (a sister that you don't like).

➤ **–aco, –aca, –acho:** These suffixes usually are pejorative, as in *libraco*, which also means "a lousy book," or *poblacho* (from *pueblo*), which means "a one-horse town." The suffix *–aco* can also be seen as an adjectival ending with no negative connotation, as in *austríaco* (Austrian,) and *polaco* (Polish.)

➤ **–ejo/a:** Add these suffixes to make things smaller and bothersome: *animal* → *animalejo* (a little irritating animal); *calle* → *calleja* (a small, uninteresting street).

Acuérdate

Do you remember how some of the names in *Don Quixote* had a double meaning? Well, now you can see how Alonso Quijano used an augmentative suffix when he changed his name from Quijano to *Quixote*. The suffix makes his name bigger and stronger.

Miscellaneous Suffixes

Now let's look at the final suffixes in this chapter:

➤ **–ería:** This refers to a place where items are made or sold: *zapatería*; (shoe store or factory); *mueblería* (furniture store or factory). You already know *pizzeria* from Italian.

➤ **–dad:** This one corresponds to *–ity* in English. With it, you can create abstract nouns from adjectives: *generoso* (generous) → *generosidad* (generosity); *sensible* (sensitive) → *sensibilidad* (sensitivity.)

➤ **–aje:** This makes nouns from verbs and other nouns: *hospedar* (to provide with accommodations) → *hospedaje* (lodging); *aprendiz* (apprentice) → *aprendizaje* (apprenticeship).

➤ **–al, –tal:** These suffixes indicate a tree or grove: *manzana* → *manzanal* (apple orchard); and *café* → *cafetal* (coffee plantation). They can also be used figuratively to express abundance: *dinero* → *dineral* (a whole field of money).

➤ **–anza:** With this, you can make nouns from some verbs: *enseñar* → *enseñanza* (instruction).

Acuérdate

Le dio un telefonazo could also be a slangy way of saying "She gave him a phone call." Context, context, context!

It sometimes corresponds to *–ance* in English: *ordenar* (to order) → becomes *ordenanza* (ordinance).

➤ **–dura:** This suffix indicates the effect of an action: *picar* (to puncture; to bite) makes *picadura,* (a puncture or insect bite).

➤ **–ense:** This indicates place of origin: *nicaragüense* means "Nicaraguan."

➤ **–eo:** This indicates collective nouns, such as *papeleo,* which means "paperwork."

➤ **–ero:** This suffix has a variety of uses that expand on the meaning of the root word: *sombra* (shade) → *sombrero* (hat); *vaca* (cow) → *vaquero* (cowboy).

➤ **–eza:** With this, you can make abstract nouns from adjectives: *bello* (pretty) → *belleza* (beauty); *rico* (rich) → *riqueza* (richness or wealth).

Acuérdate

One good thing about knowing the Spanish suffixes is that you can avoid wasting time with your dictionary trying to look up suffixed words. Many of these words won't be in your dictionary anyway. If you know the definition of the root word, you will often be able to figure out what the suffixed word means without any additional research.

➤ **–edo/–eda:** These suffixes make collective nouns, often with trees: *roble* (oak tree) → *robledo* (oak grove); *álamo* (poplar tree) → *alameda* (poplar grove).

➤ **–erio:** This suffix appears in nouns derived from verbs or other nouns: *ministro* (government minister) → *ministerio* (government ministry); *imperar* (to rule; to prevail) → *imperio* (empire).

➤ **–ero, –era, –dero, –dera:** In nouns and adjectives, these suffixes express the idea of a trade, instrument, or place: *pan* → *panadero* (baker); *coche* → *cochera* (car port, or garage); *lavar* → *lavadero* (laundry room); *ropa* → *ropero* (wardrobe).

➤ **–ado, –ido:** These suffixes can express a certificate or degree, a similarity to a root word, or a sound: *dolor* (pain) → *dolorido* (painful); *doctor* → *doctorado* (Ph.D.); *maullar* (to meow) → *maullido* (a cat's meow).

➤ **–oso/–osa:** In adjectives derived from nouns or verbs, these suffixes indicate abundance of a condition: *furia* → *furioso* (furious); *contagiar* → *contagioso* (contagious).

➤ **–dor, –dora:** These suffixes show up in adjectives derived from verbs: *hablar* → *hablador/a* (talkative). They also appear in some nouns: *inspectar* → *inspector/a* (inspector).

Haz Clic Aquí

For a more complete list of suffixes, visit www.arcom.net/belca/como_esc/c_sufijos.html, or search for "Spanish suffixes" and surf through the generated Web sites.

Acuérdate

The common verb ending *–ear* is often used with coined verbs. as in *bacupear,* which means "to back up a computer file."

➤ **–és/esa:** These indicate place of origin or the language from that place: *danés* (Danish/Danish language); *escocés (*Scottish); *holandés (*from Holland/Dutch language).

➤ **–ada:** This one is similar to the English suffix *–ful,* as in *cuchara* (spoon) → *cucharada* (spoonful).

➤ **–udo, –uda:** In adjectives, these express abundance: *lana* (wool) → *lanudo* (wooly); *barba* (beard) → *barbudo* (a man with a big beard).

➤ **–ez:** This suffix shows up in abstract nouns, as in *escaso* (scarce) → *escasez* (scarcity).

➤ **–izo, –iza:** These suffixes appear in adjectives derived from other adjectives: *rojo* → *rojizo* (reddish); *enfermo* (sick) → *enfermizo* → (sickly).

Risa del Día

This chapter is getting pretty long, so your *chiste* for today will have to be short. I couldn't find any jokes about *artesanos*, probably because artisans are held in such high esteem. This joke is a bit off the wall:

> *El esposo se está bañando:*
>
> *María, ¿dónde está el champú?*
>
> *Ahí, delante de ti …*
>
> *Pero es que es para cabello seco y yo lo tengo mojado.*

Vocabulario Útil:

➤ **bañarse:** to bathe

➤ **delante de ti:** in front of you

➤ **cabello:** hair

➤ **seco:** dry

➤ **mojado:** wet

El Cuiz

Please provide the Spanish for these words. If you cheat, I'll steal your *piñata* and eat all its delicious contents by myself:

1. following _____

2. peacock _____

3. owl _____

4. potter _____

5. pots for *piñatas* _____

6. fitting; appropriate _____

7. quality figure _____

8. step _____

9. to choose _____

10. design _____

11. page _____

12. blank _____

13. afterward _____

14. newspaper _____

15. construction paper _____

16. thick _____

17. to cover _____

18. frame _____

19. end to affix; to glue on _____

20. around _____

21. whether it be _____

22. ribbon _____

23. sparkle; brilliance _____

24. to say goodbye _____

25. to hang; to hold _____

26. to break _____

27. to spin around _____

28. depth perception _____

29. wet _____

Tareas

1. Research Mexican handicrafts, either on the Internet or in your local library, and see what appeals to you. If you've got some extra cash, you can purchase *artesanías* from catalogs or over the Web.

2. Choose 20 vocabulary words (nouns and adjectives) and practice adding some of the suffixes that you learned here to these words. Then try to guess what they might mean, using the explanations here as your guide. If you know a native Spanish-speaker, ask that person how your newly "suffixed" words sound.

The Least You Need to Know

➤ Mexico produces many beautiful handcrafted objects known as *artesanías*.

➤ If you can't travel to Mexico, you can see and purchase *artesanías* over the Internet.

➤ Some Spanish suffixes do not have an equivalent cognate with an English suffix.

➤ Suffixes can be diminutive, augmentative, pejorative, adjectival, or nominative (make more nouns). They can also be used to create terms of endearment.

Los Viajes

I have some good news and some bad news. The good news is that there is no *lectura* in this chapter. You needed a break from all those readings, anyway. I've axed the dreaded *"El Cuiz,"* too. Even the grammar section is short. *¡Qué suerte!*

Of course, there is a price to pay for my generosity: This chapter contains challenging dialogues. Your mission, should you choose to accept it, is to read each dialogue aloud and see how much of it you understand. Underline or highlight any words that are new or unknown to you. Then read the English translation to see how you did.

Diálogo I: En el Aeropuerto Internacional de San José, Costa Rica

Mike has just arrived in San José, Costa Rica (not California!). Here is his conversation with the immigration officer:

Mike: *Buenas tardes, señor.*

El agente: *Buenas tardes. ¿De dónde es?*

Mike: *Soy de Australia.*

El agente: *Su pasaporte, por favor.*

Mike: *Sí, cómo no. Aquí lo tiene.*

El agente: *Muy bien. ¿Cuál es el motivo de su viaje a Costa Rica.*

Mike: *Será un viaje de placer. Tengo amigos aquí en San José, y he venido a vistarlos. También me gustaría hacer un viaje alrededor del país. Me encantaría ver los volcanes.*

El agente: *Claro, los volcanes son muy interesantes. ¿Por cuántos días permanecerá usted en el país?*

Mike: *Hasta el 3 de marzo. O sea, son 30 días en total, más o menos.*

El agente: *Bien. Su visa vencerá en 60 días. Espero que su estadía sea agradable.*

Mike: *Gracias. Disculpe, ¿me puede decir una cosa?*

El agente: *A ver …*

Mike: *¿Qué hora es aquí? Quiero ajustar mi reloj.*

El agente: *Ya son las 11:45.*

Mike: *Gracias, señor. Usted es muy amable.*

El agente: *No hay de qué.*

Translation:

Mike: Good afternoon, sir.

The agent: Good afternoon. Where are you from?

Mike: I'm from Australia.

The agent: Your passport, please.

Mike: Yes, of course. Here you go ("here you have it").

The agent: Very good. What is the reason for your trip to Costa Rica?

Mike: It will be a pleasure trip. I have friends here in San José, and I've come to visit them. I'd also like to take a trip around the country. I'd love to see the volcanoes.

The agent: Sure, the volcanoes are very interesting. How many days will you remain in the country?

Mike: Until March 3rd. In other words, it'll be 30 days all together, more or less.

The agent: All right. Your visa will expire in 60 days. I hope that you have a pleasant stay.

Mike: Thank you. Pardon me. Can you tell me something?

The agent: All right … ("let's see what it is …").

Mike: What time is it here? I want to adjust my watch.

The agent: It's 11:45 now.

Mike: Thank you, sir. You are very kind.

The agent: Don't mention it ("there is no need to thank me").

Acuérdate

If you are planning to travel, find out ahead of time what the visa requirements are for the countries you plan to visit. In most cases, you'll just need a valid passport. However, for some countries you may be required to have all your paperwork taken care of ahead of time.

If you found any words that were new or difficult in the previous dialogue, write them down. Look them up in your dictionary to see if these words have any secondary meanings.

Gramática: Interrogatives

You have already encountered most of these, so this may be a review. But just in case, let's take a quick look at those "question words" *una vez más*.

Notice that these interrogatives have *tildes* on them. I'll explain why they are required in a minute:

Interrogatives

Interrogative	Translation
¿quién?	who? or whom? (singular)
¿quiénes?	who? (plural)
¿qué?	what? or which? (singular and plural)
¿cuál?	which?
¿cuáles?	which? (plural)
¿cuándo?	when?
¿dónde?	where?
¿cómo?	how?

continues

Interrogatives (continued)

Interrogative	Translation
¿cuánto?	how much?
¿cuántos?	how many?
¿por qué?	why?

Here are a few sentences using interrogatives:

➤ **¿Quiénes estaban ahí en ese momento?** Who (plural) was there at that moment?

➤ **¿Quién va a llamar mañana?** Who will be calling tomorrow?

➤ **¿Qué tengo que hacer?** What do I have to do?

➤ **¿Dónde está la estación de policía más cercana?** Where is the nearest police station?

➤ **¿Cómo era el hombre que le asaltó?** What was the man like ("look like") who mugged you?

Cultura Latina

If you are looking for accommodations, it is quite acceptable to ask the receptionist to show you the room before you decide to take it. In Guatemala I once ended up in a room with a broken bed (no mattress), no bathroom facilities, and two rabid dogs just across the hall barking furiously at me through a half-torn chicken wire gate, ready to tear me to shreds at any moment. Guess I should have asked to see the room first ....

Now, as I mentioned before, you have no doubt seen some of these very same words without the *tilde*. This is because these words also work as relative pronouns. And what is a relative pronoun? Just a little word that hooks two clauses together: "the man *who* came to dinner"; "the house *which* is yellow"; "the person *whom* I saw yesterday."

To better illustrate this point, let's see what English would look like if we used *tildes* to distinguish between interrogatives and relative pronouns:

➤ *Where* do you live?

That's the house *where* I live.

➤ *Who* robbed you?

That's the guy *who* robbed me.

➤ *Which* guy is it?

I already told you *which* guy it is.

➤ *When* did this happen?

It happened *when* I was going home.

➤ *Why* did he do it?

I don't know *why* he did it.

➤ *How* did it happen?

I don't know *how* it happened.

See what I mean? In Spanish, when these words function as question words, you need to write the *tilde* on them. When they don't, the *tilde* isn't necessary.

Diálogo II: **El Planetario de Madrid**

Here we have a tourist asking for directions:

El turista: *Disculpe, señor.*

El madrileño: *Sí, dígame. ¿En qué le puedo ayudar?*

El turista: *Muchas gracias, señor. Es que soy turista y estoy en Madrid por primera vez.*

El madrileño: *Muy bien. ¿A dónde quiere ir?*

El turista: *Voy al Planetario de Madrid. Quiero ver el nuevo programa. Se llama La Vida Más Allá de la Tierra.*

El madrileño: *¡Qué casualidad! Soy astrónomo. Sé perfectamente donde está el planetario.*

El turista: *No me diga. Entonces, ¿cómo se llega al lugar?*

El madrileño: *Mire, si quiere ir en el metro, súbase en la línea 6. Bájese en la estación de Méndez Álvaro. Si va a ir en autobús, puede tomar la línea 148, que es la que va de la Plaza de Callao al Puente de Vallecas.*

El turista: *Muy bien. Muchísimas gracias por su ayuda. Ahí veo una parada de autobuses.*

El madrileño: *Espero que disfrute del programa. Adiós.*

El turista: *Adiós.*

Ten Cuidado

The *tildes* on the interrogatives don't change their pronunciation; they are important only when writing the language. There is no need to say these words any differently. But don't forget to write the *tildes* when these words are used as interrogatives.

Acuérdate

Remember that the words for "why" and "because" are practically the same. Literally, *¿por qué?* means "for what?" When written as one word and without the *tilde*, *porque* means "because." So, *¿Por qué lo hiciste?* means "Why did you do it?"; *Porque sí* means "Just because."

Ten Cuidado

Remember that when *que* is used in expressions of emotion or surprise, you must write the *tilde*: *¡Qué bonita!* means "How pretty!" *¡Qué lástima!* means "What a shame!" *Que* also requires a *tilde* when used as a question word. But don't write the *tilde* when it is used as a relative pronoun: *El hombre que vive aquí* means "the man who (or "that") lives here."

Translation:

The tourist: Excuse me, sir.

Person from Madrid: Yes, tell me, how can I help you?

The tourist: Thank you very much, sir. You see, I'm a tourist and I'm in Madrid for the first time.

Person from Madrid: All right. Where are you trying to get to?

The tourist: I'm going to the Madrid Planetarium. I want to see the new program. It's called "Life Beyond the Earth."

Person from Madrid: What a coincidence! I'm an astronomer. I know perfectly well where the planetarium is.

The tourist: You don't say. So, how do you get to the place?

Person from Madrid: Look, if you want to go by metro, you're going to get on line 6. Get off at the Méndez Álvaro station. If you're going to go by bus, you can take line 148, which (is the one that) goes from the Plaza de Callao to Puente de Vallecas.

The tourist: Very good. Thank you very much for your help. I see a bus stop over there.

Person from Madrid: I hope you enjoy the program. Goodbye.

The tourist: Goodbye.

Algo Nuevo

The verb *controlar* borders on being a false *amigo*, as it usually means "to check or inspect." When tickets are checked on an airplane or bus, it is known as *control de boletos*. If someone says "*Necesito controlar su boleto,*" he doesn't mean "I need to control your ticket," but simply "I need to check it to see if you actually paid for this trip."

Risa del Día

If you've ever lost your luggage during a trip, you'll appreciate the following *chiste:*

Un hombre en el mostrador de una aerolínea, despachando su equipaje:

—Mire, quiero que me manden la valija grande a Londres. La más chiquita a Miami. Los dos bolsos de lona mándemelos a Río y el baúl a Beirut.

Disculpeme, pero eso no es posible, señor.

—¿Cómo que no?, si ya lo hicieron la última vez que viajé … ¡y sin mi permiso!

Vocabulario Útil:

- ➤ **mostrador:** counter
- ➤ **aerolínea:** airline
- ➤ **despachar:** to dispatch; to take care of; to send
- ➤ **equipaje:** luggage
- ➤ **valija:** suitcase
- ➤ **Londres:** London
- ➤ **lona:** canvas; cloth
- ➤ **baúl:** chest
- ➤ **¿Cómo que no?:** "What do you mean it isn't?"

El Cuiz

Today's quiz is cancelled due to inclement weather. Lucky you! Feel free to create your own if you want to practice the vocabulary in this chapter.

Tareas

1. Review both the Spanish and the English translations of the four dialogues in this chapter, and write down any words or phrases that are new or interesting to you. Use your dictionary for additional definitions.

2. Create questions asking "who, what, where, when, why," and so on. Use the examples in this chapter as a guide, and consult your dictionary for additional words. Don't forget to write those *tildes*.

Acuérdate

Bajar means "to get down," but from a vehicle, it means "to get off." If you want the bus driver to let you out, yell *¡Baja!* or *¡Bajan!* (not *¡Bajo!*).

The Least You Need to Know

➤ Interrogative pronouns and relative pronouns are the same, except that the interrogatives need *tildes*.

➤ The *tildes* do not change the pronunciation of the interrogative words.

➤ When looking for accommodations, it is quite acceptable to ask the receptionist to show you the room before you decide to take it.

Part 5

Money, Science, Politics, and Transportation

¡Felicitaciones! *You've almost made it to the end ....*

This part contains some of the most challenging lecturas *in the book. We'll look at computers, business correspondence, a political document, and other complex texts.*

After you finish the book, I strongly suggest that you go back and read some of the earlier lecturas *again. You'll be amazed at how much easier they are now. Once you feel comfortable with the* lecturas *in the book, you'll be more than ready to tackle Spanish at an advanced level.* ¡Buena suerte!

El Comercio

In This Chapter

➤ *Lectura:* correspondencia mercantil

➤ *Gramática:* Polite Phrases and Expressions

➤ *Diálogo:* en el banco Bantico

➤ Idiot's guide to idioms

The United States is Latin America's most important trading partner. Each year the United States imports billions of dollars in goods and raw materials from Latin America and Spain, including textiles, footwear, fruits, vegetables, wine, precious metals, and minerals, just to name a few. The United States also exports many products to the Spanish-speaking world, in addition to the millions of dollars spent annually by American tourists traveling "south of the border."

El Comercio

In 1993, Canada, Mexico, and the United States signed a mutual trade agreement known as the North American Free Trade Agreement (NAFTA), thus creating what has been called the "largest free-trade zone in the world." Many U.S. companies have set up assembly plants across the Mexican border, known as *maquiladoras* (or simply as *maquilas*). A significant number of American-owned high-tech companies have also established sizable operations in many Latin American countries, as well as in Spain.

Even if you never find yourself in a position to conduct official business in Spanish, a basic familiarity with the kind of language used for business purposes can come in

Haz Clic Aquí

For more online information about doing business in Latin America or Spain, visit one of these Web sites: www.compassmg. com/g_las.htm, www.ivey. uwo. ca/success/current_issue.htm, or www.nal.usda.gov/atmic/pubs/ srb9412.htm#1. You can also search for "business + Spain + Latin America" for additional Web sites.

handy. Even the smallest merchant likes to talk about trade and the economy. And if you ever need to correspond with a company or an educational institution, you should know the basics of formal correspondence. So, let's begin the final part of this book with a *lectura* related to commerce. Later, we'll look at some courteous expressions that can help you to better communicate in any professional setting.

Lectura: Correspondencia Mercantil

In Spanish, as in English, the kind of language used in official business can be a little difficult to understand. But the good news is that most business correspondence tends to be rather formulaic, using the same openings, closings, and cordialities throughout. Remember to have your dictionary on hand as you read the text, and note any words or phrases that you find difficult.

Industrias Agrícolas Echeverría S.A. de C.V.
Fertilizantes—Maquinaria Pesada—Sistemas de Irrigación
Teléfono: 52 5 546 30 41 ; Fax 52 5 546 30 39
Parque Industrial del Norte
Apartado Postal 195
Torreón, Coah.
C.P. 27170, México

Torreón, Coah., el 23 de junio de 2000

Estimados Señores:

Nos complace referirnos a su atenta carta del día 5 de este mes para proporionarles la infomación que se sirven solicitar:

Economía General: *Ha mejorado sensiblemente, según los últimos informes proporcionados por instituciones tan serias como el Banco Nacional de México y el Crédito Comercial S.A.*

Ventas a Plazo: *Como una consecuencia de la recuperación económica, numerosas granjas están intensificando sus operaciones a plazo. Puede observarse al respecto en la "Estadística Comercial", que el volumen de las ventas aumentó en forma muy apreciable durante el mes pasado, y hay gran optimismo.*

Importaciones: *Puede considerarse que, a medida que vaya desarrollándose la industria nacional, el capítulo de importaciones ha de reducirse en importancia, porque el país producirá cuanto necesite para su consumo. El gobierno está decidido a facilitar el establecimiento de nuevas industrias y a impartir amplia protección a las existentes.*

Confiamos en que la información anterior sea de utilidad para las resoluciones que ustedes tomen en el caso de que nos hablan.

Quedando a su entera disposición para cualquier consulta, los saludamos muy atentamente.

Juan José Sarabía Martínez Gerente del Depto. de Ventas

Vocabulario Útil:

➤ **mercantil:** mercantile; business (adjective)

➤ **maquinaria pesada:** heavy machinery

➤ **parque industrial:** industrial park

➤ **apartado postal:** P.O. box

➤ **Coah.:** Coahuila (a state in Mexico)

➤ **C.P.:** "*Código Postal*" (postal code)

➤ **Estimados Señores:** Esteemed Sirs

➤ **nos complace:** It is our pleasure ("It pleases us")

➤ **atenta carta:** kind letter

➤ **proporionar:** to provide

➤ **se sirven:** here, "are requested"

➤ **sensiblemente:** appreciably; considerably

➤ **informe:** report

➤ **serio:** serious; legitimate

➤ **venta a plazo:** installment plan

➤ **recuperación:** recuperation; up-swing

➤ **volumen:** volume; amount

➤ **aumentar:** to increase; to expand

Acuérdate

Another way to say "it is my (our) pleasure to do X" in a business letter (in addition to *nos complace*) is *me (nos) es grato* plus infinitive: *Nos es grato contestar su atenta carta ...* means "It is our pleasure to respond to your kind letter ...." You wouldn't say this in conversation, but you may see it in a business letter.

➤ **optimismo:** optimism

➤ **desarrollarse:** to develop

➤ **capítulo:** chapter; period

➤ **reducirse:** to be reduced

➤ **facilitar:** to facilitate; to make easier

➤ **establecimiento:** establishment

➤ **impartir:** to impart

➤ **amplio:** broad; wide-ranging

➤ **existente:** current; existing

➤ **confiar en:** to trust

➤ **anterior:** previous

➤ **utilidad:** usefulness; of use

➤ **resolución:** decision; resolutions

➤ **quedando:** remaining

➤ **a su disposición:** at your disposal

➤ **saludar:** to greet; to give salutations

➤ **atentamente:** sincerely

Algo Nuevo

You will see the letters *S.A.* (sometimes with *de C.V.*) after the names of many businesses. These letters stand for *Sociedad Anónima (de Capital Variable)*, which means "Anonymous Society of Variable Capital." In plain English, it means "Incorporated." So, *Industrias Agrícolas Echeverría S.A. de C.V.* would translate as "Echeverria Agricultural Industries, Inc."

Análisis del Texto

¡Excelente! Now let's take a closer look:

➤ *el 23 de junio de 2000*

Notice the form for writing the date: *el* + "day" + *de* + "month" (no capital letter) + *de* + "year."

➤ *Estimados Señores*

Acuérdate

If you send a letter and you're not sure to whom it should be addressed, you can use *A quien corresponda*, which means "To whom it may concern." Notice the use of the subjunctive—because you don't know whom it concerns, you need to put the verb in the subjunctive to allow for this uncertainty.

Most business letters begin with *Estimados señores* .... This is much more formal than *Queridos*, which means "Dear" and implies affection. You can sometimes omit the *estimado* part if you want and just write *Señores*. This would include both men and women (I know it isn't fair ...). If you are addressing a woman, it would, of course, be *estimada*.

➤ *Nos complace referirnos a su atenta carta*

Almost all business letters are *atenta*. This extends to the closing as well: *atentamente* means "sincerely" or "kindly."

➤ *se sirven solicitar*

In formal writing, the verb *servir* has a secondary meaning of "to please" or "to be so kind as to": *Sírvase reponder lo más pronto que sea factible* means "Please reply (take the liberty of replying) as soon as it becomes feasible." In this example, it is understood that

the responses to various questions have been requested, and the *se sirven* makes the tone of the
letter more polite.

> ➤ *según los últimos informes proporcionados por
> instituciones tan serias*

Here, *últimos* would be translated as "latest" rather
than "last."

> ➤ *en forma muy apreciable*

Here again we see the avoidance of the *–mente*
adverb. This could have been written as *apreci-
ablemente*, but the *en forma construction* is more
manageable in Spanish. Nonetheless, an accurate
translation would read "appreciably," not "in an
appreciable form."

> ➤ *a medida que vaya desarrollándose la industria
> nacional*

Literally, this means "as the national industry may
go developing itself." No, that doesn't make sense.
Let's see what's going on. First, that subjunctive
(*vaya*) is there because the writer is speculating as
to how things may develop and therefore must use
the subjunctive to reflect this "unknown quantity."
Second, the *ir* + present participle suggests motion
and progress, although the sentence could also
have been written with *a medida que se desarolle la
industria nacional*. But the use of *ir* suggests a period of time during which progress may be noted.
A better translation is, "to the extent to which the
national industry (may) develop over time."

> ➤ *ha de reducirse en importancia*

Haber + de + infinitive in this sentence means about
the same thing as the verb *deber*: *Ha de ser posible* means
"It should be possible."

> ➤ *el país producirá cuanto necesite para su consumo*

Here's another subjunctive construction. We do not know how much the country will
need, so the subjunctive allows for this uncertainty. You could translate this as "The
country will produce whatever amount it may need (but we don't know how much)."

Ten Cuidado

The word for "colleague" is
colega. It's a nice word to use in
a business or educational setting.
Just remember that the word
doesn't change to *colego* when
addressing a man; *estimados cole-
gas* would be the way to address
a mixed group. Say *una colega* if
you are addressing a woman.

Acuérdate

The word *serio* has several meanings. It can mean "serious" or
"grave," but it also can mean
"reliable" and "respectable." If
you say that a person is *serio/a*,
this would mean that he or she
seemed "worried" or even "de-
pressed."

293

➤ *El gobierno está decidido*

The verb *decidir* does mean "to decide," but in this context we might venture to translate this as "the government is resolute" rather than "decided."

➤ *Confiamos en que la información anterior sea de utilidad para las resoluciones que ustedes tomen en el caso de que nos hablan*

Translated, this means, "We trust that the preceding information may be useful vis-à-vis the decisions that you may make (more subjunctive) with respect to the issues under discussion." The word *sea* is the subjunctive of *ser* and is needed here because of the hope and uncertainty of the statement.

➤ *Quedando a su entera disposición para cualquier consulta, los saludamos muy atentamente*

Here the letter reads, "Remaining at your entire disposal for any consultation (questions, advice, and so on), we greet you (send salutations) most sincerely."

Algo Nuevo

The verb *arreglar* literally means "to arrange," but it can be extended to mean "to work something out" or "to fix things up." Use *arreglar* any time you need something repaired, fixed, worked out, or lined up: *¿Me podría arreglar un viaje a Galicia?* means "Could you fix up a trip for me to Galicia?"; *Voy a arreglar mis cosas* means "I'm going to get my stuff in order"; and *Mi auto está descompuesto. Lo voy a tener que arreglar pronto* means "My car is out of commission. I'll have to fix it soon." The nominative form of this verb is *arreglo*: *El comerciante llegó a un arreglo con sus clientes*, as in "The merchant came to an arrangement with his clients."

Gramática: Polite Phrases and Expressions

This section contains numerous courteous expressions that you should learn by heart. You're probably already familiar with some of them. That's ok. It's always a good idea to have these phrases at the tip of your tongue whenever you meet someone, especially in a business setting.

Things to Say When Being Introduced

When you first meet someone, don't just greet them with *Hola* or *Buenos días* (*tardes, noches*). Try using one of the following polite expressions; it will be greatly appreciated:

➤ **Mucho gusto:** Nice to meet you

➤ **Un placer:** A pleasure

➤ **Encantado:** Charmed (said by men, usually to women)

➤ **Encantada:** Charmed (said by women to anyone)

➤ **Me da mucho gusto conocerlo/la:** Nice to meet you

➤ **El gusto es mío:** The pleasure is mine (if the other person says *mucho gusto* to you first)

➤ **(Your name), a sus órdenes:** "at your service"

➤ **(Your name), para servirle:** "at your service"

The last two are mostly used by men. *Encantado* (said if you're a man) and *encantada* (if a woman) are also quite popular. *El gusto es mío* is a good response if someone says *Mucho gusto* to you first. Be careful not to respond with *Sí* to *El gusto es mío* (I've heard this!), which would mean, "Yes, the pleasure *is* all yours, I'm sure."

"Of Course"

Here are three ways to say "of course." They're good responses to a question when the answer is obviously going to be "yes":

➤ *Sí, cómo no*

➤ *Sí, por supuesto*

➤ *Sí, desde luego* (used mostly in Spain)

Cultura Latina

Although many of these polite expressions may seem to you as an unnecessary formality, I promise that they won't impede the spontaneity of your conversations. It is difficult to be too polite in Spanish, at least in the beginning. In fact, these courteous phrases will actually help you break the ice so that you can really start communicating with people.

Acuérdate

Remember that the gender-specific ending of *encantado/a* must match *your* gender, not the gender of the person whom you are addressing (*encantar* = "to enchant"). If a man were to say *encantada* to a woman, he would be saying: "You must be very enchanted to meet me, handsome devil that I am ...." (That's probably not the best way to make a good first impression, guys.)

For "of course not," try these:

➤ *No, de ninguna manera* (No, in no way)

➤ *No, no puede ser* (No, that can't be)

Algo Nuevo

Business culture in the Spanish-speaking world is very different from that of the United States, Canada, and England. For one thing, the "get it done yesterday" perspective of many businessmen and -women in the United States is not as common in Latin America or Spain. A business meeting may not start "on time" by American or European standards. Issues about money, sales, or contract negotiations may be postponed until the eating, drinking, and other social activities have all been concluded.

Polite Forms for Asking Questions

When doing business, you'll often find that at some point you will want to pose a question. Here's a list of courteous phrases you can use to ensure that you get the answers you need. The translations are all a bit on the literal side. In reality, all these expressions basically mean "please." Let's take a look:

➤ *Poder hacer el favor de* + **infinitive:** This means "to be able to do the favor of X," as in: *¿Me podría hacer el favor de decir el precio por kilo?* ("Could you [do me a favor and] tell me what the price is per kilo?"). You can also use it without *poder*, as in *Hágame el favor de decirme su dirección y teléfono durante el día.* ("Do me the favor of telling me your address and daytime phone number.")

➤ *Poder ayudar con ...:* This is translated as "to be able to help with ...," as in: *¿Me puede ayudar con el idioma, por favor?* ("Can you please help me with the language?").

➤ *Poder decir una cosa ...:* This means "To be able to tell someone something," as in: *Disculpe, ¿me podría decir una cosa? ¿Cuánto van a cobrarme por el manejo, envío, y los impuestos?* ("Pardon me. Could you tell me something? How much are they going to charge me for handling, shipping, and taxes?")

➤ *Permitir hacer una pregunta:* "To be permitted to ask a question," as in *Señorita, ¿me permite hacerle una pregunta? ¿Cuál es su número de seguro social?* ("Miss, may I ask you a question please? What is your Social Security number?")

➤ *Tener la bondad de + infinitive:* "To be so good as to …," as in *Señora, ¿no puede usted tener la bondad de decirme su nombre y apellido?* ("Madam, would you please be so kind as to tell me your first and last name?")

➤ *¿No le importa si + conjugated verb:* This means "Do you mind if I …?" as in: *¿No le importaría si enviamos la mercancía el viernes?* ("Would you mind if we sent the merchandise on Friday?").

"Thank You" and "You're Welcome"

I know that you already know how to say "Thank you" and "No, thank you" and "You're welcome." But it can't hurt to have a few more phrases to expand on what you already know. After you say *Gracias,* consider adding one of the following phrases:

After *Gracias,* add …

➤ **muy amable:** (you are) very kind

➤ **por su ayuda/paciencia:** for your help/patience

➤ **por su atención:** for helping me

➤ **por todo:** for everything

➤ **Estoy muy agradecido/a por su tiempo:** I'm very grateful for your time

➤ **Espero que no haya sido molestia:** I hope that it hasn't been too much trouble

When someone says *Gracias* to you, you should respond with one of the following:

➤ **De nada:** You're welcome.

➤ **Por nada:** You're welcome.

➤ **No hay de qué:** Don't mention it.

➤ **No faltaba más:** "It goes without saying."

➤ **No se preocupe:** Don't worry about it.

➤ **A sus órdenes:** At your service.

➤ **A la orden:** At your command (mostly in the Caribbean).

➤ **Para servirle:** At your service.

➤ **A usted (por su cortesía/paciencia):** Thank *you!* (for your courtesy/patience)

Ten Cuidado

The verb *molestar* is a false cognate. It doesn't mean "to molest" as we now use this word in English. *Molestar* simply means "to bother" or "to cause inconvenience." Thus, the expression *No se moleste* does not mean "Don't molest yourself," but rather "Don't trouble yourself or create any unnecessary inconvenience in your life on my behalf."

Cultura Latina

Yes, you can say *de nada* all day for "you're welcome." But I suggest that you try using the more formal expressions now and then. Your efforts to be courteous will not go unappreciated. Don't forget that you can always add *señor* or *señora* to the end of most courteous phrases: *A sus órdenes, señora.*

Ten Cuidado

The expression *Que le vaya bien* is popular, especially in Mexico, but it is usually said to people leaving by those remaining behind. Don't say *Que le vaya bien* when you are the one leaving (I've done this—it's embarrassing). If you're leaving, say *Adios.* If you're staying behind, you can say *Adios, que le (te, les) vaya bien.*

When someone wishes something good for you (such as *Buena suerte,* which means "Good luck"), respond with one of the following:

➤ **Gracias, igualmente:** Thanks, same to you.

➤ **Que le vaya bien:** Good luck (may it go well for you).

➤ **Gracias, muy amable:** Thanks, you are very kind.

Diálogo: En El Banco Bantico S.A.

Here's a conversation in a Costa Rican bank between Bridget O'Kelly and various people there. This time the dialogue is followed by a "Vocabulario Útil" section only:

Cajero: *Buenas tardes, señorita. ¿En cómo le puedo ayudar?*

O'Kelly: *Buenas tardes. Soy Bridget O'Kelly y quisiera abrir una cuenta corriente y otra de ahorros.*

Cajero: *Está muy bien. Con todo gusto. Nomás que aquí sirve sólo a los que ya tienen sus cuentas. Tiene que pasar a la ventanilla tres. Ahí la pueden atender.*

O'Kelly: *Muy bien. Gracias. (Va a la ventanilla tres)*

Cajero: *Buenas tardes, señora.*

O'Kelly: *Señorita.*

Cajero: *Ah, sí. Señorita. Perdón. ¿En qué puedo servirle?*

O'Kelly: *Quiero abrir dos cuentas, una corriente y la otra de ahorros.*

Cajero: *Bien, ¿de dónde es usted?*

O'Kelly: *Soy de Irlanda.*

Cajero: *Bienvenida a Costa Rica. Espero que le guste su estadía aquí. A ver, ¿tiene usted su pasaporte y permiso para trabajar en Costa Rica?*

O'Kelly: *Sí señor, aquí los tiene.*

Cajero: *Gracias. ¿Me espera un momentico por favor?*

O'Kelly: *Sí, cómo no.*

Mientras espera O'Kelly, llega una señora costaricense y se pone delante de ella. Le da sus papeles al cajero, y comienza a hablar con él de una forma muy cordial.

O'Kelly: *Perdone, señora, pero fíjese que hay fila ¿eh?*

La señora: *Ay, perdón, señorita. Lo que pasa es que pensé que usted ya había terminado.*

O'Kelly: *No se preocupe, pero es que no he terminado todavía.*

La señora: *Bueno, Gustavo (dirigiéndose al cajero), tengo prisa. Saludos a tu mamá de mi parte. Nos vemos mañana.*

Cajero: *Que te vaya bien, tía.*

O'Kelly: *Ahora, ¿qué pasa con mis cuentas?*

Cajero: *Todo está bien, señorita. He aquí los paples para abrir las cuentas. Llene las dos solicitudes y pasa por favor a la ventanilla cinco.*

O'Kelly: *¿A otra ventanilla? Bueno, está bien. Muchas gracias.*

Cajero: *A sus órdenes.*

Cultura Latina

Spanish-speakers tend to have a slightly different perception of time and punctuality than Anglos. Arriving somewhere "on time" may mean being "late" by up to several hours. In many cases, a 2:00 business meeting in Latin America might not begin until 3:00 (although this is changing in some sectors). If you're in doubt, you can ask *¿A la hora en punto?* ("Should I arrive exactly at the specified hour?")

Acuérdate

The word for "a line or queue" in Spanish is *una fila; hacer fila* means "to wait or get in line/ queue." You may also hear the word *cola* (literally, "tail") and *hacer cola*. Both words are correct; *cola* seems to be more popular in South America.

Vocabulario Útil:

➤ **cajero/a:** teller; cashier; clerk

➤ **quisiera:** would like; might like

➤ **cuenta corriente:** checking account

➤ **cuenta de ahorros:** savings account

➤ **con todo gusto:** "with pleasure"

➤ **ventanilla:** window (not always with glass)

➤ **Irlanda:** Ireland

➤ **bienvenido:** welcome

➤ **estadía:** stay; visit

➤ **saludos:** greetings

➤ **de mi parte:** on my behalf

➤ **he aquí:** here; I have here

➤ **llenar:** to fill out

Algo Nuevo

Though considered substandard by purists, in Latin America you'll hear *nomás* ("*no más*"), an adverb meaning "just" or "only. *Vaya nomás a la tienda y ahí lo va a poder compar* means "Just go the store and you'll be able to buy it there"; *Así nomás* means "Just like that (as easy as that)." You may also hear *nada más*, which means essentially the same thing.

Idiot's Guide to Idioms

As promised, each chapter in this final part of the book contains a list of idiomatic phrases for you to memorize. The translations are not literal; instead, you'll find the English equivalent expression. You may want to look up any new words. However, you don't have to because most of these are highly idiomatic (a word that linguists use when a phrase doesn't make any sense):

➤ **A buen hambre no hay pan duro:** Beggars can't be choosers.

➤ **ahogarse en un vaso de agua:** to make a mountain out of a molehill

➤ **al azar:** at random

➤ **al cantar del gallo:** at the crack of dawn

➤ **Al hierro caliente batir de repente:** Strike while the iron is hot.

➤ **Antes que te cases mira lo que haces:** Look before you leap.

➤ **al pie de la letra:** to the letter

➤ **a pedir de boca:** to your heart's content

➤ **A quien madruga, Dios le ayuda:** The early bird catches the worm.

➤ **a toda costa:** at all costs

Risa del Día

Sometimes doing business in another language is not as easy as you might think. If you need something translated into Spanish for business purposes, make sure that you hire a qualified professional. Also, if you plan to market a product in a Spanish-speaking country, have your advertising reviewed by a native speaker of that country before you release the material. Cutting corners can be embarrassing. Even the big companies end up making huge mistakes sometimes. Take a look at these:

➤ In the 1970s, General Motors failed miserably to market the Chevy Nova car in Latin America. It's no wonder—in Spanish, *"No va"* means, of course, "It doesn't go."

➤ The Dairy Association's huge success with the campaign "Got Milk?" prompted them to expand advertising to Mexico. It was soon brought to their attention the Spanish translation read "Are you lactating?" (*¿Tiene leche?*)

➤ An American T-shirt maker in Miami printed shirts that promoted the Pope's visit for the Spanish market. Instead of "I saw the Pope" (*el Papa*), the shirts read "I Saw the Potato" (*la papa*).

➤ Frank Perdue's chicken slogan, "It takes a strong man to make a tender chicken," was translated into Spanish as "It takes an aroused man to make a chicken affectionate." (*tierno* means tender, but with living things, it means "sweet and affectionate.")

Acuérdate

Technically, the verb *fijar* means "to stick on" and can be used, like *pegar*, for adhering or posting things to walls, and so on. But as a reflexive verb, it means "to pay attention" or "to look at" or "to consider," or even "what do you think of that?" It is often used as a filler: *Fíjate que ya no tengo dinero* means "You see, I don't have any money left."

Ten Cuidado

Atender (*atiendo, atiendes*) doesn't mean "to attend"; it means "to serve or help." If you enter a store and can't find anyone to help you, ask *¿Quién atiende aquí?* for "Who's here to help the customers?" The noun *atención* sometimes means "attention" in the English sense, but it can also mean "assistance."

➤ When Parker Pen marketed its ball-point pen in Mexico, the ads were supposed to have read, "It won't leak in your pocket and embarrass you." The company thought that the word *embarazar* (to impregnate) meant to "embarrass," so the ad read: "It won't leak in your pocket and make you pregnant!"

➤ When American Airlines wanted to advertise its new leather first-class seats in the Mexican market, it translated its "Fly In Leather" campaign literally, which meant "Fly Naked" in Spanish! (The word *cuero* does mean "leather," but in the phrase *vuela en cuero,* it hints at nakedness.)

El Cuiz

Give the Spanish equivalents. Cheating will result in the immediate bankruptcy (*bancarota*) of your company and no more special discounts (*descuentos*):

1. here, "are requested" _____
2. appreciably; considerably _____
3. reports _____
4. Esteemed Sirs _____
5. "It is our pleasure" _____
6. kind letter _____
7. installment plan _____
8. recuperation; up-swing _____
9. industrial park _____
10. P.O. box _____
11. chapter; period _____
12. to be reduced _____
13. to increase; to expand _____
14. appreciable _____
15. to impart _____
16. broad; wide-ranging _____
17. current; existing _____
18. to trust _____
19. usefulness; of use _____
20. decision; resolutions _____
21. to facilitate; to make easier _____
22. establishment _____

23. stay; visit _____
24. greetings _____
25. here; I have here _____
26. sincerely _____
27. teller; cashier; clerk _____
28. would like; might like _____
29. checking account _____
30. disposal _____
31. savings account _____
32. "with pleasure" _____
33. window (not always with glass) _____
34. to fill out _____

Tareas

1. Using the letter as a guide, write a short letter to a business, asking for the price of some product. You can borrow (steal) the openings and closings of the letter from the example here. It's all very formulaic ....

2. Spend some extra time learning the courteous expressions discussed in this chapter. Do whatever it takes. I guarantee that it will be time well spent and that these polite phrases will open up many doors to you—even if your Spanish is less than perfect.

The Least You Need to Know

➤ The United States is the number 1 trading partner for Latin America.

➤ Business culture in Spain and Latin America is very different from that of the United States—negotiations and discussions about money are often put off until the end of your visit.

➤ Courteous expressions, in addition to the basic *Gracias* and *De nada,* can open doors for you and are a must when doing business.

➤ If you're writing for the Spanish-speaking market, have all translations done (or reviewed) by a professional translator, or suffer the consequences.

La Tecnología

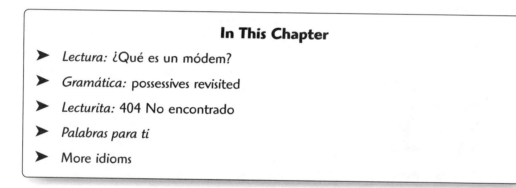

In This Chapter

➤ *Lectura:* ¿Qué es un módem?

➤ *Gramática:* possessives revisited

➤ *Lecturita:* 404 No encontrado

➤ *Palabras para ti*

➤ More idioms

For many of us, computers have become an integral part of our daily lives. In fact, I am writing these words on my home computer right now—and boy, am I glad that that whole Y2K thing is over ....

La Tecnología y el Mundo Latino

While it is certainly true that much of the Spanish-speaking world remains under-developed, the number of Spanish-speakers who are online or who use computers on a daily basis is growing steadily every year. Even in some of the most remote areas, computer technology is rapidly integrating itself into everyday life. As international trade and communication continue to expand, a knowledge of computers and computer terminology will become increasingly important. So, I thought that this would be a good time to introduce you to some Spanish technospeak.

Ten Cuidado

Be aware that the computer terminology in your bilingual dictionary may be unreliable. Part of the problem is that computer terms change so often that it's almost impossible for the lexicographers to keep up with it all. For more accurate terminology, search for *glosarios de términos de la informática* on the Internet.

Cultura Latina

There are three words for computer in Spanish. In Latin America, both *computadora* and *computador* are used, although the feminine *computadora* seems slightly more popular. In Spain, people say *ordenador*. If you read a text about computers and see the word *ordenador* used throughout, you can be sure that the material was intended for the Spanish market.

Lectura: ¿Qué Hace el Módem?

Here is a short *lectura* that discusses how a modem works. The passage will expose you to the kind of language you'll be faced with if you ever need to read a computer-related text in Spanish:

> *La computadora (computador, ordenador) consiste en un aparato digital que funciona al encender y apagar interruptores electrónicos. Las líneas telefónicas, de lo contrario, son dispositivos análogos que envían señales en forma de un corriente continuo. Como consecuencia de ello, se necesita un módem para unir el espacio entre estos dos tipos de dispositivos. El módem envía los datos digitales de la computadora a través de líneas telefónicas análogas. Puede lograr esto modulando los datos digitales para convertirlos en una señal análoga; es decir, el módem varía la frecuencia de la señal digital para formar una señal análoga continua. Y cuando el módem recibe señales análogas a través de la línea telefónica, hace el opuesto: demodula, o quita las frecuencias variadas de la onda análoga para convertirlas en impulsos digitales. De estas dos funciones, modulación y demodulación, surgió el nombre del módem.*

> *En la mayoría de los casos, su computadora viene con alguna clase de software de comunicaciones y un gran número de programas fabricados por terceros que están disponibles para uso con el módem. Debido a que el módem solamente funciona en versiones, debería asegurarse de comprar programas de software de comunicaciones que son compatibles con las versiones de sus aplicaciones y con el sistema operativo.*

Vocabulario Útil:

- ➤ **consistir:** to consist
- ➤ **aparato:** machine; device
- ➤ **encender:** to turn on
- ➤ **apagar:** to turn off
- ➤ **interruptor:** switch
- ➤ **de lo contrario:** "on the other hand"
- ➤ **dispositivo:** device
- ➤ **análogo:** analog
- ➤ **señal:** signal
- ➤ **corriente:** current
- ➤ **continuo:** continuous
- ➤ **consecuencia:** result; consequence
- ➤ **ello:** that; all of that
- ➤ **unir:** to unite; to link
- ➤ **a través de:** across

- ➤ **lograr:** to achieve
- ➤ **modular:** to modulate
- ➤ **es decir:** "that is to say ..."
- ➤ **variar:** to vary; to fluctuate
- ➤ **frecuencia:** frequency
- ➤ **recibir:** to receive
- ➤ **el opuesto:** the opposite
- ➤ **onda:** wave
- ➤ **impulso:** impulse
- ➤ **mayoría:** majority
- ➤ **alguna clase:** some kind
- ➤ **software de comunicaciones:** communication software
- ➤ **terceros:** third parties
- ➤ **debido a:** due to
- ➤ **asegurarse:** to make sure
- ➤ **sistema operativo:** operating system

Algo Nuevo

You will find that Spanish has adopted many English words directly into its computer vocabulary: *el software, el hardware, el mouse, el monitor,* and *el módem.* This has been partly due to the fact that until relatively recently, most technical manuals, as well as the computer applications themselves, were written only in English. So, all the Spanish-speaking computer programmers had to learn the English words. Also, because there are so many Spanish-speaking countries, the adoption of the English terms has allowed for greater uniformity in the use of these terms from place to place.

Análisis del Texto

Now let's take a look at a few selected parts of the *lectura:*

➤ *al encender y apagar*

You've seen the *al* + infinitive before. It means "upon" or "when you do X."

➤ *de lo contrario*

This translates as "on the other hand," even though one might argue that "on the contrary" would be closer to the Spanish. Usually, "on the other hand" is *por el otro lado* in Spanish. But sometimes you have to read between the lines. *De lo contrario* can also mean "if not," as in: *Creo que el técnico va a poder reparar el problema. De lo contrario, voy a tener que comprar un nuevo módem.* ("I think that the technician is going to be able to fix the problem. If not, I'm going to have to buy a new modem.")

➤ *como consecuencia*

Here, *como* means "as," not "how." That's why there's no *tilde.*

➤ *líneas telefónicas análogas*

Acuérdate

On a Mac computer, make the letter *ñ* by hitting Option + *n* and then *n* again. On an IBM-compatible PC with a Windows operating system, make *ñ* by hitting Crtl + Shift + ˜ and then *n*, or by holding down the Alt key and hitting 0241 on the number pad (release Alt after you key 0241). You will probably have to use the 0241 method when writing *ñ* in e-mail and over the Internet.

This means "analog telephone lines." So why couldn't this have been *líneas análogas telefónicas*? Well, that also would have been a possibility. However, putting the word *telefónicas* at the end would have changed things a bit. In Spanish, the last word in a series of adjectives has the most impact. If I say *líneas análogas telefónicas,* I would be setting up a comparison between the analog phone lines and the analog "something else" lines. But with *análogas* coming last, the emphasis is on the fact that the telephone lines are analog, not that the analog lines are telephone lines.

➤ *puede lograr esto modulando*

Just a reminder that the present participle form of *modular (modulando)* needs to be translated here as "by modulating."

➤ *en la mayoría de casos*

Yes, this means "in the majority of cases," but you could probably be a bit more loose with the translation and just say "Most of the time …."

Algo Nuevo

The pronoun *ello* is a little-used but very handy way to say "all of that." When you are discussing a variety of points and wish to group them together as a whole, you can use *ello*. So, if I'm talking about my life story—my childhood, my adolescence, my first computer, and so on—I can wrap all that history together with *ello: A pesar de ello, he podido mantener una perspectiva muy optimista* means "In spite of all of that (my entire life's experience), I have still been able to maintain a positive perspective."

Gramática: Possessives—I Got Mine, You Got Yours

You've probably already learned most of these. But as always, a little review won't kill you. The possessives are pretty easy. Just remember that when more than one thing is being "possessed," an –s must be added for the plural.

Note also that these do not have *tildes* on them. This is important because *tú* means "you," while *tu* means "your." In the *nosotros* and *vosotros* form, you must match the gender and number to those of the noun:

Possessives, Singular and Plural

Singular	Plural	Definition
mi	*mis*	my
tu	*tus*	your
su	*sus*	his/her/your/its
nuestro	*nuestros*	our (masculine nouns)
nuestra	*nuestras*	our (feminine nouns)
vuestro	*vuestros*	you all's (masculine nouns)
vuestra	*vuestras*	you all's (feminine nouns)
su	*sus*	their (you all's)

Algo Nuevo

To make *tildes* on an IBM-compatible keyboard running a Windows operating system, hold down the Ctrl key, hit ` (which usually appears above the Tab key), and then release. Now type the letter (*a, e, i, o, u*) on which you want the *tilde* to appear. You may also use the following combinations on your number pad while holding down the Alt key: 0225 = *á*; 0233 = *é*; 0237 = *í*; 0243 = *ó*; 0250 = *ú*; and 0252 = *ü*. Release the Alt key after entering the number. As with the *ñ*, you will probably have to use the Alt + number combinations when writing the specialized characters in e-mail and in HTML stuff.

Ten Cuidado

Be careful not to overdo it with possessives when talking about the things that belong to you. It is quite common to use the definite articles (*el, la, los, las*) rather than the possessives in many cases. Don't talk about everything as "*mis carros, mi perro, mi casa, mi comida, mi ropa*"—you'll give the impression that you're *egoísta* (selfish). When ownership is obvious or implied, the article works just fine.

Here are a few examples of possessives:

➤ **Él es mi papá, y ella es mi mamá:** He is my dad, and she is my mom.

➤ **Nuestra computadora es nueva, pero nuestro software es viejo:** Our computer is new, but our software is old.

➤ **Mi casa es su casa:** My house is your house.

➤ **Su red está sobrecargada:** Your (his/her) network is overloaded.

➤ **Vuestros monitores son muy antiguos:** Your monitors are very out-of-date.

In addition to these possessives, there is a second set of possessives called possessive adjectives. In English, we also make this distinction when we say "my car" and "the car is mine." These work the same as other adjectives:

Possessive Adjectives, Plural and Singular

Singular	Plural	Definition
mío/mía	*míos/mías*	mine
tuyo/tuya	*tuyos/tuyas*	your
suyo/suya	*suyos/suyas*	his, hers, your
nuestro/nuestra	*nustros/nuestras*	our
vuestro/vuestra	*vuestros/vuestras*	you all's (familiar)
suyo/suya	*suyos/suyas*	their; you all's

Here are a few more examples:

➤ **Todos los archivos de la carpeta tuya se han borrado:** All the files in your folder have been erased.

➤ **Este disquete es mío, pero el otro es de Óscar:** This floppy disk is mine, but the other one is Oscar's.

➤ **Oye, ¿son tuyos estos documentos?** "Hey, are these documents yours?"

➤ **Su disco duro puede archivar más datos que el nuestro:** His (her) hard drive can store more data than ours.

Lecturita: 404 No Encontrado

If you're trying to log on to a Spanish Web site and are having trouble, you may come across the following message. I thought I'd give you the translation just in case:

Acuérdate

Some English-speakers have trouble remembering that the possessive adjectives match the gender of the object owned, not the gender of the person speaking. So there's no need to feel uncomfortable saying *la casa es mía* if you're a man, or *el coche is mío* if you're a woman. Possessive adjectives have nothing to do with *your* gender, just the gender of your possessions.

> *El servidor Web no puede encontrar el archivo o la secuencia de comandos que ha solicitado. Compruebe la dirección URL para asegurarse de que la ruta de acceso es correcta. Póngase en contacto con el administrador del servidor si el problema persiste.*

Translation:

> The Web server cannot find the file or script you asked for. Please check the URL to ensure that the path is correct. Please contact the server's administrator if this problem persists.

Palabras Para Ti

The following list introduces you to some basic computer terminology in Spanish. In some cases, you may find that the English word is more common than the Spanish word—even in Spain. Still, it never hurts to know the terms in both languages:

➤ **bandwidth:** *ancho de banda*

➤ **baud:** *baudio*

➤ **BIOS (Basic Input Output System):** *Sistema Básico de Entrada/Salida*

➤ **bookmark:** *marca*

➤ **button:** *botón*

➤ **browser:** *navegador*

➤ **CD (compact disc):** *disco compacto*

➤ **chat:** *charla*

➤ **to delete:** *borrar*

➤ **DNS (Domain Name System):** *Sistema de nombres de dominio*

Haz Clic Aquí

It should come as no surprise that you can find many computer-related Web sites on the Internet. For general terminology (in Spanish), visit www.geocities.com/Athens/Parthenon/4206/glosario.htm#N, or navegante.expreso.com.pe/ayuda/glosario.htm You can also do a search for *informática* (which is the real word for "computer-related stuff").

➤ **DOS (disk operating system):** *sistema operativo de disco*

➤ **floppy disk:** *diskete; disco*

➤ **file:** *archivo*

➤ **frame:** *estructura*

➤ **gateway:** *puerta de acceso*

➤ **GIF (Graphics Interchange Format):** *Formato grafico de intercambio*

➤ **GUI (graphic user interface):** *Interfaz gráfico de usuario*

➤ **hard drive:** *disco duro*

➤ **home page:** *página principal o inicial de un sitio Web*

➤ **host:** *"host"; anfitrión*

➤ **HTML (Hypertext Markup Language):** *Lenguaje de marcas de hypertexto*

➤ **HTTP (Hypertext Transfer Protocol):** *Protocolo de tranferencia hypertexto*

➤ **key:** *tecla*

➤ **keyboard:** *teclado*

➤ **LAN (local area network):** *Red de area local*

➤ **link:** *enlace*

➤ **monitor:** *monitor*

➤ **mouse:** *"el mouse"; ratón*

➤ **motherboard:** *placa matriz; "el motherboard"*

➤ **printer:** *impresora*

➤ **to push (a button):** *oprimir; presionar; aplastar*

➤ **RAM (random access memory):** *Memoria de acceso aleatorio*

➤ **ROM (read only memory):** *Memoria solo de lectura*

➤ **to run a program:** *ejecutar*

➤ **to save:** *guardar; archivar*

➤ **scanner:** *escáner*

➤ **SPAM:** *"Bombardeo" con correo electrónico*

➤ **URL (uniform resource locator):** *Localizador uniforme de recursos*

➤ **WAN (wide area network):** *Red de area amplia*

Idiot's Guide to Idioms

Now that you'll be able to say "There's more than one way to skin a cat" in Spanish, I'm sure your life will be complete. Notice that the word *gato* does not appear in the Spanish version (*pulga* means "a flea"):

➤ **boca abajo:** face down

➤ **boca arriba:** face up

➤ **borrón y cuenta nueva:** to turn over a new leaf

➤ **buscar una aguja en un pajar:** to look for a needle in a haystack

➤ **Cada quien tiene su manera de matar pulgas:** There's more than one way to skin a cat.

➤ **caminar con pies de plomo:** to go with caution

➤ **caer bien (me cae bien):** to like (a person)

➤ **caer mal:** to dislike (a person)

➤ **Caras vemos, corazones no sabemos:** You can't judge a book by its cover.

➤ **cerrar los ojos a la realidad:** to bury one's head in the sand

➤ **criar cuervos, que te sacarán los ojos:** to bite the hand that feeds you

➤ **dar en el clavo:** to hit the nail on the head

➤ **De eso ni hablar:** That's out of the question.

➤ **dejar mucho que desear:** to leave much to be desired

Cultura Latina

Internet use among Latin Americans as a whole has increased substantially over recent years and is expected to reach 35 million in 2001. In Spain, the number is expected to reach 10 million.

Acuérdate

For Macintosh computers, use your Option key in combination with the other keys to produce the *tildes*. You can also pull down the Apple menu and open the Key Caps menu to see how to make these symbols. If you're working in Microsoft Word, you can always pull down the Insert menu, open Symbols, and find the special characters there. It's slower, but it works.

Risa del Día

Throughout history people have always needed somebody else to tease or make jokes about. In *el Cono Sur*, *argentinos* and *uruguayos* love to pick on Spaniards, whom they call collectively (and sometimes lovingly) *gallegos* or "Galicians" (even though all Spaniards obviously do not come from Galicia). Elsewhere, Peruvians and Ecuadorians trade insults, as do Mexicans and Guatemalans, Colombians and Venezuelans, Costa Ricans and Nicaraguans, and so on. Other countries pick on *Argentinos*, *Cubanos*, *gringos*, or just about any nationality they can think of.

This situation may be unfortunate, but luckily between Latins these jokes are usually made in good fun. Everyone seems to get their revenge sooner or later by hurling the same jokes back at the people who first told them. Still, it is true that the idea of "political correctness" has yet to take hold in most sectors of the Spanish-speaking world.

In an effort to be "PC" (that's politically correct, not "personal computer"), I'm going to insert my Spanish name, *Esteban*, where you would normally see *argentinos*, *gallegos*, *gringos*, and so on. You can insert whomever you want; the jokes remain the same.

1. *¿Cómo se sabe si Esteban acaba de usar una computadora?*

   Si el monitor está lleno de liquid paper.

2. *Esteban pide una pizza a domicilio y le preguntan:*

   —*¿En cuantos pedazos quiere que la cortemos?*

   ¿6 ó 12?

   —*Hombre, pues 6 nada más, yo no como tantos.*

3. *¿Por qué hay hielo sobre un televisor? ... porque Esteban intentó congelar la imagen.*

The following joke had to stay in the original. No offense meant to any Spaniards out there ....

Un avión de Iberia llegando a Ezeiza:

—*Aquí torre de control torre de control ... ¿cuál es su posición?*

—*Pues, aquí estamos con José sentados delante de los relojitos.*

So, to be fair ...

¿Para qué los argentinos le ponen azúcar a la almohada?

... para tener dulces sueños.

Acuérdate

For ¡ and ¿, use the following combinations if you're working on an IBM-compatible PC: Ctrl + Alt + Shift + ! = ¡; Ctrl + Alt + Shift + ? = ¿. On the number pad, it's Alt + 0161 for ¡ and 0191 for ¿. On a Mac, pull down the Key Caps menu to add these characters.

Vocabulario Útil:

➤ **a domicilio:** for home delivery

➤ **pedazo:** piece

➤ **congelar la imagen:** to freeze the image

➤ **Iberia:** Spanish national airline

➤ **Ezeiza:** main airport in Buenos Aires

➤ **dulces sueños:** sweet dreams

El Cuiz

Give the equivalent Spanish words. Cheating will result in a crashed hard drive and the loss of all your data.

1. switch _____

2. continuous _____

3. result; consequence _____

4. to turn off _____

5. device _____

6. analog _____

7. to consist _____

8. across _____

9. to vary; to fluctuate _____

10. machine; device _____

11. to turn on _____

12. signal _____

13. to achieve _____

14. frequency _____

15. some kind _____

16. communication software _____

17. to modulate _____

18. current _____

19. that; all of that _____

20. to unite; to link _____

21. wave _____

22. the opposite _____

23. third parties _____

24. piece _____

25. impulse _____

26. majority _____

27. to receive _____

28. to remove _____

29. due to _____

30. to make sure _____

Acuérdate

You will hear *un PC* ("pay say") or *una PC* for "personal computer." Both genders are acceptable. For a laptop or notebook, the word *laptop* is also used in Spanish, as is *computadora (ordenador) portátil* (portable computer).

Tareas

1. Sit at a computer and try to name the basic parts in Spanish. If you don't know something, go online and see if you can find it. Then try to make the special Spanish characters á, é, í, ó, ú, ü, ñ, ¿, and ¡.

2. Talk about all the things that you own. Then talk about other people's stuff. Practice using the possessives with these sentences. Refer to the examples and explanations for guidance.

The Least You Need to Know

➤ It is useful to be familiar with computer terminology in Spanish.

➤ Many English words have been adopted into Spanish, but it's always best to know both the Spanish and English terms.

➤ Possessives such as *mi, tu,* and *su* are invariable with respect to gender, but *nuestro, vuestro, mío, tuyo,* and *suyo* must match the gender of the noun possessed. All possessives must match for singular or plural.

➤ Don't overuse the possessives *mi* and *mis;* it sounds odd in Spanish. Use the definite articles when ownership is obvious.

La Política

It's no wonder that the Spanish-speaking world has long been a hotbed of political activity. Both Spain and Latin America have been plagued by civil wars, revolutions, counterinsurgencies, military dictatorships, foreign invasions, corruption, debt, hyper-inflation—the list goes on. The last 50 years have been especially tumultuous politically for nearly every Spanish-speaking country.

Pero Las Cosas Han Mejorado

In spite of its political troubles, things have begun to look up in recent years for *el mundo hispanohablante.* Francisco Franco's nearly 40 years as Spain's *generalísimo* ended with his death in 1975. Since then, Spain's constitutional monarchy has made great strides toward democratic reform. In 1996, control of the Spanish parliament changed hands peacefully in a free and open election when Felipe González and his *Partido Socialista Obrero Español,* or PSOE (Spanish Socialist Workers' Party), lost to José María Aznar and the *Partido Popular.*

Many of the political instabilities that Latin America faced during the 1980s and 1990s have also turned around. In the wake of peace accords and free elections, Central America has finally put an end to most guerilla activity and right-wing counter-insurgencies. The countries of *el Cono Sur* have returned to democracy after decades of military dictatorships. Mexico's ruling party, the PRI, may soon lose its nearly 80-year hold on power as opposition parties such as the PAN (National Action Party) continue to win gubernatorial elections across the country. Even Cuba, which has long been politically and economically isolated from much of the West, has opened its doors to limited foreign investments and free enterprise.

Nevertheless, the Spanish-speaking world still has numerous obstacles to overcome in the political arena, and politics undoubtedly will continue to be an ever-present element in the lives of Spaniards and Latin Americans for many years to come.

Haz Clic Aquí

For an up-to-date look at the political situations of Spain and several Latin American countries, visit the official Web site of the United Nations at www.un.org. Both English and Spanish are language options. If the information you need isn't there, perform a search under the name of the country you are interested in. Every Spanish-speaking country maintains its own official Web site.

Lectura: La Constitución de la República de Cuba

The following *lectura* is from the preamble to Cuba's Constitution. Of course, you are free to agree or disagree with what it says. The text was not chosen for political reasons, but rather because it seemed perfect for this topic—it is filled with political rhetoric and challenging vocabulary. To make your first reading easier, you can skip ahead to the "Vocabulario Útil" section later in this chapter and skim over the vocabulary words before you read it. Have your dictionary in hand, and don't forget to take your time.

Preámbulo:

Nosotros, Ciudanos Cubanos;

herederos y continuadores del trabajo creador y de las tradiciones de combatividad, firmeza, heroísmo y sacrificio forjadas por nuestros antecesores; por los aborígenes que prefirieron muchas veces el exterminio a la sumisión; por los esclavos que se rebelaron contra sus amos; por los que despertaron la conciencia nacional y el ansia cubana de patria y libertad; por los patriotas que en 1868 iniciaron las guerras de independencia contra el colonialismo español y los que en el último impulso de 1895 las llevaron a la victoria de 1898, que les fue arrebatada por la intervención y ocupación militar del imperialismo yanqui;

por los obreros, campesinos, estudiantes e intelectuales que lucharon durante más de cincuenta años contra el dominio imperialista, la corrupción política, la falta de derechos y libertades populares, el desempleo y la explotación impuesta por capitalistas y terratenientes;

por lo que promovieron e integraron y desarrollaron las primeras organizaciones de obreros y de campesinos, difundieron las ideas socialistas y fundaron los primeros movimientos marxista y marxista-leninista; por los integrantes de la vanguardia de la generación del centenario del natalicio de Martí, que nutridos por su magisterio nos condujeron a la victoria revolucionaria popular de Enero; por los que, con el sacrificio de sus vidas, defendieron la Revolución contribuyendo a su definitiva consolidación; por los que masivamente cumplieron heroicas misiones internacionalistas;

Guiados

por el ideario de José Martí y las ideas politico-sociales de Marx, Éngels y Lenin;

Apoyados

en el internacionalismo proletario, en la amistad fraternal, la ayuda, la cooperación y la solidaridad de los pueblos del mundo, especialmente los de América Latina y del Caribe;

Decididos

a llevar adelante la Revolución triunfadora del Moncada y del Granma, de la Sierra y de Girón encabezada por Fidel Castro que, sustentada en la más estrecha unidad de todas las fuerzas revolucionarias y del pueblo, conquistó la plena independencia nacional, estableció el poder revolucionario, realizó las transformaciones democráticas, inició la construcción del socialismo y, con el Partido Comunista al frente, la continúa con el objetivo final de edificar la sociedad comunista;

Conscientes

de que todos los régimenes sustentados en la explotación del hombre por el hombre determinan la humillación de los explotados y la degradación de la condición humana de los explotadores; de que sólo en el socialismo y el comunismo, cuando el hombre ha sido liberado de todas las formas de explotación: de la esclavitud, de la servidumbre y del capitalismo, se alcanza la entera dignidad del ser humano;

Cultura Latina

José Julian Martí (1853–1895) was a Cuban writer and patriot whose poetry, political prose, and eventual death in battle made him the martyred symbol of Cuban aspirations of independence.

y de que nuestra Revolución elevó la dignidad de la patria y del cubano a superior altura;

Declaramos

Nuestra voluntad de que la ley de leyes de la República esté presidida por este profundo anhelo, al fin logrado, de José Martí:

"Yo quiero que la ley primera de nuestra República sea el culto de los cubanos a la dignidad plena del hombre."

Vocabulario Útil:

Here are some vocabulary words to help you with this *lectura:*

➤ **preámbulo:** preamble

➤ **ciudadano:** citizen

➤ **heredero:** inheritor

➤ **continuador:** person who continues

➤ **creador:** creative

➤ **combatividad:** fighting spirit

➤ **firmeza:** firmness

➤ **heroísmo:** heroism

➤ **sacrificio:** sacrifice

➤ **forjar:** to forge; to shape

➤ **antecesor:** forefather; ancestor (formal)

➤ **aborígenes:** native peoples

➤ **exterminio:** extermination

➤ **sumisión:** submission

➤ **esclavo:** slave

➤ **rebelarse:** to rebel

➤ **ansia:** longing; wish (formal)

➤ **arrebatar:** to steal; to rob

➤ **imperialismo:** imperialism

➤ **yanqui:** Yankee; of the United States

➤ **obrero:** worker

➤ **luchar:** to fight

➤ **dominio:** dominion

➤ **definitivo:** final; definitive

➤ **popular:** popular; of the people

➤ **explotación:** exploitation

➤ **terrateniente:** landholder

➤ **promover:** to promote

➤ **difundir:** to broadcast; to publish

➤ **fundar:** to found

➤ **integrante:** someone who belongs to a group

➤ **centenario:** hundred-year anniversary

➤ **natalicio:** birth (formal)

➤ **nutrir:** to nurture

➤ **magisterio:** teaching

➤ **masivamente:** en masse

➤ **ideario:** ideas; ideology

➤ **guiar:** to guide

➤ **apoyar:** to support

➤ **internacionalismo:** internationalism

➤ **llevar adelante:** to promote; to bring forward

320

➤ **triunfador:** triumphant

➤ **encabezado por:** led by

➤ **sustentar:** to sustain; to hold

➤ **estrecho:** close; narrow

➤ **pueblo:** here, "the people"

➤ **al frente:** to the foreground;
   in the lead

➤ **objetivo:** goal; objective

➤ **edificar:** to edify; to construct

➤ **regímenes:** governments; regimes

➤ **liberar:** to free; to liberate

➤ **servidumbre:** servitude

➤ **alcanzar:** to reach

➤ **entero:** entire; whole

➤ **ser humano:** human being

➤ **voluntad:** will

➤ **presidido por:** to be presided
   over by

➤ **anhelo:** wish; desire; hope

➤ **culto:** reverence; worship

➤ **plena:** open; full

Análisis del Texto

Now let's take a closer look at a few excerpts from the *lectura:*

➤ *Nosotros, Ciudanos Cubanos*

There really isn't any better translation for this than "We, the Citizens of Cuba." You could also say, "We, the People of Cuba."

➤ *tradiciones de combatividad, firmeza, heroísmo y sacrificio forjadas por nuestros antecesores*

Notice that the *forjadas* refers to *tradiciones*. With all these extra words in the sentence, it's easy to get confused. Remember, the gender and number of *forjadas* links it back to the feminine plural of *tradiciones.*

➤ *prefirieron muchas veces el exterminio a la sumisión*

If you prefer one thing over another in Spanish, it's *preferir + a*, as in: *Prefiero la democracia al totalitarismo* ("I prefer democracy over (to) totalitarianism").

➤ *por los que despertaron la conciencia nacional*

The *los que* translates as "those who."

Acuérdate

The word for "patriot" is *patriota*. There is no change to *patrioto*. You must say *un patriota*, or *una patriota*. The word also can be used as an adjective, where again, there is no change. Of course, you will have to add *–s* whenever you're talking about something in plural.

321

➤ *que lucharon durante más de cincuenta años contra*

If you are fighting against something, it's *luchar contra,* as in: *Luchó contra la pobreza de su país* ("She fought against the poverty in her country"). The word *durante* does mean "during," but with time expressions, as in the previous phrase, it usually means "for."

➤ *por lo que promovieron e integraron y desarrollaron las primeras organizaciones de obreros y de campesinos*

Notice here how the subject comes after the conjugated verb. The subject here is actually *las primeras organizaciones.* Because Spanish verbs are linked to their subject by conjugation, placement of the subject may be at the end of the sentence, unlike in English, where the subject nearly always comes before the verb. Don't let this throw you off.

You can also see that in Spanish, you can say "promoted and integrated and developed," where in English, we would prefer to avoid too many "ands" and just say "promoted, integrated, and developed." Also, in a similar way, the second half "… of workers and of peasants" is worth mentioning. We English speakers would prefer not to repeat the second "of," but in Spanish, it is acceptable to say *de esto y de eso y del otro.*

➤ *por los integrantes de la vanguardia de la generación del centenario del natalicio de Martí, que nutridos por su magisterio nos condujeron a la victoria revolucionaria popular de Enero*

Here again we have a situation where the gender and number of the adjective links it back to something far away. The word *nutridos,* which means "nurtured," modifies *integrantes,* which means "members." How do I know this? Because *nutridos* is in the masculine plural form, and the only other masculine plural noun it could possibly modify is *integrantes.* Yes, gender and number continue to be our friends.

Castro marched into Havana in January 1959, and this event is often called "the January Revolution." Translated, the sentence would read: "… by the members of the vanguard of the one hundredth anniversary of the birth of Martí, who, nurtured by his teachings, brought us to the popular Revolution of January."

Algo Nuevo

When you're faced with a difficult passage in Spanish that you can't understand, pause, take a deep breath, and try to answer the following question: "Who is doing what to whom?" If you can figure out who or what the subject is, and who or what the object is, you can set this part aside and then start to decipher the other words. Spanish sentences have a tendency to become long and circuitous at times, and even native speakers occasionally need to read a sentence more than once to understand what's going on. Don't feel bad if you do, too.

> ➤ *Decididos a llevar adelante la Revolución triunfadora del Moncada y del Granma, de la Sierra y de Girón encabezada por Fidel Castro*

Time for a quick history lesson ....

On July 26, 1953, the Moncada army barracks in Santiago de Cuba were attacked by a revolutionary force led by Castro. The engagement, though unsuccessful, marked the beginning of the Cuban Revolution. Castro's forces became known as the 26th of July Movement. Castro was captured and sentenced to prison; he ultimately fled to Mexico.

Granma, believe it or not, actually comes from the English word "Grandma" (yes, "grandmother") and refers to an old boat that brought Castro back to Cuba in 1956. Today, it is the name of the country's official Communist Party newspaper. The *Sierra* refers to *la Sierra Maestra,* the mountains from which Castro organized and launched many of his revolutionary activities. Giron refers to *Playa Girón,* the beach that was the scene of the failed CIA-backed Bay of Pigs invasion of 1961.

Translated, this section would read: "Determined to bring forth the triumphant Revolution of the Moncada, the Grandma, of the Sierra (Maestra), and of Girón (Bay of Pigs), led by Fidel Castro ...."

> ➤ *la continúa con el objetivo final de edificar*

Make sure that you don't read the *la* as a definite article "the." That would really throw you off. The *la* is acting as a pronoun and refers back to *la construcción del socialismo* (see the sixth paragraph in the *lectura*).

Ten Cuidado

The word *régimen* is an unreliable cognate in English. *Régimen* is a cognate of "regime," which in English usually means "an oppressive government." In Spanish, it just means "government or administration" and isn't necessarily a negative word. Interestingly, when talking about food, *un régimen* is "a diet," as in "to go on a diet to lose weight."

Acuérdate

Remember that the definite article is required with most abstract nouns or when you are speaking in general about a specific subject. So, *la libertad* = "liberty," and *el baile* = "dancing in general."

➤ *sustentados en la explotación del hombre*

The *en* here should be translated as "by," rather than "on" or "in." So, this would read: "sustained by the exploitation of men." Remember that *el hombre* here means "men and women in general," not "the man." It may not be politically correct, but Spanish rarely is when it comes to gender.

➤ *Yo quiero que la ley primera de nuestra República sea*

Just a reminder: The *sea* must be in the subjunctive because it is preceded by the *Yo quiero*.

Gramática: Sorting Out Those Homonyms

You were already introduced to a few homonyms (words that are pronounced the same but are written differently) when we discussed *tildes* and the monosyllabic pronouns vs. possessives way back in the beginning of this book. Now we'll take a look at a few more homonyms in Spanish and see how the slight variation in spelling can make a big difference in what words mean. Some of the words in the following list are "true homonyms" in that they would be pronounced exactly the same by everyone and in all cases. Others are only homonyms in Latin America. You'll also see that the *tilde* (or lack thereof) can make a big difference.

The following list is not complete (that would require an entire book all to itself) but will nonetheless give you an idea of the kinds of spelling variations that you may come across, and highlight the types of spelling errors you should do your best to avoid:

Monosyllabic homonyms

➤ a (preposition)/**ha** (from *haber*)

➤ as ace (in cards)/**has** (from *haber*)

➤ ¡Ay! (an exclamation)/**hay**: there is/are

➤ ¡Eh! (an exclamation)/**he** (from *haber*)

➤ **oí** I heard/**hoy**: today

➤ **ahí**: there/**hay**: there is/are

Two-syllable homonyms:

➤ **aré** *(from arar)* to plow/**haré**: I will do

➤ **arte**: art/**harté**: I got fed up with

➤ **asar**: to cook; to broil/**azar**: random

➤ **baso** (from *basar*) to base/**vaso**: a drinking glass

➤ **bello**: beautiful/**vello**: body hair

➤ **bienes**: goods/**vienes**: (from *venir*) you come

➤ **botar**: to throw/**votar**: to vote

➤ **basar**: to base/**bazar**: market

➤ **barón**: baron or nobleman/**varón**: male

➤ **basto**: ordinary/**vasto**: vast; extensive

➤ **casar**: to marry/**cazar**: to hunt

➤ **echo** (from *echar)* to toss/**hecho**: *(from hacer)* done

➤ **calló**: he/she/it fell silent/**cayó**: he/she/it fell down/**callo**: a callus on the skin

➤ **errar**: to miss (not hit)/**herrar**: to shoe a horse

Three-syllable homonyms:

➤ **avía**: (from *aviar)* to prepare/**había**: (from *haber*)

➤ **ávido**: eager/**habido**: (from *haber*)

➤ **ablando, ablandar**: to soften/**hablando**: talking

➤ **abría**: (from *abrir*)/**habría**: (from *haber*)

➤ **alado**: winged/**halado**: (from *halar*) to haul

➤ **aprender**: to learn/**aprehender**: to apprehend

➤ **arroyo**: small river/**arrollo**: (from *arrollar*) to carry away

➤ **bacilo**: a microorganism/**vacilo**: (from *vacilar*) to vacillate

➤ **bestia**: beast/**vestía** (from *vestir*) to dress

Acuérdate

Bastante means "enough," and *demaciado* means "too much." In some contexts, however, they can also mean "a lot." So, *Los políticos son demaciado corruptos* may not mean "The politicians are too corrupt," but rather "they are very corrupt." Also, *Los yanquis tienen bastante dinero* might not mean "The Yankees have enough money," but rather "They have a lot of money."

Idiot's Guide to Idioms

Here are some more idioms and expressions to add to your collection:

➤ **El que no se tira al agua no pasa el río:** Nothing ventured, nothing gained.

➤ **en bandeja:** on a silver platter

➤ **en menos de lo que canta un gallo:** faster than a speeding bullet

➤ **en resumidas palabras:** in short

➤ **entre la espada y la pared:** between a rock and a hard place

➤ **en un abrir y cerrar de ojos:** in the blink of an eye

➤ **Eso es harina de otro costal:** That's a horse of a different color.

➤ **estar al margen:** to be out of the loop

➤ **estar echando chispas:** to be hopping mad

➤ **estar hasta la coronilla:** to be fed up

➤ **Hay gato encerrado:** I smell a rat.

➤ **Genio y figura hasta la sepultura:** Old habits die hard.

➤ **Hablando de la caída de Roma:** Speak of the devil ....

➤ **Hombre prevenido vale por dos:** Forewarned is forearmed.

Algo Nuevo

In Spanish, both *conservador* ("conservative") and *liberal* exist in a political context. But believe it or not, these words are actually unreliable cognates. With respect to the economy, *conservador* in Spanish implies that the government would "conserve" its control over the economy, which is different from the "small government, free market, and local control" that we tend to associate with conservatives. Conversely, a *liberal* government in Spanish implies that the government would maintain a hands-off approach to the economy, allowing for less government control, lower taxes, and more free enterprise.

Risa del Día

It is no wonder that with all the political instability the Spanish-speaking world has had to endure, politicians are not always held in the highest regard. As you might imagine, much of the humor surrounding politics and politicians is far too *verde* to tell here. These two jokes are a bit watered down.

By the way, in the second joke, *Pepito* is the same personage as the *Jaimito* you met in previous jokes:

➤ Escuela para políticos

Desde afuera de la escuela para políticos se escuchaba:

—*¡Corrupto! ... ¡Incapaz! ... ¡Coimero! ... ¡Ladrón!*

Y un hombre le dijo a otro:

—*Caramba, ¿a quien insultan tanto?*

—*No son insultos, sólo están pasando lista.*

➤ Gatos revolucionarios

Una maestra cubana dice a los niños que hagan una composición con un tema de la revolución y al terminar manda a Pepito a que lea la suya:

—*Yo tengo una gata que ayer tuvo cinco gaticos y todos los gaticos son revolucionarios.*

La maestra, al ver que Pepito sabía que hasta los gaticos deben ser revolucionarios, propone al director de la escuela que llame al inspector para que oiga la composición. Pasados tres días llega el inspector a la escuela y la maestra muy diligente le pide a Pepito que lea su composición y Pepito lee:

—*Yo tengo una gata que hace cinco días tuvo cinco gaticos y tres son revolucionarios.*

Al oír esto, la maestra reacciona rápidamente y le dice:

—*Pepito, la primera vez que leíste tu composición dijiste que todos los gaticos eran revolucionarios, ¿qué pasó?*

—*Bueno maestra, es que dos ya abrieron los ojos.*

Vocabulario Útil:

➤ **corrupto:** corrupt

➤ **incapaz:** incapable

➤ **coimero:** someone who accepts bribes

➤ **ladrón:** thief

➤ **caramba:** "my goodness"

➤ **insultar:** to insult

➤ **insulto:** insult

➤ **pasar lista:** to take roll call

➤ **tema:** topic; issue; theme

➤ **mandar mandor:** to order; to have someone do something

➤ **la suya:** his

➤ **gatico:** kitten (*gatito* also possible)

➤ **proponer:** to propose; to suggest

➤ **pasados:** here, "after"

➤ **diligente:** diligent

➤ **hace cinco días:** five days ago

➤ **reaccionar:** to react

➤ **abrir los ojos:** to open one's eyes; "to realize the truth"

Acuérdate

The word *tema* is a cognate of "theme" but can be heard in everyday conversation as meaning "issue, question, subject, or topic." It can also be used as a filler to begin a statement, as in: *El tema es que el gobierno no respeta la voluntad del pueblo* ("The issue is that the government doesn't respect the will of the people").

El Cuiz

Please provide the Spanish. If you cheat, your local government will be overthrown by rebel forces:

1. heroism _____

2. citizen _____

3. sacrifice _____

4. creative _____

5. to rebel _____

6. imperialism _____

7. fighting spirit _____

8. dominion _____

9. final; definitive _____

10. slave _____

11. worker _____

12. to found _____

13. someone who belongs to a group _____

14. to fight for _____

15. popular; of the people _____

16. landholder _____

17. to promote _____

18. to broadcast; to publish _____

19. to support _____

20. triumphant _____

21. sacrifice _____

22. ideas; ideology _____

23. to guide _____

24. goal; objective _____

25. government _____

26. to sustain; to hold _____

27. to reach _____

28. entire; whole _____

29. close; narrow _____

30. party (political) _____

31. wish; desire; hope _____

32. incapable _____

33. someone who accepts bribes _____

34. thief _____

35. to insult _____

36. corrupt _____

37. to react _____

38. human being _____

39. topic; issue; theme _____

40. to propose; to suggest _____

Tareas

1. Go online or visit your favorite library and research the political situation of the Spanish-speaking country that most interests you.

2. Obtain a text in Spanish about a political event or issue (go online or check in a Spanish-language publication), and underline any words that are unfamiliar to you. Or, if you want to start with English, take a political text from your local newspaper and underline some words that you wouldn't know how to say in Spanish. Either way, when you have a list of at least 15 words, try to translate them into the other language using your dictionary.

3. Spend some time reviewing the homonyms you learned in this chapter. Notice how the addition or change of one letter or *tilde* can make a big difference in what a word means.

The Least You Need to Know

➤ Politics have been a hot topic in the Spanish-speaking world for a long time.

➤ There has been considerable progress in recent years toward increasing political stability in Latin America.

➤ Numerous homonyms exist in Spanish; even the smallest changes in spelling or accentuation can mean a difference in the meaning of a word.

Chapter 27

La Medicina

In This Chapter

➤ *Lectura:* Complicaciones Neuro-vasculares Periféricas en el Diabético

➤ *Gramática:* reviewing reflexive verbs

➤ Continuing the idiot's guide to idioms

There is currently a great demand in the United States for bilingual health care practitioners. If you are considering a career in health care, you'll have little difficulty finding a job if you can speak both Spanish and English.

Although many of us find the jargon used by doctors to be a big headache, the good news is that much of the "doctor-ese" used by English-speaking doctors is the same in Spanish because both languages use Latin and Greek roots to form such words. Of course, while it's great to recognize that *angiopatía* means "angiopathy" in English, if you don't know what "angiopathy" means, the cognate is of little help. Sometimes you'll need to look up the meaning of a word, even if you know what the equivalent is in English. Still, even if you have no interest in medicine, I invite you to read the following medical-related text.

Lectura: Complicaciones Neuro–vasculares Periféricas en el Diabético

The following medical text is not too bad. If it causes you any discomfort, take two *aspirinas y llámame en la mañana:*

> *Actualmente es poco común que un enfermo fallezca de coma o cetoacidosis diabética. No obstante, en un 70 por ciento de los casos existen serias complicaciones vasculares. Las alteraciones vasculares que dan origen al pie diabético están presentes en mayor o menor grado en el 80 por ciento de los diabéticos que tienen más de 10 años de evolución. Es digno de recordarse que en 1934 se afirmó en forma contundente y clara: Las complicaciones más graves en el pie se pueden evitar siguiendo unas cuantas reglas básicas en la educación del paciente.*

> *Una de cada cinco internaciones hospitalarias de diabéticos es por lesiones en el pie. El riesgo de amputación es 15 veces mayor que en pacientes no diabéticos y ocupa 50 a 70 por ciento de las amputaciones no traumáticas que se efectúan en hospitales generales. De aquí que, el explorar en forma rutinaria el pie del diabético cada vez que asiste a consulta para el control metabólico, constituye el método ideal de prevención al permitir la detección de las lesiones en forma temprana.*

> *Las dos lesiones básicas que se presentan en alguna etapa de la evolución de la diabetes son la neuropatía y la angiopatía. Pueden encontrarse aisladas aunque lo más común es que se asocien, y que médica y clínicamente se vea que predomina alguna de las dos. La neuropatía produce una pérdida de sensibilidad y una pérdida del sentido de posición del pie. La neuropatía motora afecta a todos los músculos del pie y en ocasiones provoca deformaciones características; la neuropatía de los nervios vaso-motores da falsamente un pie caliente a pesar de existir un riego sanguíneo defectuoso.*

> *Las infecciones son muchas veces no detectables hasta que la extremidad, e incluso la vida estén amenazadas. El paciente diabético no suele percibir la progresión de la úlcera y los signos y síntomas de la infección no se manifiestan hasta más tarde.*

Vocabulario Útil:

➤ **periférico:** peripheral

➤ **actualmente:** currently; these days

➤ **enfermo:** here, "a person who is ill"

➤ **fallecer:** to pass away; die (kinder than *morir*)

➤ **un coma:** a coma

➤ **diabético:** diabetic (adjective and noun)

➤ **no obstante:** nonetheless

➤ **alteración:** change; alteration

➤ **dar origen:** to originate

➤ **mayor o menor:** more or less; about

➤ **digno:** worthy

➤ **afirmarse:** to affirm; to maintain

➤ **contundente:** conclusively; convincingly

➤ **regla:** rule

➤ **educación:** instruction

➤ **internación:** admission (to a medical facility)

➤ **hospitalario:** hospital (adjective)

➤ **lesión:** injury; wound

➤ **riesgo:** risk

➤ **ocupar:** to occupy

➤ **no traumático:** nontraumatic

➤ **efectuarse:** to be performed

➤ **de aquí que:** thus

➤ **el explorar:** exploring

➤ **rutinario:** routine

➤ **asistir:** to attend; to go to

➤ **consulta:** consultation

➤ **metabólico:** metabolic

➤ **detección:** detection

➤ **etapa:** stage

➤ **neuropatía:** neuropathy

➤ **angiopatía:** angiopathy

➤ **aislado:** isolated

➤ **asociarse:** here, "to be found together"

➤ **predominar:** to predominate

➤ **pérdida:** loss

➤ **sensibilidad:** sensitivity

➤ **sentido:** feeling

➤ **motor:** motor (adjective)

➤ **en ocasiones:** sometimes; occasionally

➤ **riego:** here, "supply"

➤ **sanguíneo:** blood (adjective)

➤ **defectuoso:** defective

➤ **manifiestar:** to show; to manifest

Análisis del Texto

Time to perform a physical exam on our little *lectura:*

➤ *es poco común que un enfermo fallezca*

Fallezca is the subjunctive of *fallecer*. Even though it is not common for people to die from this condition, it is still possible and could happen from time to time. The uncertainty and possibility of the statement requires *fallezca* instead of *fallece*.

➤ *10 años de evolución*

I might have understood this as "evolution" the first time I read it, too. Obviously, though, these patients aren't "evolving." You need to see beyond the obvious cognate here and think of the secondary meanings of this word, such as "progression" or "development."

Acuérdate

The verb *soler* (*suelo, sueles,* and so on) + infinitive means "to usually ...": *Suele tener muchos problemas médicos* means "He usually has a lot of medical problems." *Soler* is not used too often in conversation. The verb *acostumbrar* and the verbal phrase *tener el costumbre de* tend to be more common.

Ten Cuidado

Remember that *actualmente* is a false friend. It means "these days" and "in the present time," not "actually."

➤ *siguiendo unas cuantas reglas básicas*

Here, *siguiendo* needs to be translated as "by following." Remember that *cuánto,* as an interrogative (question word), is left in the singular gender-neutral form, but must match gender and number when used adjectivally. Translation: "by following a few basic rules."

➤ *una de cada cinco internaciones hospitalarias de diabéticos*

Here we have the "four out of five doctors" construction. Note that *una* is feminine because it is linked to *internaciones*. Translation: "one out of every five hospital admissions of diabetics."

Algo Nuevo

In this *lectura,* we have a fine example of "*el* + infinitive" in *el explorar en forma rutinaria*. In Spanish, it is possible to create nouns from verbs by using the masculine singular article *el* plus an infinitive verb. This is not generally the preferred construction where a more common noun exists; I wouldn't say *el trabajar* for "work" when I can simply say *trabajo*. But if I wanted to express the idea of "working with Spanish-speaking patients" as a singular idea, I could say *el trabajar con pacientes de habla hispana*.

➤ *a pesar de existir*

The phrase *a pesar de* means "in spite of." It can be followed by *que* when there is another clause after it: *A pesar de que Juan está enfermo* = "In spite of the fact that Juan is ill." In cases of doubt or uncertainty, the verb may be in the subjunctive mood: *A pesar de que el médico pueda tratarlo* = "In spite of the fact that the doctor may be able to treat him." It can also be followed by an infinitive (without the *que*): *A pesar de haber intentado curarlo, el pobre falleció* = "In spite of having tried to cure him, the poor guy passed away."

➤ *e incluso*

Don't forget that the word *y* becomes *e* before *i*, *y*, and *hi*. And *o* becomes *u* before *u* and *hu*. Just a reminder ....

Gramática: Reviewing Reflexive Verbs

Reflexive verbs usually are covered in basic Spanish textbooks. But this chapter offers a good opportunity to review those reflexives with a different perspective.

Esteban's Guide to Reflexive Verbs

When you wash yourself, talk to yourself, or ask yourself a question, your actions are considered reflexive: "I talk to myself." In other words, when the object of a verb (in this case, "myself") is the same as the person doing the action (in this case, "I"), we have a reflexive construction. So, while "The dog bit Bob" is not reflexive, "The dog bit his tail (his own tail)" is.

Many introductory textbooks make a big deal out of reflexive verbs, as if they were creatures all to their own. However, most reflexive verbs aren't "reflexive verbs" at all, but simply reflexive constructions using regular old verbs. What makes them reflexive is that the indirect object pronoun (INDOP)—or sometimes just the direct object pronoun (DOP)—and the person doing the action of the verb are one and the same. That's all there is to it.

As you know, a "reflexive verb" is written as an infinitive with *se* attached to it:

➤ **lavarse:** to wash oneself

➤ **preguntarse:** to ask oneself

➤ **tocarse:** to touch oneself (such as your nose)

➤ **cuidarse:** to take care of oneself

➤ **bañarse:** to bathe oneself

Acuérdate

When a *–mente* adverb is followed by a second (or third) *–mente* adverb, only the last in the series actually takes the *–mente* suffix. In the *lectura*, you saw *médica y clínicamente*. This should be understood as "medically and clinically." Another example: *Te quiero profunda y eterna y cariñosamente* means "I love you deeply, eternally, and affectionately."

Acuérdate

When the object of a verb is part of your body, the construction is as follows: *Me lavo las manos* ("I wash myself the hands"). While *Yo lavo mis manos* would be understood, it is not the correct construction for Spanish.

As a quick review, here are those reflexive pronouns again:

The Reflexive Pronouns

Pronoun	Example
me	*me lavo*
te	*te lavas*
se	*se lava*
nos	*nos lavamos*
os	*os laváis*
se	*se lavan*

Notice how the conjugations of the verb follow the changes in the pronoun. This is our big clue to reflexiveness, unlike many other DOPs and INDOPs, where the verbs don't conjugate according to the object pronoun, but according to who or what was doing the action.

Take a quick look at the following example to see what I'm talking about:

➤ **Te amo:** I love you. (not reflexive)

➤ **Te aman:** They love you. (not reflexive)

➤ **Te amamos:** We love you. (still not reflexive)

➤ **Te amas:** You love yourself. (Finally, we have a reflexive—the *te* and the *tú* are linked because they are both in the second person singular.)

Algo Nuevo

There is a construction in Spanish that looks like a reflexive but is actually an expression of mutuality ("each other"). When you see *se* + third person plural, you may be dealing with such a construction: *Los novios se besan* means "The boyfriend and girlfriend kiss each other" (not "they kiss themselves"). When you come across one of these, pay attention to the context of the sentence. For example, *Los niños se lavan* could mean "The children are washing themselves" or "The children are washing each other."

So why is *te amas* reflexive? There is no reflexive verb jumping into the picture out of nowhere. It's the same old *amar*. But the construction is reflexive because the person doing the action (*tú*) and the object of that action (*te*) are one and the same. Yes, we could say that the reflexive verb here is *amarse*, but that doesn't matter—the construction is the important thing.

Many verbs that are reflexive in Spanish are not reflexive in English (and vice versa). However, the idea of yourself being the object is still understandable if you stretch your imagination a little:

➤ **preocuparse**: to worry (oneself)

➤ **sentarse**: to sit down (to sit yourself down)

➤ **preguntarse**: to wonder (to ask yourself)

➤ **lastimarse**:   to hurt (yourself)

➤ **emborracharse**: to get (yourself) drunk

➤ **encontrarse**: to be (to find yourself)

There are exceptions:

➤ **enamorarse**: to fall in love (not with yourself)

➤ **sentirse**: to feel (not "to feel yourself," but to feel in terms of your health and/or emotional state)

➤ **irse**: to leave (not to leave yourself)

You'll find that your dictionary will give you definitions for reflexive verbs, but in reality very few verbs exist *only* as reflexives. So, my advice is that you not think of these verbs as "reflexive verbs" but rather as reflexive constructions using regular old verbs when the subject and object are the same.

Here are some additional examples to show you what I mean:

➤ **Me lastimé la espalda**: I hurt my back.

➤ **¿Cómo se siente?**: How do you feel?

➤ **Tengo que irme**: I have to leave.

Acuérdate

If you are injured and need to cry for help, yell *¡Socorro!* (In English we have the word "succor.") Yes, *ayuda* also means "help," but isn't quite as shoutable as *socorro*: *¡Socorro! Me he caído y no puedo levantarme!* means "Help, I've fallen and I can't get up!" By the way, Socorro is also a town south of Albuquerque, New Mexico.

Acuérdate

The verb *dormir* means "to sleep," but when it's reflexive (*dormirse*) it means "to fall asleep." It's a subtle difference, as in *Siempre duermo bien, pero anoche no pude dormirme*, which means "I always sleep well, but last night I couldn't fall asleep."

Acuérdate

You know that *ir* means "to go." Add the reflexive *se*, and it becomes *irse* ("to leave"). Perhaps the idea is "to go and take yourself with you." Who knows ....

Haz Clic Aquí

Visit the Web sites www. geocities.com/CollegePark/ Campus/2024/verb23.html and www. chass. utoronto.ca/spanish_ portuguese/spa220/gramatica.html for additional explanations about reflexive verbs. Both sites are excellent resources.

➤ **Me pregunto si eso va a ser posible:** I wonder (ask myself) if that is going to be possible.

➤ **Me duele el codo y no quiero tocármelo:** My elbow hurts and I don't want to touch it.

➤ **Mis amigos quieren que yo me emborrache, pero yo no lo voy a hacer:** My friends want me to get drunk, but I'm not going to do it.

➤ **El hombre no quiso sentarse:** The man refused to sit down.

Diálogo: No Me Siento Bien

No matter how fascinating your surroundings may be, being sick is never fun. In this *diálogo*, Kathy has gotten ill during a trip to Colombia and has gone to the doctor in search of relief. She's a bit of a hypochondriac, so you'll get to hear about a lot of different illnesses, both real and imagined:

El médico: *Buenas tardes, señora.*

Kathy: *Señorita.*

El médico: *Ay perdón, señorita. ¿Cómo se siente el día de hoy?*

Kathy: *Ay, doctor, no me siento nada bien.*

El médico: *¿Qué le pasa?*

Kathy: *Bueno, cada vez que salgo para hacer algo me enfermo.*

El médico: *No me diga. A ver. ¿Cuáles son sus síntomas?*

Kathy: *Tengo hinchazón en la mano izquierda, ampollas en el pie derecho, y un sarpullido en la espalda. Y ando muy mal del estomago, doctor. Tengo dolores de cabeza y de la garganta. Me siento mareada e inquieta. Tengo mucha tos, y estornudo todo el tiempo. Creo que tengo también la ictiricia, la hepatitis, la alta presión, la diabetes, e inclusive el cáncer pulmonar. Ya va para dos días que tengo ... usted sabe ... la diarrea. ¿Usted cree que voy a morirme?*

El médico: *Pues, no sé. Déjeme examinarla primero.* (La examina el médico. Parece que no tiene nada.) *Bueno, no creo que se vaya a morir. De hecho, me parece que usted es una persona físicamente muy sana. Vamos a ver si no le podemos quitar lo de la diarrea. ¿De acuerdo?*

Kathy: *Sí, está bien.*

El médico: *¿Quisiera que le prepare un té de manzanilla?*

Kathy: *¿Té de mazanilla? No puede ser. ¿En serio?*

El médico: *No, señorita. Se lo dije en broma. Estudié la medicina en la Clinica Mayo en Minnessota y en el Hopsital de la Universidad de Stanford en California. Le voy a dar una reseta para unas pastillas. Puede ir a la farmacia para comprar la medicína. Tome dos tres veces al día hasta que se sienta mejor.*

Kathy: *Bueno, y si todavía estoy mal, ¿qué debo hacer?*

El médico: *Llame al consultorio para hacer una cita.*

Kathy: *Pues, espero que estas pastillas me hagan efecto. ¿Pero qué voy a hacer para las otras enfermedads que tengo?*

El médico: *Conozco a un buen psicólogo.*

Ten Cuidado

Be aware that the *se* passive (*Se habla español* = "Spanish is spoken") can look like a reflexive construction. Usually the context of the statement will tell you what's going on. Spanish can't speak itself, obviously, but *Juan se habla* would mean "Juan is talking to himself."

Translation:

The doctor: Good afternoon, Madam.

Kathy: Miss.

The doctor: Oh, sorry, Miss. How do you feel today?

Kathy: Oh, doctor, I don't feel well at all (*nada* here means "at all").

The doctor: What's wrong (with you)?

Kathy: Well, every time I go out to do something I get sick.

The doctor: You don't say. Let's see. What are your symptoms?

Kathy: I've got swelling in my left hand, blisters on my right foot, and a rash on my back. And I've got stomach problems, doctor. I have headaches and (pain in my) throat. I feel dizzy and uneasy. I cough a lot, and I sneeze all the time. I think I also have jaundice, hepatitis, high blood pressure, diabetes, and even lung cancer. It's been nearly two days that I've had—you know—diarrhea. Do you think I'm going to die?

The doctor: Well, I don't know. Let me examine you first. (The doctor examines her; she looks fine.) Well, I don't think that you're going to die. In fact, you seem to be a very healthy person, physically. Let's see if we can't take care of (remove) the diarrhea. Agreed?

Kathy: Yes, all right.

The doctor: Would you like me to make you some chamomile tea?

Kathy: Chamomile tea? That can't be right. Are you serious?

Haz Clic Aquí

If you are interested in medical terminology, visit http://usuarios. bitmailer.com/rafabravo/ busmedline.html. You can access the site's *glosario médico* and surf the links to other Spanish-language publications about medicine.

The doctor: No, Miss. I was just kidding (I said it to you in jest). I studied medicine at the Mayo Clinic in Minnesota and at Stanford University Hospital in California. I'm going to give you a prescription for some pills. You can go to the pharmacy to buy the pills. Take two three times a day until you feel better.

Kathy: All right, and if I still feel bad, what should I do?

The doctor: Call the office to make an appointment.

Kathy: Well, I hope these pills are effective (on me). But what am I going to do about the other illnesses I have?

The doctor: I know a good psychologist.

Idiot's Guide to Idioms

Here are some more idioms and sayings to help you expand your Spanish vocabulary:

➤ **ir al grano:** to come to the point

➤ **largarle a otro el mochuelo:** to pass the buck

➤ **llover a cántaros:** to rain cats and dogs

➤ **llovido del cielo:** a godsend

➤ **los que mandan:** the powers that be

➤ **más pobre que una rata:** poor as a church mouse

➤ **Más vale un pájaro en la mano que cien volando:** A bird in the hand is worth two in the bush.

➤ **Más vale prevenir que lamentar:** Better safe than sorry.

➤ **matar la gallina de los huevos de oro:** to kill the goose that lays the golden egg

➤ **meter planca:** to pull strings (to have influence)

➤ **No es nada del otro mundo:** It's nothing to write home about.

➤ **Ojos que no ven, corazón que no siente:** Out of sight, out of mind.

➤ **por un pelo:** by the skin of one's teeth

Cultura Latina

Folk remedies, homeopathy, and herbal medicines are all quite popular in Latin America. Depending on where you are, you may be offered a traditional remedy for your ailments, such as chamomile tea (*té de manzanilla*) or *las ventosas* (suction cups applied to the skin to draw out disease). You may or may not believe in such practices, but for some people they are part of everyday life.

Risa del Día

The doctor/patient joke is classic in Spanish:

➤ Paciente olvidón ....

—*Doctor, doctor ... ¿cómo sé si estoy perdiendo la memoria?*

—*Eso ya se lo dije ayer.*

➤ Más allá del oficio ....

Un hombre va a la consulta del medico y le dice:

—*¡Doctor, me he caído y me duelen mucho las piernas!*

El doctor después de examinarlo le dice:

—*No se preocupe, no es nada. Dentro de unos días ya estará usted trabajando.*

—*Caramba Doctor, qué maravilla, además de curarme ¿me dará trabajo?*

➤ Consejos dentales, y de moda

Un hombre va al dentista y le dice:

—*Doctor, tengo los dientes muy amarillos, ¿que me recomienda?*

¡Corbata marrón!

➤ Respuesta inesperada

Una paciente le dice a su médico:

—*Doctor, ¡la pierna que me operó me quedó más corta!*

Y el médico le responde:

—*No se preocupe señora, le puedo hacer la misma operación en la otra pierna.*

Acuérdate

The prefix *in–* often corresponds to "un–" in English. So, *inesperado* is "unexpected," and *intocable* would be "untouchable."

Vocabulario Útil:

➤ **olvidón:** forgetful

➤ **perder:** to lose

➤ **corbata:** a tie

➤ **marrón:** brown

➤ **más allá:** beyond

➤ **oficio:** trade; duty

➤ **maravilla:** a wonder; a marvelous thing

➤ **curar:** to cure

➤ **consejo:** advice

➤ **inesperado:** unexpected

El Cuiz

Provide the Spanish equivalents. If you cheat, your HMO will deny your benefits for all your medical bills:

1. to originate _____

2. progression _____

3. worthy _____

4. currently; these days _____

5. a person who is ill _____

6. to pass away; die (kinder than *morir*) _____

7. admission (to a medical facility) _____

8. hospital (adjective) _____

9. nonetheless _____

10. to affirm; to maintain _____

11. exploring _____

12. routine _____

13. conclusively; convincingly _____

14. rule _____

15. injury; wound _____

16. risk _____

17. traumatic _____

18. to be performed _____

19. thus _____

20. consultation _____

21. sensitivity _____

22. stage _____

23. isolated _____

24. blood (adjective) _____

25. defective _____

26. loss _____

27. feeling _____

28. to show; to manifest _____

29. trade; duty _____

30. advice _____

31. forgetful _____

32. unexpected _____

Tareas

1. Using the examples in this chapter, create sentences with reflexive constructions. You don't have to look up reflexive verbs for this exercise. Remember that almost any old verb can be used reflexively.

2. Research a topic that relates to medicine, anatomy, or health care and create a vocabulary list from words that interest you.

The Least You Need to Know

➤ Medical jargon tends to be the same in both English and Spanish.

➤ Reflexive infinitives have a *se* on the end.

➤ You can recognize a reflexive construction when the subject and the object are the same.

➤ Reflexive verbs are often just regular old verbs placed in a reflexive construction.

Chapter 28

Transportación e Infraestructura

In This Chapter

➤ *Lectura:* los medios de transporte e infraestructura de Venezuela

➤ *Gramática:* Esteban's final advice on cognates

➤ Your final idiot's guide to idioms

Much of the development taking place in Latin America today involves the improvement of infrastructure. Economic reforms can go only so far if goods and services can't be moved from place to place in a timely manner. Food and basic supplies won't be distributed to the areas most in need if roads are inadequate or nonexistent; products cannot be received or shipped without a well-maintained system of roads, airports, rail service, and harbors. Even tourism, which has become a viable alternative to industrialization in some areas of the Spanish-speaking world, must be supported by airports, highways, and sanitation systems to ensure the access and safety of the tourists that each country hopes to attract. Ultimately, the natural environment (*el medio ambiente*) will be irreparably compromised if development is not undertaken wisely and with great care.

With this in mind, I thought that a chapter about infrastructure and transportation would be a good way to finish this book. So, here we go ....

Lectura: Los Medios de Transporte e Infraestructura de Venezuela

Your last *lectura* discusses the infrastructure of Venezuela and the country's plans to make improvements:

Cultura Latina

Most Spanish-speaking countries have at least one national airline. Some of the more well-known airlines are Lan Chile, Aerolíneas Argentinas, Mexicana, Aero-México, Iberia, TAME (Ecuador), Avianca (Colombia), Lasca (Costa Rica), and TACA (Honduras and other Central American countries).

Transporte Marítimo: *La ley que crea el Consejo Nacional de Puertos y el Instituto Nacional de Puertos, adscribe a éste, ocho puertos: Puerto Sucre, Puerto Carúpano, Puerto de Guanta, Puerto El Guamache, Puerto Guaranao, Puerto La Guaira, Puerto de Maracaibo y el Puerto de Puerto Cabello* (Author's note: These are all names of places. Don't worry about them). *Los tres últimos son los más importantes en cuanto al volumen de carga de exportación e importación.*

También existen numerosos puertos privados que son generalmente de empresas industriales (aluminio, petroleras, mineras, cementeras y de productos químicos) para la carga y descarga de sus insumos y materias primas.

Servicio Aéreo: *Venezuela mantiene conexión aérea con casi todos los países del mundo, directa o indirectamente a través de las operadoras instaladas en el país. Las líneas aéreas venezolanas aunadas a las principales líneas internacionales permiten una estructura confiable para importar y exportar. Los itinerarios son autorizados por el Ministerio de Transporte y Comunicaciones tanto para el transporte internacional de carga como para el de pasajeros.*

Red de Carreteras: *De los 77.785 km. de carretera 22.780 son asfaltadas y 24.720 son pavimentadas. En Venezuela existen líneas de transporte terrestre con excelente infraestructura, las que conjuntamente con las empresas transportistas menores permiten una disponibilidad de servicio de transporte de carga terrestre de aproximadamente 80 empresas. Las principales ciudades de Venezuela se comunican con una amplia red de carreteras asfaltadas, esta red está conformada por las autopistas Caracas-La Guaira, Caracas-Valencia, Valencia-Puerto Cabello, Ciudad Bolívar-Upata, Autopista Centro Occidental, Autopista del Llano José Antonio Paéz (sin concluir), Autopista de Oriente (en ampliación).*

Ferrocarril: *Existen 439 km. La única línea comercial existente conecta Puerto Cabello (geográficamente al centro de la costa venezolana) con Barquisimeto. Está en proyecto el desarrollo de la Red Nacional de Ferrocarriles, la cual dependerá del Instituto Autónomo Ferrocarriles del Estado (FERROCAR).*

346

Administración y Desarrollo de Infra-estructuras: Más de treinta proyectos se están abriendo a la inversión privada nacional y extranjera a través del régimen de concesiones. Esto representa una oportunidad importante para compan[td]ías internacionales al proporcionarles campo en el desarrollo de obras públicas y servicios asociados. El gobierno de Venezuela busca otorgar diez autopistas, cuatro carreteras y caminos, un puente de tres kilómetros sobre el Río Orinoco y dos canales de navegación. Cuatro puertos y dos aeropuertos, así como varios servicios de transporte aéreo y terrestre se abrirán también a la inversión privada. La Ley de Concesiones para el Otorgamiento de Obras y Servicios Públicos contempla el otorgamiento de obras y servicios públicos existentes, y su mantenimiento, gerencia y explotación, concediendo al inversionista la posibilidad de cobrar tarifas y peajes.

Haz Clic Aquí

If you're interested in reading more about development and infrastructure of Latin American countries, visit the following Web sites: www.alojo.com/ongs/sin_imagenes/iinfraes.htm, www.alcaldia.com/plandesarrollo/transporte.html, or www.iadb.org/sds/utility.cfm/151/SPANISH/pub/81 You can also search for "*infra-estructura y desarrollo*" to find other sites.

Vocabulario Útil:

- ➤ **crear:** to create
- ➤ **medios:** means (noun)
- ➤ **marítimo:** maritime; of the sea
- ➤ **consejo:** council; advisory board
- ➤ **puerto:** port
- ➤ **adscribir:** to ascribe
- ➤ **insumos:** supplies; consumables
- ➤ **materias primas:** raw materials
- ➤ **aéreo:** air (adjective)
- ➤ **operadora:** here, airline operator
- ➤ **aunar:** to combine; to hook up with
- ➤ **confiable:** dependable
- ➤ **itinerario:** schedule
- ➤ **carga:** load; freight
- ➤ **carretera:** roadway; highway

- ➤ **terrestre:** by land
- ➤ **infraestructura:** infrastructure
- ➤ **conjuntamente:** in partnership with; together
- ➤ **disponibilidad:** availability
- ➤ **empresa:** company; firm
- ➤ **comunicarse:** here, "are connected"
- ➤ **red:** network
- ➤ **conformar:** to constitute; to make up
- ➤ **autopista:** highway
- ➤ **en ampliación:** being enlarged
- ➤ **ferrocarril:** rail; train
- ➤ **existente:** in existence
- ➤ **en proyecto:** projected

Acuérdate

Remember that *sin* ("without") can take an infinitive verb. These phrases should be translated as "without X-ing," as in: *sin saber* ("without knowing") and *sin tener* ("without having"). Occasionally, "not yet X-ed" sounds better: *sin conluir* means "not yet completed."

Ten Cuidado

The English word "investment" shows us why we cannot always employ cognates as a way to fumble through Spanish. The verb *investir* does not mean "to invest," but "to swear in or inaugurate." *Investar* doesn't exist. Investment and the verb "to invest" are *inversión* and *invertir*, respectively. If you say *Quiero investir mi dinero*, that would mean "I want to inaugurate my money," which obviously makes no sense.

➤ **desarrollo:** development

➤ **inversión:** investment

➤ **régimen:** here, plan

➤ **campo:** field

➤ **obras públicas:** public works

➤ **otorgar:** to authorize

➤ **contemplar:** to stipulate

➤ **otorgamiento:** authorization

➤ **cobrar:** to charge money

➤ **tarifa:** fee

➤ **peaje:** toll

Análisis del Texto

Now let's take a look at the more interesting parts of the *lectura:*

➤ *la ley que crea el Consejo Nacional de Puertos y el Instituto Nacional de Puertos, adscribe a éste*

Here's a trick question: Why is *éste* masculine if it refers to *ley?* Well, because it doesn't refer to *ley*, but rather to *consejo*. Now, if *éste* had been *ésta,* then, yes, it would have had to be linked back to *ley*. See how important gender is?

➤ *también existen numerosos puertos privados*

Numerosos, when it means "numerous," almost always comes before the noun. You could say *una familia numerosa* for "a large family," but in the plural, *numerosa* tends to come first. This is also the case with the similar adjective *varios* (several).

➤ *servicio aéreo*

The adjective *aéreo* means "air," as in *correo aéreo* ("air mail"). Don't say *correo de aire* or *servicio de aire*, which would actually mean "mail made out of air" or "service made out of air." On the other hand, you can't say *bolsa aérea* for "the airbag" in your car, which is *bolsa de aire*. Go figure ....

➤ *tanto para el transporte internacional de carga como para el de pasajeros*

If you aren't already familiar with the *tanto/como* construction, learn it now: *Tanto los automóviles como las motocicletas pasarán por el puente* means "Both the cars and the motorcycles will go over the bridge." The phrase above would translate as: "Both for the international transportation of freight as well as for passengers." The *el* in *el de* functions as a pronoun for *transporte*. Note the gender link.

➤ *existen líneas de transporte terrestre con excelente infraestructura, las que conjuntamente con las empresas transportistas menores permiten*

The *las que* part would translate simply as "which." So, this would be: "there are lines of ground transportation with excellent infrastructure, which, along with the smaller transportation companies, allow for …."

➤ *está en proyecto el desarrollo de la Red Nacional de Ferrocarriles*

It is not uncommon to see a helping verb and a noun used together. We do the same thing in English, where "to make progress" and "to progress" mean about the same thing. Here we see *está en proyecto*. The verb *proyectar* also exists and means about the same thing. Both would be translated in English as "planned" or "projected."

➤ *al proporcionarles campo*

Campo does mean "country," and *quiero pasar un día de campo* could mean "I want to go for a picnic." But in our example here, *campo* means more "an opportunity to become a participant in the field." *Proporcionar* means "to supply or offer." Colloquially, it can be used as "to get hold of," as in *Por fin logré proporcionarme un vehículo* ("I was finally able to get a car").

Acuérdate

The phrase *así como* is a nice way to say "as well as" in Spanish: *Obtuve mi licencia de conducir, así como la registración de mi vehículo* means "I obtained my driver's license, as well as the registration for my vehicle."

Acuérdate

Many less common "verb + noun" phrases may not be in your dictionary. You'll find the common ones, such as *tener éxitio* ("to be successful") and *hacer frío* ("to have cold weather"), but some, such as *estar en proyecto*, may be missing. If you're stuck, look up both the noun and the verb; based on the examples given, try to understand what is meant by way of context.

Algo Nuevo

You know that the verb *buscar* means "to look for," but it has a few other secondary meanings as well. In some contexts, *buscar* means "to try to achieve," as in: *un programa que busca mayor inversión en el sector público* ("a program that aims to achieve a greater investment in the public sector"). It can also be followed by an infinitive: *El gobierno busca ortogar la construcción* means "The government is attempting (trying, setting out) to authorize the construction." *Buscar* can also mean "to get or pick up," as in *Te voy a buscar en el aeropuerto* ("I'm going to pick you up at the airport").

Gramática: Esteban's Final Advice About Cognates

Yes, Spanish and English really do share a lot of words. Most of these words come from our "dead amigos" of Latin and Greek. The prefixes and suffixes that you learned in this book will help you tremendously in recognizing and producing words that are cognates in both languages. Cognates can help you understand many Spanish words with minimal effort. They can also help you produce new Spanish words practically out of thin air. But as with most things in *la vida,* there's a catch. Read on to learn more ....

Algo Nuevo

Linguists divide cognates into several subcategories, depending on how similar the words are to each other. For the purposes of this book, we can define a cognate as any word that looks reasonably similar in both languages and that means about the same thing. Some of these *amigos* are written exactly the same in both languages, while others require you to work a little harder.

Recognizing Cognates

While there are some words in Spanish and English that are identical, more words are nearly the same in both languages except for a slight change in spelling. In many cases, the only difference between the Spanish word and the English word is the addition or change of a vowel at the end of the word, or the use of only one consonant where the consonants are doubled in the English word ("committee" = *comité* in Spanish). A *th* in English may be written as a *t* in Spanish; *t*'s may be *d*'s, and *ph*'s are written as *f*'s. There may also be additional changes here and there to compensate for the bizarre way we spell in English:

➤ *carro*

➤ *rata* (yes, "a rat")

➤ *senador*

➤ *democrata*

➤ *republicano*

➤ *crema*

➤ *vitamina*

➤ *aspirina*

➤ *calandario*

➤ *fotografía*

➤ *excelente*

➤ *guitarra*

➤ *teléfono*

➤ *presidente*

➤ *autor*

➤ *grupo*

➤ *americano*

➤ *medicina*

➤ *lampa*

➤ *automóvil*

➤ *banco*

➤ *catedral*

➤ *diferente*

➤ *elegante*

➤ *famoso*

Algo Nuevo

Some Spanish words are cognates of uncommon English terms. For example, the Spanish verb for "to end" is *terminar*. It is a cognate of "to terminate," a word that you know but might not use every day. The Spanish word for someone who walks in his sleep is *sonámbulo*. The verb "to somnambulate" exists in English and means "to walk in your sleep." It's not a common word, but if you already knew it, you're in luck. When you hear a Spanish word, you may have to go through several synonyms for the same English word before you actually locate the cognate.

Many Spanish words that begin with *es–* have an English *amigo*. If you remove the *e* (and possibly the final vowel), the cognate becomes even clearer:

➤ **espacio:** space

➤ **especia:** spice

➤ **especial:** special

➤ **espía:** spy

➤ **esquí:** ski

➤ **estudiar:** study

➤ **estimado:** esteemed (careful, sometimes the *e* stays)

➤ **estupendo:** stupendous

➤ **estúpido:** not so stupendous

Some cognates don't always jump out and bite you on the nose. You may need to study such words a bit before you can recognize them:

➤ **champú:** shampoo

➤ **silla:** seat

➤ **humedad:** humidity

➤ **ejecutar:** to execute

Ten Cuidado

In many words in English, an internal consonant is doubled: *appendix, commemorate, assessment,* and so on. In Spanish, doubled consonants are very rare. The only exception is the doubled *cc* in words such as *acción.* Otherwise, if the consonant is doubled in the English word, don't double it in the Spanish cognate. You'll be right 99 percent of the time.

Words that end in *–um* in English tend to end in *–o* in Spanish:

➤ **gymnasio:** gymnasium

➤ **acuario:** aquarium

➤ **auditorio:** auditorium

The ending *–a* is common in Spanish and may correspond to *–e* (or nothing) in English:

➤ **persona:** person

➤ **agricultura:** agriculture

➤ **causa:** cause

➤ **dama:** lady

➤ **disciplina:** discipline

➤ **gasolina:** gasoline/petrol

➤ **forma:** form

➤ **planeta:** planet

➤ **idiota:** idiot

➤ **mapa:** map

There are many other ways to recognize a cognate. The more Spanish you read and hear, the better you will become at recognizing these *amigos*. But read on to see why things aren't as simple as all that ….

False Cognates

Yes, it is true that many words in Spanish and English look similar and mean the same thing, but cognates can also lead you astray. Some *amigos* may have a long list of secondary meanings that do not exist in the first language. These can be considered as unreliable cognates because they may serve you well in some situations, but not in others.

Algo Nuevo

For an example of an unreliable cognate, let's look at the verb *cancelar*. In many cases, you will be able to get by with *cancelar* when you want to say "to cancel." However, in Spanish, *cancelar* has a secondary meaning of "to pay off in full." You can say *Quiero cancelar esta factura* for "I want to pay off this bill." If you're not careful, you could misunderstand this as "I want to cancel this bill," which wouldn't mean the same thing and could lead to problems. Cognates are indeed very useful, but you must be careful when using them; don't assume that the words are always full cognates just because they look or sound similar.

Other false friends can have entirely different (or even opposite) meanings than the one you are thinking of. You must always verify either by the context or your dictionary that a cognate really does mean what you think it does. Here are a few examples:

➤ **asistir:** to attend (not "to assist")

➤ **caro:** expensive (not "car")

➤ **fábrica:** factory (not "fabric")

➤ **flor:** flower (not "floor")

➤ **librería:** bookstore (not "library")

➤ **colegio:** elementary school (not "college")

➤ **horno:** oven (not "horn")

Acuérdate

Don't forget that although a cognate may look the same, it will be pronounced very differently in each language.

Haz Clic Aquí

Check out these Web sites for more information on how to learn more about cognates: mwn.net/infomac/app/ss/emeec. html and www.opengroup.com/ open/labooks/welcome.shtml. If these don't work out, search for "Spanish cognates." As always, the Internet is an excellent resource for Spanish.

➤ **constipado:** a stuffy nose (not "constipated")

➤ **curioso:** strange (not "curious" like a cat)

➤ **sensible:** sensitive (not "sensible")

➤ **apuntar:** to write down (not "to appoint")

➤ **restar:** to subtract (not "to rest")

➤ **pan:** bread (not "pan")

➤ **sopa:** soup (not "soap")

➤ **familiar:** having to do with family (not "something you already know a lot about")

So, Now What?

At this point, you're probably feeling both elated and frustrated. First I tell you about all these cool free words, and then I say that you can't always trust them and should always make sure they aren't false *amigos*. Well, I know it's frustrating. Tell you what—here's my advice.

When you speak Spanish, you can figure that about 70 percent of the time, your instincts about cognates will lead you in the right direction (at least close enough for you to get your idea across). So, go ahead and use a cognate when it occurs to you. If you need to say "communication" and haven't learned the Spanish word yet, try *comunicación* and see what happens. If someone doesn't understand you, they'll let you know. Even if the cognate you choose isn't 100 percent correct, it may be a lot better than saying nothing at all.

Nevertheless, when it's *your* turn to understand Spanish rather than produce it, you might want to be even more cautious. Don't assume that you know exactly what is meant by a word just because you think you recognize it. You may indeed be right, but too many people have gotten into a lot of trouble by blithely using cognates as a way to muddle through Spanish. If the subject at hand is important, make sure that you really understand what the words mean. Follow your instincts, but let your dictionary be your guide.

La Última Palabra ...

You may have heard or seen people (Hollywood movies are nororious for this) who take this *amigo* concept a bit too far, believing that they can somehow conjure up Spanish by making their English sound Spanish: "I want-o to buy-o a Mexican-o blanket-o. How much-o cost-o?" Nice try, but that isn't Spanish, and talking like that is a bad idea and an embarrassment to those English-speakers who are really trying to learn the language correctly. I may be a complete idiot, but I will personally vigorously slap with a wet tortilla anyone who goes around talking like that after having read this book!

Ten Cuidado

Remember: You can use cognates as an aid to communication and for building up your vocabulary, but *not* as a way to fumble through the language.

Idiot's Guide to Idioms

Here's your last list of idiomatic expressions. There are many more where these came from. If you are so inclined, you may purchase books that contain hundreds of these sayings and idioms at many bookstores and online:

➤ **quitarse un peso de encima:** to take a load off one's mind

➤ **saber nadar y guardar la ropa:** to sleep with one eye open

➤ **salir de Guatemala entrar en Guatapeor:** out of the frying pan into the fire

➤ **ser plato de segunda mesa:** to play second fiddle

➤ **sin que conste en acta:** off the record

➤ **sin ton ni son:** without rhyme or reason

➤ **tener en cuenta:** to bear in mind

➤ **toparse con la horma de sus zapatos:** to meet one's match

➤ **venir como anillo al dedo:** to fit like a glove

Risa del Día

I think I've heard this one in English, too. It's a humorous commentary on management. It's also full of useful vocabulary:

Un tipo volaba en un globo. De pronto se percata que estaba perdido. Maniobra y desciende un poco.

Divisa a un hombre abajo en la calle. Baja un poco y le grita:

"¡Oiga!, ¿podría usted ayudarme? Prometí a un amigo que me encontraría con él a las 2:00; tengo media hora de atraso, y no sé donde estoy ...."

"Claro que puedo ayudarle. Usted se encuentra en un globo de aire caliente, flotando a unos 30 metros encima de esta calle. Está entre los 40 y los 42 grados de latitud Norte y entre los 58 y los 60 grados de longitud Oeste."

"¿Así? ¿Acaso es ingeniero usted?"

"Sí señor. Lo soy, ¿cómo lo supo?"

"Porque todo lo que Ud. me ha dicho es técnicamente correcto, pero aún no sé qué debo hacer con la información que dio y el hecho es que continuo perdido."

"¡Ahh ...! ¿Y usted debe de ser un gerente ...?"

"En efecto lo soy. Pero... ¿como lo averiguó?"

"¡Muy fácil: No sabe ni dónde está, ni para dónde va. Hizo una promesa que no tiene idea de cómo cumplir y espera que ahora otro le resuelva el problema. De hecho, está exactamente en la misma situación en que se hallaba antes de encontrarnos ... pero ahora, por algún motivo, resulta que eso es culpa mía!"

Vocabulario Útil:

- ➤ **tipo:** guy; man (literally, "type")
- ➤ **globo:** balloon
- ➤ **percatarse:** to perceive
- ➤ **maniobrar:** to maneuver
- ➤ **divisar:** to sight; to make out
- ➤ **atraso:** lateness
- ➤ **encontrarse:** to find oneself
- ➤ **grados:** degrees
- ➤ **ingeniero:** engineer
- ➤ **aún:** still; yet

- ➤ **gerente:** manager
- ➤ **en efecto:** in reality; "as a matter of fact"
- ➤ **averiguar:** to find out
- ➤ **ni:** neither; nor
- ➤ **resolver:** to resolve
- ➤ **de hecho:** in fact
- ➤ **hallarse:** same as *encontrarse*
- ➤ **motivo:** reason
- ➤ **culpa:** fault

Algo Nuevo

As you probably know, the verb *deber* means "should" or "ought to" and is followed by an infinitive: *Tú debes ir a la fiesta* ("You should go to the *fiesta*"). When followed by *de*, *deber* means "must be," as in *Las llaves deben de estar en el pasillo* ("The keys must be [I suppose] in the hall"). But unlike its English counterparts, *deber* can also take the conditional or past subjunctive forms: *debería hacerlo, debiera hacerlo*. It's best to simply think of these as more polite ways of telling people what they should do: *Usted debería ir al concierto* means "You should go to the concert." You'll go crazy trying to translate these as "could should," "would should," and "might should."

El Cuiz

Spanish, please …. Cheating will result in the closure of all airports, harbors, and rail services:

1. council; advisory board _____
2. export _____
3. import _____
4. supplies; consumables _____
5. means _____
6. maritime; of the sea _____
7. to combine; to hook up with _____
8. dependable _____
9. port _____
10. raw materials _____
11. air (adjective) _____
12. schedule _____
13. by land _____
14. highway _____
15. load; freight _____
16. company; firm _____

17. infrastructure _____

18. in partnership with; together _____

19. projected _____

20. development _____

21. network _____

22. investment _____

23. government; plan _____

24. availability _____

25. in existence _____

26. balloon _____

27. public works _____

28. to authorize _____

29. lateness _____

30. fee _____

31. toll _____

32. to perceive _____

33. to maneuver _____

34. manager _____

35. in reality; "as a matter of fact" _____

36. degrees _____

37. engineer _____

38. still; yet _____

39. to find out _____

40. reason _____

41. fault _____

Tareas

1. Write down all the English words that you can think of in 10 minutes that end with *–tion* or *–um*. Change the *t* in *–tion* to *c,* and write a *tilde* on the *–ó*, making *–ción*. You have just created a list of words that are likely candidates for Spanish. Now, with your dictionary, verify some of the words that you have created. Although some may not have worked out (or may have needed *s* instead of *c*) this exercise is extremely valuable and will dramatically increase the number of Spanish words that you know.

Ten Cuidado

If you're driving up a hill on a narrow road, you must yield and let those coming down pass first. In some areas, watch for live-stock, and other "unexpected" road hazards. In rural areas, buses may stop unexpectedly whenever there is a passenger. Bottom line: *Ten cuidado,* always.

The Least You Need to Know

➤ Much of the development currently taking place in Latin America has to do with improving infrastructure.

➤ Cognates can help you understand and create many new words.

➤ Many cognates have secondary meanings that aren't present in the other language.

➤ Generally, cognates will share enough of the same meaning to get your point across (about 70 percent), but you should always check with your dictionary to be safe.

Basic Grammar Resource

For your convenience, I have included some basic grammar in this appendix. If you don't find what you're looking for here, consult your beginning instructional text.

Phonetic Names of Letters

Sooner or later, you will need to spell something for someone, such as your name or home town. So, it's a good idea to know the names of the letters in Spanish. In the following list, *ay* sounds like "day," "way," and "say." The combinations *ch* and *ll* are no longer considered as one letter.

- ➤ *a*—ah
- ➤ *b*—bay (*bay larga; bay grande; bay de "burro"*)
- ➤ *c*—say; thay
- ➤ *d*—day
- ➤ *e*—ay
- ➤ *f*—ehfay
- ➤ *g*—hay
- ➤ *h*—ahchay
- ➤ *i*—ee (*ee lahteenah*)
- ➤ *j*—hotah
- ➤ *k*—kah
- ➤ *l*—ehlay
- ➤ *m*—ehmay

➤ *n*—ehnay

➤ *ñ*—ehnyay

➤ *o*—oh

➤ *p*—pay

➤ *q*—coo

➤ *r*—ehray

➤ *rr*—ehrrrray, or "dohblay ehray"

➤ *s*—ehsay

➤ *t*—tay

➤ *u*—oo

➤ *v*—vay (*vay corta; vay chica;* "*vay de vaca*")

➤ *w*—oovay (dohblay oo; vay dohblay)

➤ *x*—ehkees

➤ *y*—ee greeaygah

➤ *z*—setah; thayta

Present Indicative

These are your basic conjugations:

–ar Verbs

Pronoun	Ending	Conjugation
yo	–*o*	First person singular
tú	–*as*	Second person singular familiar
él, ella, usted	–*a*	Third person singular/ second person formal
nosotros/as	–*amos*	First person plural
vosotros/as	–*áis*	Second person plural familiar
ellos, ellas, ustedes	–*an*	Second and third person plural

–er and –ir Verbs

Pronoun	Ending	Conjugation
yo	*–o*	First person singular
tú	*–es*	Second person singular familiar
él/ella/usted	*–e*	Third person singular/ second person formal
nosotros/as	*–emos* (*–imos* for—*ir* verbs)	First person plural
vosotros/as	*–éis*	Second person familiar
ellos, ellas, ustedes	*–en*	Second and third person plural

Preterite Endings

These are the endings for the preterite, or "simple past." (Wonder why they call it simple when it can be so difficult?)

Regular –ar Verbs

Ending	Infinitive	Example
–é	*hablar*	*hablé*
–aste	*pagar*	*pagaste*
–ó	*cantar*	*cantó*
–amos	*contar*	*contamos*
–asteis	*mandar*	*mandasteis*
–aron	*comprar*	*compraron*

–er and –ir Verbs

Ending	Infinitive	Example
–í	*comer*	*comí*
–iste	*salir*	*saliste*
–ió	*vivir*	*vivió*
–imos	*entender*	*entendimos*
–isteis	*meter*	*metisteis*
–ieron	*decidir*	*decidieron*

When forming the preterite, don't forget the Spanish spelling rules. As with the subjunctive, the addition of some endings may require that an orthographic convenience be used to match the spelling to the pronunciation. For example, *pagar* becomes *pagué* in the *yo* form of the preterite because the *g* would be soft next to that *e*. We prevent that by inserting a *u*. You should still consider these verbs as regular.

If the verb stem ends in a vowel, the *i* in *–ieron* becomes *y*. So, *leer* becomes *leyeron* in the third person plural preterite tense because its stem is *le–*.

Imperfect Past Endings

They call this the "imperfect," but really, there's nothing wrong with it:

–ar Verbs

Ending	Example
–aba	*hablaba*
–abas	*cantabas*
–aba	*pagaba*
–ábamos	*contábamos*
–abais	*cantabais*
–aban	*compraban*

–er and –ir Verbs

Ending	Example
–ía	*vivía*
–ías	*comías*
–ía	*sentía*
–íamos	*pedíamos*
–íais	*metíais*
–ían	*sabían*

The first person and third person singular forms look the same, but the context usually makes it clear what's going on. Pronouns and names can also be added for clarity.

Irregular Imperfects

Imagine being both imperfect and irregular at the same time. What a life ....

Luckily, only three common verbs take an irregular imperfect form: *ser*, *ir*, and *ver*.

➤ **ser**—*era, eras, era, éramos, erais, eran*

➤ **ir**—*iba, ibas, iba, íbamos, ibais, iban*

➤ **ver**—*veía, veías, veía, veíamos, veíais, veían*

Tú Command Forms (Imperative Mood)

To tell someone to "speak," simply say *habla* (don't forget to be nice and add *por favor* now and then). Any DOPs and INDOPs are glued right on to the imperative verb, which will necessitate the addition of a *tilde* to maintain the correct stress (*habla*, *háblame*, and so on):

Forming Commands

Verb	Command	Definition
comer	*Come.*	Eat.
vivir	*Vive.*	Live.
cantar	*Cántala.*	Sing it.
escribir	*Escríbeme.*	Write me.
dar	*Dámelo.*	Give it to me.
contar	*Cuéntaselos.*	Tell them to him.

For the irregular *tú* commands, see the reference card in the beginning of the book. Also, remember that when you tell someone *not* to do something, you must use the subjunctive.

Stem-Changing Verbs

Here are a few examples of those stem-changers. Remember that these changes are not seen in the *nosotros* and *vosotros* forms of the verbs.

Some Stem-Changing Verbs

Verb	Yo Form	Change
contar	*cuento*	$o \rightarrow ue$
mostrar	*muestro*	$o \rightarrow ue$
poder	*puedo*	$o \rightarrow ue$
volver	*vuelvo*	$o \rightarrow ue$
jugar	*juego*	$u \rightarrow ue$
querer	*quiero*	$e \rightarrow ie$
perder	*pierdo*	$e \rightarrow ie$
pensar	*pienso*	$e \rightarrow ie$
pedir	*pido*	$e \rightarrow i$
repetir	*repito*	$e \rightarrow i$

Future and Conditional Tense Endings

For most verbs, just add the future ending right onto the infinitive. Notice how these endings, with the exception of the *nosotros* form, are all accented on the last syllable:

Future Tense

Ending	Conjugation
–é	*hablaré*
–ás	*cantarás*
–á	*sentirá*
–emos	*viviremos*
–éis	*comeréis*
–án	*pensarán*

Conditional Tense

Ending	Conjugation
–ía	*pensaría*
–ías	*comprarías*
–ía	*tocaría*
–íamos	*creeríamos*
–íais	*jugaríais*
–ían	*beberían*

For the irregular future and conditional stems, consult the reference card at the beginning of the book.

"Go" Verbs

Remember that these take the "go" part only in the first person indicative. However, in the present subjunctive, these verbs maintain the "go" part throughout:

"Go" Verbs

Verb	Yo Form
hacer	*hago*
poner	*pongo*
oír	*oigo*
salir	*salgo*
tener	*tengo*
traer	*traigo*
venir	*vengo*

Some have stem changes:

"Go" Verbs with Stem Changes

Verb	Yo Form
decir	*digo*
seguir	*sigo*

Subjunctive Endings

It's almost like putting the wrong ending on the verb. Build it around the *yo* form. If there's a stem change, it will also show up here (except in *nosotros* and *vosotros* forms).

–ar Verbs

Ending	Verb	Subjunctive	Definition
–e	*hablar*	*hable*	I may speak
–es	*cantar*	*cantes*	you may sing
–e	*dudar*	*dude*	he/she/you may doubt
–emos	*pensar*	*pensemos*	we may think
–éis	*sentar*	*sentéis*	you all may sit
–en	*tomar*	*tomen*	they/you all may take

–er and –ir Verbs

Ending	Verb	Subjunctive	Definition
–a	*creer*	*crea*	I may believe
–as	*vivir*	*vivas*	You may live
–a	*correr*	*corra*	he/she/it/you may run
–amos	*vender*	*vendamos*	we may sell
–áis	*meter*	*metáis*	you all may insert
–an	*comer*	*coman*	they/you all may eat

Again, if a verb is a "go" verb or has some other change in the *yo* form, it maintains this throughout the subjunctive.

Verbs That Change Forms and the Subjunctive

Verb	*Yo* Form	Example
tener	*tengo*	*tenga*
traer	*traigo*	*traigas*
oír	*oigo*	*oiga*
salir	*salgo*	*salgamos*
hacer	*hago*	*hagan*
decir	*digo*	*digas*
conocer	*conozco*	*conozcáis*
poner	*pongo*	*pongamos*

For the irregular present subjunctives, refer to the reference card at the beginning of the book.

Demonstratives

Here are the pointing words. Remember, when used as adjectives there is no *tilde*. When used as pronouns, the *tilde* is required (except for the neuters):

➤ Masculine singular nouns:

  ➤ **este:** *este sombrero*—"this hat"

  ➤ **ese:** *ese reloj*—"that watch"

  ➤ **aquel:** *aquel edificio*—"that building far away"

➤ Feminine singular nouns:

  ➤ **esta:** *esta flor*—"this flower"

  ➤ **esa:** *esa alfombra*—"that carpet"

  ➤ **aquella:** *aquella mujer*—"that woman far away"

➤ Masculine plural nouns:

  ➤ **estos:** *estos platos*—"these plates"

  ➤ **esos:** *esos zapatos*—"those shoes"

  ➤ **aquellos:** *aquellos hombres*—"those men far away"

➤ Feminine plural nouns:

  ➤ **estas:** *estas muñecas*—"these dolls"

  ➤ **esas:** *esas camisas*—"those shirts"

  ➤ **aquellas:** *aquellas playas*—"those far-away beaches"

The gender of the demonstrative pronoun links it to the nouns in question. You can often translate these as "this one," "that one," and even "these ones" in English:

➤ Masculine singular:

> ➤ **éste:** "this one"
>
> ➤ **ése:** "that one"
>
> ➤ **aquél:** "that one far away"

➤ Feminine singular:

> ➤ **ésta:** "this one"
>
> ➤ **ésa:** "that one"
>
> ➤ **aquélla:** "that one far away"

➤ Plurals:

> ➤ **éstos:** "these"
>
> ➤ **éstas:** "these"
>
> ➤ **ésos:** "those"
>
> ➤ **ésas:** "those"
>
> ➤ **aquéllos:** "those far away"
>
> ➤ **aquéllas:** "those far away"

➤ Neuter demonstrative pronouns:

> ➤ **esto:** "this (concept)"
>
> ➤ **eso:** "that (concept)"
>
> ➤ **aquello:** "that" (not used very often in conversation)

Other Books

There are literally hundreds of books in circulation today about Spanish—far too many to list here. Many are excellent. Some are not so good. Check out what's available for free at your local library before you *gastar dinero*. If you plan to purchase a book, spend a few minutes reviewing it to make sure that it suits your learning style. You might also consider browsing at www.amazon.com or at other book-related Web sites.

If you are studying Spanish for professional reasons, you'll find many subject-specific books on the market today. Visit your local bookstore, or go online and search for a book that relates specifically to your area of interest.

Among the many general texts available, here are a few that stand out in my mind as being exceptional:

➤ *Cassell's Colloquial Spanish: A Handbook of Idiomatic Usage,* by A. Bryson Gerrard. 3rd Revised Edition, ISBN 0-02-079430-4. Macmillan, 1981.

Ah, the book that changed my life! This used to be called *Beyond the Dictionary in Spanish.* I got hooked on it when I was in college. I might have given up on my Spanish had it not been for this little gem. While some of the information is now a bit outdated, this book will still do wonders for your Spanish and really have you speaking like a native. Not only is it full of great information, it's also fun to read. I highly recommend it.

➤ *A New Reference Grammar of Modern Spanish,* by John Butt and Carmen Benjamin. 2nd edition, ISBN 0-8442-7088-1. Edward Arnold, 1995.

The Butt and Benjamin book is one of the most comprehensive reference guides on Spanish grammar currently available. If you plan to continue your studies of this language, this book is a must.

➤ *El Pequeño Larousse Ilustrado 1999.* ISBN 9-706-07778-2. Larousse, 1999.

Although it costs about $40, this Spanish-dictionary/encyclopedia is worth every *centavo*. You'll have easy access to information in Spanish about practically everything in one single volume. It's updated every few years, so buy the newest edition you can find. Your Spanish (and knowledge of the world) will improve by leaps and bounds. You can order this book at most bookstores.

➤ *The Oxford Spanish Dictionary: Spanish-English/English-Spanish,* by Beatriz Galimberti Jarman and Roy Russell, (editors). ISBN: 0-19-864510-4. Oxford University Press, 1994.

Many excellent dictionaries have been produced, and everyone has their favorite. I'm rather partial to the Oxford version. As a professional translator and interpreter, I have found this reference to be consistently superior in giving me the words, definitions, and phrases I need. The *HarperCollins Spanish Dictionary,* by Colin Smith (ISBN 00-627-0207-6, HarperCollins, 1997), is also quite good.

Index

J-K-L

Q-R

"thank you," polite expressions, 297

"there" expressions, 214

three-syllable homonyms, 325

tico diminutive suffix, 272

ticos (Costa Ricans' nickname), 131

tildes, 29
  accentuation, 33
    Esteban's rule number 1, 33-34
    Esteban's rule number 2, 34-35
    exceptions to Esteban's rules, 35-36
  demonstrative pronouns, 92
  distinguishing one word from another, 37-38
  homonyms, 324
    monsyllabic, 324-325
    three-syllable, 325
    two-syllable, 325
  interrogatives, 281-283
  lack of for demonstrative adjectives, 92
  neuter demonstrative pronouns, 93-94
  possessives, 309-310

time
  duration expressions, *por,* 166
  unspecified future, subjunctive mood, 153

tipping (*una propina*), 188

Tomatina (festival), 209

tonada, El Festival Nacional de la Tonada (*lectura*), 83
  analysis of the text, 84-85
  vocabulary list, 83

tools, 39
  bilingual dictionaries, 40
  books, 41-42
  cassettes, 41-42
  flashcards, 42
  Internet, 40
  magazines, 41
  newspapers, 41
  television and films, 42-43
  videos, 41-42

trade agreement, 289

transitive verbs, object pronouns, 118-119

transportation, 345

trio (romantic music), 253

tú
  command forms, 365

versus *usted,* 175
  regional variations, 177
  showing respect, 175

vos in parts of Latin America, 177

two-syllable homonyms, 325

U-V

"u" (the letter), pronunciation, 18

uca pejorative suffix, 274

ucha pejorative suffix, 274

ucho pejorative suffix, 274

uco pejorative suffix, 274

udo/a suffix, 276

"ue" (the diphthong), pronunciation, 24

un ending, indefinite articles, masculine, 55

una ending, indefinite articles, feminine, 55

United States
  Hispanic perspective of living (*lectura*), 145
    analysis of the text, 146-147
    vocabulary list, 145-146
  history of Hispanics, 143-144
  statistics and demographics, 147-148

unknown but potential existence, subjunctive mood, 154

unspecified future time, subjunctive mood, 153

Uruguay, 82

usted
  commands, subjunctive mood, 150
  versus *tú,* 175
    regional variations, 177
    showing respect, 175

"v" (the letter)
  dropped pronunciation, 24
  pronunciation, 19

Vatican Web site, 206

Venezuela, 114
  infrastructure (*lectura*), 346
    analysis of the text, 348
    vocabulary list, 347-348

ver verbs, irregular imperfect form, 135

verbana (open-air celebration), 211

verbs
  conjugation, 70
    helping, 73-74
    imperfect past tense, 364
    ir, 74-76
    irregular imperfect tense, 365
    present indicative, 71
    present indicative tense, 362-363
    se, 76
    stem-changing, 72-73
  estar, 103
    with adjectives, 104-105
    with nouns, 103-104
    with past participles, 105-106
  hay, preterite simple past form, 106-107
  helping, *haber* ("to have"), 213
  infinitive form, 69
    commands, 69
    object of another verb, 70
  reflexive, 335-337
    infinitive plus *se,* 335
  ser, 103
    with adjectives, 104-105
  with nouns, 103-104
    with past participles, 105-106
  stem-changing, 366
  tenses, 71
    conditional, 139-140
    future, 138-139
    imperfect past, 135-136
    past perfect, 137-138
    past subjunctive, 227-229
    present perfect, 74
    present progressive, 202-203
    preterite past, 134-135, 363-364
  transitive versus intransitive, object pronouns, 118-119

videos, 41-42

La Virgin de la Almudena, festivals in her honor, 212

virtual dictionaries, 40

vocabulary lists (lessons)
  bank conversation, 300
  business correspondence, 291
  computer modems, 307
  computer terminology, 312-313

W

X-Z